Selected Plays by Griselda Gambaro

Selected Plays by Griselda Gambaro

Siamese Twins (1967)
Mother by Trade (1999)
As the Dream Dictates (2002)
Asking Too Much (2004)
Persistence (2007)
Dear Ibsen, I Am Nora (2013)
The Gift (2015)

Translated and introduced by
GWEN MacKEITH

methuen | drama
LONDON • NEW YORK • OXFORD • NEW DELHI • SYDNEY

METHUEN DRAMA
Bloomsbury Publishing Plc
50 Bedford Square, London, WC1B 3DP, UK
1385 Broadway, New York, NY 10018, USA
29 Earlsfort Terrace, Dublin 2, Ireland

BLOOMSBURY, METHUEN DRAMA and the Methuen Drama logo are trademarks of
Bloomsbury Publishing Plc

First published in Great Britain 2022

Copyright © Griselda Gambaro, 2022
Translation © Gwen MacKeith, 2022

Introduction © Gwen MacKeith, 2022

The authors have asserted their right under the Copyright, Designs and Patents Act, 1988,
to be identified as authors of this work.

For legal purposes the Acknowledgements on p. 207 constitute an extension of
this copyright page.

Cover design by Rebecca Heselton
Cover image: Portrait of Griselda Gambaro, 08/10/2010
© Basso Cannarsa/Opale/Bridgeman Images

All rights reserved. No part of this publication may be reproduced or transmitted in any form or by any means, electronic or mechanical, including photocopying, recording, or any information storage or retrieval system, without prior permission in writing from the publishers.

Bloomsbury Publishing Plc does not have any control over, or responsibility for, any third-party websites referred to or in this book. All internet addresses given in this book were correct at the time of going to press. The author and publisher regret any inconvenience caused if addresses have changed or sites have ceased to exist, but can accept no responsibility for any such changes.

All rights whatsoever are strictly reserved and application for performance etc. should be made before rehearsals by professionals and by amateurs to the respective copyright holders. No performance may be given unless a licence has been obtained.

A catalogue record for this book is available from the British Library.

A catalog record for this book is available from the Library of Congress.

ISBN: HB: 978-1-3502-3364-5
       PB: 978-1-3502-3363-8
       ePDF: 978-1-3502-3365-2
       eBook: 978-1-3502-3366-9

Typeset by RefineCatch Limited, Bungay, Suffolk
Printed and bound in Great Britain

To find out more about our authors and books visit www.bloomsbury.com
and sign up for our newsletters.

Contents

Introduction 1
Siamese Twins (1967) 15
Mother by Trade (1999) 51
As the Dream Dictates (2002) 69
Asking Too Much (2004) 103
Persistence (2007) 121
Dear Ibsen, I Am Nora (2013) 143
The Gift (2015) 181
Acknowledgements 207

Introduction

It is a great pleasure and a privilege to present this anthology of plays in translation by Griselda Gambaro, one of Argentina's most important and prolific dramatists. Gambaro is also a playwright of international significance whose bold and philosophical plays have much to say to the new contexts they find themselves in. This collection joins a constellation of translations into English and, with the exception of *Siamese Twins* (1967), offers works which were written and produced in the more recent phases of Gambaro's creative output. While only a sample of Gambaro's considerable theatrical corpus (some forty-eight plays), this publication comes with the hope that it will further understanding in the anglophone world of her extraordinary theatre, which is all too seldom performed on the English-speaking stage.

Born in La Boca, Buenos Aires, in 1928 into a family of second-generation Italian immigrants, Gambaro is the youngest of five children and the only girl. From a working-class family, the young Griselda Gambaro educated herself through reading literature which was available from her local public library. She began with writing fiction and a number of her early plays began in narrative form. She has continued to write novels and short stories alongside drama, and has described alternating between the two genres in her pattern of writing; after a period of working on a play, she turns her attentions to the more introspective demands of writing fiction. She lives in Don Bosco, a suburb of Buenos Aires, where she conducts her industrious writing life. Gambaro's diverse and original readings of classical Western literature form a rich substrate in her work which she combines with an acute power of observation of the world around her and a close scrutiny of herself and others.

In the early 1960s, Gambaro became involved with the Instituto Torcuato Di Tella, an avant-garde cultural institute formed in Buenos Aires in 1958. The Di Tella was a breeding ground for all kinds of artistic experimentation. This included the visual arts, happenings, cinema, music and theatre. Griselda Gambaro's play *El Desatino* (*The Blunder*) (1965) was the second theatrical production to be staged at the institute. The magazine *Confirmado* in response described Gambaro as '*un prodigio de originalidad y frescura*' / 'a wonder of originality and freshness' (9 September 1965). The institute achieved international renown and Gambaro's series of four plays established her as a dramatist of note: *Las paredes* (*The Walls*) (1964), *El desatino* (*The Blunder*) (1965), *Los siameses* (*The Siamese Twins*) (1967) and *El campo* (*The Camp*) (1971). These plays which, on the face of it, are absurd in nature, provoked a reception of her work which saw their locus as being Eurocentric and, even amongst the Argentine left, out of touch with a current Argentine reality. However, with particular reference to the plays of this period, the speculation about the influences of Pinter, Ionesco, Beckett and Artaud have been put several times to Gambaro in interview over the years to which she has always countered with her affirmation that it is her reading of the classics which has shaped her work, alongside the indelible imprint of the specifically Argentine theatrical tradition of the *grotesco criollo*, a profoundly social theatre.

The dramatist Armando Discépolo (1887–1971) is widely identified as the figurehead of the theatre of the *grotesco criollo* and Gambaro hails him as being to Argentina what Shakespeare is to Britain (Gambaro 2014: 129). Discépolo himself was an actor and a director, as well as a dramatist and translator who brought many key foreign works into Spanish, including by Shakespeare, Chekhov and Pirandello. He developed a distinctively Argentine stage language and performative vocabulary for his tragicomedies. Tragicomedy inevitably evokes other theatre traditions, including the theatre of Luigi Pirandello and the Italian grotesque. Pirandello's play *Six Characters in Search of an Author* toured to Buenos Aires on two occasions, in 1923 and 1927 and enjoyed great success. And yet any appropriation of Pirandello's '*umorismo*' takes on a very *criollo* identity as it intersects with the existing theatrical traditions of the Hispanic world and is transformed by its new context. The popular one-hour *sainete* was the comic form widely practised by theatre companies between 1890 and 1930 in Argentina. This had been imported from Spain and enjoyed great popularity right up until the 1960s. Consisting of a one-act farce, the *sainete* was a light satirical piece which often depicted stereotypical characters of the day and recognisable scenarios in comical ways. In this sense, the *sainete* was somewhat caricatured in its content. This repertoire of stereotypical characters and scenarios was elaborated upon by Discépolo, however, and the nature of the humour took on a different behaviour. Beneath the comedy in the *grotesco criollo* there is always its counterpart, a rumbling melancholy. This lends a true psychological depth and interiority which was absent in the traditional *sainete* (Viñas 1973: 11). Stereotypical characters can be laughed at and ridiculed but the distress at their tragic predicament looms large.

A pervasive theme in the *grotesco criollo* is one of '*fracaso*', of failure. This sense of failure is linked to the pursuit of the dream of 'Hacerse la América' ('Making Yourself in America'); crudely put, the Argentine equivalent of the 'American Dream' explored in North American drama. Discépolo creates a portrait of poverty where deception, criminality, humiliation and the corruption of loving relationships are all undeniable themes. In the 1890s puppetry was also flourishing in the theatre practice of Uruguay and Argentina (Richardson 1975: 31–4). This too infiltrated the *grotesco criollo*, informing the physicality of the actors as well as influencing the visual identity of the theatre. The instructions which Discépolo makes to his actors suggest a deliberate '*torpeza*', a malcoordination, as if movement is not generated from within but is orchestrated by external forces. Characters are not in control of their own destiny but blindly fulfil the roles assigned to them, unable to express the human face beneath the construct of their social exterior. The notion of puppetry and the mask in the *grotesco criollo* diverges from its expression in the Italian *grottesco*, however, in the sense that where the Italian playwrights maintained this idea on the level of a character's moral and ideological dilemma, in the *grotesco criollo* a more realist sociological dimension is added. It is a theatre which is not concerned with the individual but with the collective, giving expression to temperaments and collective moods, rather than developing characters within three-dimensional psychological parameters. Thus it is not a theatre of meditative speeches or monologues where characters are revealed in an especially individuated way. Stylistically, it is orchestral in the way that characters work as an ensemble. However, where the *sainete* demonstrated a palette of predictable and recognisable caricatures, the *grotesco criollo* took these caricatures and humanised them. Actors who were instrumental in the development of the *grotesco criollo* combined these prototypes with their own keen observations of real people from real communities. Thus a new style and approach to acting in Argentina became established. Once again, the heavily stylised nature of the grotesque was combined with a documentary-like counterpart which made for a fascinating aesthetic and a deeply affecting socially committed drama which could speak of the immigrant experience. For Griselda Gambaro, this legacy of the *grotesco criollo* is fundamental, and in particular her incorporation of the theatre of Armando Discépolo. Although some of the plays included in this collection show a clear departure from many of the features of the *grotesco criollo*, the dramatic sensibility endures, an aesthetic founded on ambivalence both in its expression and the response elicited in the audience; a simultaneous smile and grimace.

What Gambaro and Discépolo share as Argentine writers is their complete immersion in translated texts, Discépolo of course being himself a translator. They embody the description of the Argentine writer which Jorge Luis Borges outlined in his influential lecture of 1951, 'The Argentine Writer and Tradition'. Here Borges sought to free the Argentine writer from having to represent any artificial notion of national identity, typified by the figure of the gaucho, instead identifying the very particular access to Western literature granted to them by their Argentineness. The critic Beatriz Sarlo describes translated texts, and the practice of translation itself, as key to the development of the Argentine cultural landscape (Sarlo 1998). This is not to suggest in any way a transnational universal culture, or cultural homogeneity. Both Discépolo's and Gambaro's readings of Western literature are sent through the prism of their specifically Argentine perspective, a process through which the works are necessarily transformed. Griselda Gambaro's Argentineness can be found in her diverse readings and the way these readings find themselves into her work, not as an anxiety of influence, but with a sense of being entitled to a place at their table. The result is an intensely literary dramatist for whom the word is paramount. In her essay 'Teatro y literatura' ('Theatre and Literature') Gambaro writes:

> I try to maintain in my pieces a strong link between dramatic literature and the stage, between theatre and book. The words of the text are not chosen at random, each one is charged with its action, its sound and meaning, its embodiment, its energy. And it is in this linguistic operation that is executed from the beginning of the text, that literature and theatricality mutually enhance each other, and in great authors they form a single substance, as we see in Shakespeare.[1] (Gambaro 2014: 152)

Gambaro's dialogue with the Western literary canon is an important aspect of her radicalism. As Marguerite Feitlowitz notes in her introduction to her translations of *Las Paredes / The Walls* (1966), *Información para extranjeros / Information for Foreigners* (1972) and *Antígona Furiosa* (1986):

> The language, which incorporates quotes and echoes from Sophocles, Shakespeare and Rubén Darío, extends beyond Argentina, not only inscribing the country's history into that of the world but also forcefully asserting that Antígona was not just happening there and then but is happening, everywhere, always. (Feitlowitz 1991: 9)

---

[1] 'trato de mantener en mis piezas un vínculo fuerte entre la literatura dramática y el escenario, entre el teatro y el libro. Las palabras del texto no son elegidas al azar, cada una está cargada con su acción, su sonido y significado, su corporeidad, su energía. Y en esta operación lingüística que se ejecuta desde el inicio del texto, literatura y teatralidad se potencian mutuamente y en los grandes autores forman una única sustancia, como vemos en Shakespeare.'

In the decade of the 1970s, the misapprehension of Gambaro's work being Eurocentric and out of touch with an Argentine reality was implicitly and categorically revised when Rafael Videla's regime banned her novel *Ganarse la muerte* (1976), deeming it to be a threat to social order and the institution of family. Gambaro went into exile in Spain in 1977, returning to Argentina in 1980. In fact, Gambaro is a radical and subversive dramatist whose ethics are always at the centre of her work. She has created a fierce theatre of resistance: against state repression, against corruption, against collective amnesia. Much of the critical attention paid to Gambaro's theatre has focused on the ways in which the plays have dramatised the dynamic between victims and victimisers, and with specific reference to the Argentine social, historical and political context of dictatorship and state violence. Gambaro has been a tireless witness to her country's past, its legacy and ongoing reality, and her theatre, on some level, is always characterised by a fearless examination of political and domestic violence. Gambaro's insistent probing of this dynamic is explored by a corpus which includes many varied experimentations with theatrical form. Her works have always seen new ways of dramatising her central preoccupations. From the early works first performed in the Cultural Centre, El Instituto Torcuato di Tella in the mid-to-late 1960s to the present day, each phase of her playwriting reveals an unrelenting curiosity and determination to reinvent. She is as much theatrical innovator as she is political dramatist, or, for Gambaro, the two are intimately related.

Siamese Twins (1967)

In *Siamese Twins* of 1967, Lorenzo and Ignacio form the well-known archetypes of Cain and Abel. One brother's envy leads him to subject his more successful and independent twin to cruelty and to torture, and finally to conspire to bring about his murder. At the beginning of the play Lorenzo, having thrown a stone at a child on the street, is being chased by the child's father. The first thing we hear is the sound of his footsteps running down a corridor before he bursts onstage through a door, slamming and locking it behind him. Ignacio is some paces behind, and when he meets the shut door, he pleads to be let in because the child's father is getting close and will mistake him for Lorenzo. While Lorenzo is safe inside, he refuses Ignacio's desperate appeals to be let in and taunts his brother from behind the door. 'Answer me in writing', he says at one point, which gives a flavour of the grotesque humour which accompanies many of the cruellest moments encountered in the play. Ignacio inevitably takes the beating meant for his brother which we hear but do not see.

When Ignacio is finally admitted to the room by Lorenzo, the sadism continues. Ignacio wants to 'cut the cord' between them. He wants Lorenzo to leave the house of his parents so that he can establish his own family there. Lorenzo will have none of it; he humiliates Ignacio, eroding everything which represents his brother's wish to become separate. At the end of Act One two grotesque police officers, Nasal Man and Smiley Man, arrive at the house. Lorenzo and Ignacio imagine them to be on the trail of the man who threw a stone at a child's head and Lorenzo contrives to set Ignacio up as the culprit. Ignacio is then arrested by these officers, and taken away.

This injustice, under the direction of Lorenzo, is carried through into the second act. Ignacio is released and returns home but Lorenzo betrays his brother once again by setting him up as the perpetrator of a series of fantastical crimes and he is once again imprisoned. The rest of the play takes place around the prison where Ignacio is wrongfully incarcerated. We encounter two more grotesque characters, Old Man and Young Man, who become indifferent witnesses to the cruelties being carried out on-stage, and eventually assist in the burial of Ignacio's body which is disposed of in an unmarked grave.

Diana Taylor has pointed out that this secret assassination of an untried man, which takes place off-stage unseen by the audience, prophesises the disappearances of so-called 'subversives' which were to follow in Argentina after 1967, particularly during the repression of 1976–83 (Taylor 1991: 118). It is true that Gambaro's foreshadowing of these events seems remarkable. It is also important to note that Gambaro will not allow us the comfort of a reading of her plays as allegorical, as representations of historical episodes of state violence in Argentina. Gambaro is not only commenting on Argentina; rather, she is forcing the recognition of a psychic truth about the mentalities developed in order to carry out state violence. Gambaro's audience recognises and is implicated in these processes and forced to acknowledge that these acts of violence can happen anywhere. The strength and power of *Siamese Twins* is this deep relevance to ourselves.[2] Its ingenuity is in the unconscious pathways through which it makes contact with us, often through the black humour whereby at the height of cruelty we find ourselves laughing, however involuntarily.

It seems all the more extraordinary now that Gambaro faced a critical reception of this play at the time of its opening for turning her back on Argentine reality, and for being too indebted to the European absurd. This critique becomes absurd in itself as it characterises exactly what Gambaro's theatre *never* allows us to do: to escape any kind of reality. All of her plays subject us mercilessly to a reality which is all too relevant to our present, and we have no choice but to experience it.

Mother by Trade (1999)

Gambaro has referred to a shift in focus from her early work pre-1982 and the work which then followed whereby, while she was an outsider looking in on her earlier works, she begins to locate herself in her own plays. In an interview she described looking for 'an answer in which I, the author, am implicated; I allow myself to reflect with my own voice among my characters.' (Picon Garfield 1985: 71). The Argentine director, Silvio Lang, has directed many of Gambaro's plays, and several of the plays featured in this collection. In the prologue to Gambaro's collected works he also describes a change in tone in Gambaro's theatre which happened from the early 1990s. From then, she is not only present in her own plays but she also allows a sense of warmth to take shape which was absent in her earlier works. To be clear, this is not to be confused with sentimentalism, which would be precisely antithetical to Gambaro's drama. Lang writes in his prologue to her collected works:

---

2   Catherine Boyle first makes this observation in her essay 'Griselda Gambaro and the female dramatist: The audacious trespasser' in *Knives and Angels: Women Writers in Latin America* ed. Susan Bassnett. This comment is elaborated on here: 'What is terrifying in the writing to Griselda Gambaro is the awareness it gives us that though we wish to believe that only other people blind themselves to the real truths of life, we belong body and soul to those others' (155).

It could be said that the 1990s is the time when affect entered Gambaro's theatre. Not only because the virulence of humor and the cruelty of previous works attenuated the existence of affect, but now it seems that Gambaro recognises in affect a new name for emancipation. The intensification of affect in Gambaro is linked to a gesture: the embrace. It is not a question of any model of humanitarianism but of another kind of politics.[3] (Gambaro 2011: prologue)

This observation is critical in considering the nature of Gambaro's later works included here.

Thirty-two years after the first performance of *Siamese Twins* (and many extraordinary plays in between) comes *Mother by Trade* in 1999, a play with a cast of only women and clearly feminist in tone. In this play, unlike the cord which Ignacio wants to cut, the play poses the question of whether it is possible to repair a familial bond which has already been broken. We begin with a recipe for melodrama: a mother meets her daughter forty years after she abandoned her as an infant; the daughter discovers her mother cohabiting with her lesbian partner of twenty-five years. This script, however, resists the high emotion and comforting closure you could expect from such a premise; instead the play dramatises a stark process of truth and reconciliation between mother and daughter who are strangers to one another. There are no tears, no moving embraces, there is no healing recognition of the relationship they've never had. Rather, the unsayable is said by both sides, and, with that, the myth of maternal instinct is unflinchingly dismantled. Yet though it promises to be hard won, the possibility of a real and demythologised relationship is gradually prised open.

Matilde, the mother, was a once successful singer and has a diva personality to go with it. Eugenia, her partner, plays second fiddle, gently humanising her often stark and merciless responses to her estranged daughter, Leticia. Leticia, like her biological mother, can also be merciless in her communications, which make no allowance for her mother's fragile ego. But it is in this willingness to tell the truth, to say what is painful to hear, and for this to be heard and borne by Matilde, and by Leticia, which offers the possibility of reparation.

At the time the play was written, in the 1990s, Argentina was enjoying a period of apparent prosperity and stability after the collapse of the military junta in 1983. However, from as early as 1989, the then neoliberal Argentine president, Carlos Menem, gave controversial pardons to key military figures involved in the repression. *De profesión maternal* is underscored by a mistrust in some kinds of forgiveness, which are rendered meaningless when granted or received too casually. I mention this not as a way of explaining what the play is 'about'. The play has the potential to be about many things. However, this backdrop may be of interest merely as a flavour, one of several resonances.

Gambaro's theatre often explores the question of how trauma can be digested and integrated into a present consciousness, and she no answer to this. Rather, it seems that

---

3 'Se podría decir que la década de 1990 es el momento de la entrada del afecto en el teatro de Gambaro. No solo porque la virulencia del humor y la crueldad de las obras anteriores atenuaran la existencia del afecto, sino porque ahora pareciera que Gambaro reconoce en el afecto un nuevo nombre de la emancipación. La intensificación del afecto en Gambaro está ligado a un gesto: el abrazo. No se trata de ningún modelo humanitarista sino de otra política.'

the act of playing and trying things out, as actors might in a rehearsal, can have value as different versions of the past, and of people, are experimented with. The audience senses that Matilde is fumbling for a version of 'mother' which she can play with some degree of authenticity. *De profesión maternal* suggests that 'maternal instinct' in the fundamental relationship between mother and child is not something a woman is necessarily born with, it is what she works at, and what she creates in collaboration with the society she lives in.

As the Dream Dictates (2002)

In *As the Dream Dictates* (2002), we experience the shifting sands of characters who are mercurial, mysterious and unpredictable, and scenarios which are construed and then dissolve before our eyes.

Ana is a cleaner on a geriatric ward who longs to go on a sailing trip with her generous and benevolent brother. She cares for an old man who wants to believe his children haven't abandoned him to be cared for by an institution. However, Ana's brother, Manuel, may not be as benevolent as she dreams him to be, and the Old Man finds himself unable to sustain his confidence in children who will care for him in his old age. Ana and the Old Man find themselves helpless in the dream, and take refuge in wishful fantasies that become increasingly hollow and difficult to maintain.

In an interview, Gambaro described the first staging of the play in 2002 under Laura Yusem's direction:

> Laura's staging surprised me a bit. In the step that goes from the written work to the stage, one discovers other meanings oneself, for example that Ana's dream connects very strongly with our Argentina, which today is so pathetic. Taking the image, quite conventional in my text, of a sailboat and an island in the open sea, hers are not big dreams. On the contrary, they are related to simple tastes, such as the desire of the old man in the nursing home to eat biscuits, or to smoke a cigarette, or to attend an evening at the Colón theatre. This staging reveals more exactly in which place (or country) we are dreaming.[4]

Between 1998 and 2002 Argentina suffered a great depression, a period of instability during which there was widespread unemployment with 50 per cent of the population living below the poverty line. This resulted in social unrest and the loss of confidence in, and eventual collapse of, government. There had been jubilation when the years of

---

4 'La puesta de Laura me sorprendió un poco. En el paso que va de la obra escrita a la escena uno mismo descubre otros significados, por ejemplo que el sueño de Ana se conecta muy fuertemente con nuestra Argentina, hoy tan patética. Sacando la imagen, bastante convencional en mi texto, de un velero y de una isla en mar abierto, los suyos no son grandes sueños. Al contrario, se relacionan con gustos simples, como el deseo del viejo internado en el geriátrico de comer bizcochitos con grasa, o fumarse un cigarrillo, o asistir a una velada en el Colón. Este montaje revela más exactamente en qué lugar (o país) estamos soñando.' Taken from an interview with Griselda Gambaro by Hilda Cabrera published in *Pagina/12* on 22 August 2002, https://www.pagina12.com.ar/diario/espectaculos/6-9180-2002-08-22.html

violent repression had come to an end and Argentina had adopted the free-market politics of privatisation and financial deregulation. The neoliberal president Carlos Menem's era is remembered for the hedonist lifestyle of 'pizza and champagne' amongst the middle classes, a fragile bubble of wellbeing and prosperity which would burst when the country declared itself bankrupt in December 2001. This is perhaps the backdrop to which Gambaro refers in this interview.

The title, *Lo que va dictando el sueño*, plays on a line from a poem by Sor Juana Inés de la Cruz, 'Ya que para despedirme'. The poem is about the loss of a loved one and this poem is the goodbye. The particular lines read:

> porque va borrando el agua
> lo que va dictando el fuego

These lines roughly translated could read:

> because water is erasing
> what fire is dictating

The mourning lover's tears wash away the ink of the words she is writing, words which are dictated by human passion. This sense of being dictated to might be something akin to the truth and inescapability of unconscious forces. So too in dreaming, we are never really in charge. Our dreams, like good theatre, can face us with the things we don't want to look at, with loss. The dream in Gambaro's play is also part of reality itself, and cannot be ignored. It is humans grappling with the impossibility of questions such as how to imagine the future when there is great trauma in the past. *As the Dream Dictates* is an invitation to dream of a better future, which can only be possible when reality and dream confront one another. A bold vision of the future can only be conceived of when hollow fantasies are deconstructed and imagination is granted its true and transformative powers. Indeed, the dream, or the bad dream, might describe many of Gambaro's plays; a dream you want to wake up from because the truth it speaks is all too real. Gambaro herself makes a clear relationship between dream and the theatre:

> What the dream most dictates corresponds to the nature of theatre, to its substance. No matter how realistic a work is, the artifice of the production puts it in a place that denies that realism, only the *pretending* makes it true. [. . .] if the play speaks of how the dream is introduced into reality, how it dictates its laws; and how reality opposes the dream, fights it and sometimes destroys it, at the end of the piece the question remains: does the dream accept being destroyed? Or does it remain, autonomous, with a life of its own, so that despite this era of the 'assassinated dream', we can get closer and dream again?[5] (Gambaro 2014: 157–8)

---

5 'Lo que más dicta el sueño corresponde a la naturaleza del teatro, a su sustancia. Por más realista que sea una obra, el artificio de la representación la coloca en un lugar que desmiente ese realism, solo la *simulación* lo hace verdad. [. . .] si la obra habla de cómo el sueño se introduce en la realidad, dicta sus leyes; y de cómo la realidad se opone al sueño, lo combate y a veces lo destruye, en el final de la pieza queda el interrogante: ¿el sueño acepta ser destruido? ¿O permanece, autónomo, con vida propia, para que a pesar de esta época "asesina del sueño" nos acerquemos y volvamos a soñarlo?'

Asking Too Much (2004)

In *Asking Too Much* (2004) we encounter two characters, Mario and Elena, who return to Mario's apartment after a boozy dinner for one more drink. They appear to know each other, though how well the audience cannot be sure of. They might be colleagues at work, yet as the dialogue unfolds, there are suggestions that they may know each other far more intimately than the category of 'colleagues' would suggest. For the most part, the two characters address one another in the formal '*usted*' form which the Spanish language affords. However, when both characters lapse into the informal form of address, the 'tú' form, or, in the Argentine context, '*el voseo*', this introduces an ambiguity about the nature of who they are to one another.[6] Though Elena does her best to divert it, the conversation keeps coming back to the same theme: how does a couple separate when one person has stopped loving while the other continues to do so? Mario has been abandoned, perhaps by Elena, although he refers to this woman in the third person. Elena has found a new relationship after a separation and is happy. Mario does his best to engage Elena's conscience, her sense of responsibility for the one she has left. Elena won't save his feelings or pretend that she feels things which she no longer feels. She is unapologetic and says what is difficult to hear, knowing she causes pain and in the face of his veiled suicidal threats. Elena is free to discover a new and emancipated narrative, while Mario has the record with the story of failed romantic love on repeat. This is redolent of the lyrics of many Argentine tangos in which an inevitably callous woman abandons her lover who sings of the suffering she has caused, even taking pleasure in this sadness. Elena offers a riposte to this male lament so enamoured by popular culture.

At times, the characters of Mario and Elena seem like actors who are exploring their respective roles. They replay speeches, they question the authenticity of one another's performance of affect. Through the character of Elena, the play expresses a wish to get beyond the scripted roles of gender, of victims and abusers, self-pity, narratives which might constrain and mutilate our growth. Elena is attempting to find a new language and voice to stand up to a toxic discourse about the partnerships made between men and women. Mario spins a gun on his fingertip, a menacing prop which, combined with a latent violence and references to suicide, hang in the air like a poisonous cloud. And it is suggested that this prop, supposedly unloaded, may discharged at the end of the play. *Asking Too Much* is a mysterious and enigmatic play which attempts to renegotiate the terms of human attachments and how we choose to narrate our shared histories.

Persistence (2007)

Persistence chooses its setting in the real life event of the 2004 Beslan massacre in Russia. It imagines three Chechnyan rebels before and after they take the children hostage. It might be unexpected that an Argentine dramatist would take this Russian context as the

---

6   This is a problem of translation which might be resolved dramatically, rather than linguistically, given that English does not have an equivalent distinction in forms of address.

setting for her play. However, it tells us something important about Gambaro's approach and the way in which we should approach her writing, that 'the insights she unearths do not only speak for Latin America' (Boyle 1990: 145). The British theatre director Simon Usher, in response to this play, writes:

> There are many plays attempting to tackle the subject of Islamic terrorism on English stages, but none which enter the hearts and minds of the protagonists in the way Gambaro does here. The play is not a comment on terrorism or global politics, but rather it shows us how human beings arrive at solutions to their circumstances through a remorseless logic. These solutions can be extraordinarily harsh and cruel. By demonstrating this without an intrusive political perspective the play has the space to become a modern tragedy. Like Euripides in *Medea* or Shakespeare in *Macbeth*, Gambaro shows us human beings for whom the unthinkable solution of killing children, in this case massacring them, becomes a reality.

Persistence is a four-hander for three men and one woman: Zaida, her husband Enzo and her brother Boris, and 'Silent Man', a character who is always present but never speaks. Zaida and Enzo have lost a child in an bomb attack by the Russians. His body was found with an arm missing. The loss of their son under brutal circumstances fuels their zealous commitment to the cause of the Chechyan rebels in a bid to take not just an eye for an eye but children for children. Boris is Zaida's brother who is involved in the planning of the attack, albeit as a reluctant participant. Boris finds his sister dehumanised by her grief and seeks to revive her humanity. Enzo and Zaida's marriage seems devoid of love. Enzo's main concern is that he should father another child, a son, who can grow up to join their ranks as a freedom fighter. Enzo is hostile towards Boris and critical of his doubt and lack of commitment to the cause, suspecting him of wanting to desert. They return from the massacre at the school and Boris has lost his gun. He plans to leave before he is accused of desertion but before he does so, he and Zaida have a conversation in which he implores her to remember the son she lost, and to hold the little box of stones the child collected when he was alive. Zaida refuses, though they share some tender moments as they revisit the childhood of their memories. Boris resolves to leave as he cannot support fighters who are willing to kill children, or kill children himself. When he turns his back to take some water for his journey, Zaida plunges a knife in his back and murders him.

Persistence, though inspired by real events, does not attempt any kind of realism. It is a poetic play with the figure of the Silent Man who is defined by his slow physicality and wordless commentary on the action in the play. His cryptic presence and silent movements seem to give expression to the indigestible elements represented on stage. *Persistence* is a play which goes to the heart of human tragedy and explores how, when rage has had no reprieve, the terrorist imagination might inhabit each one of us.

Dear Ibsen, I Am Nora (2014)

One of the ways in which Gambaro invigorates her stagecraft is in dialogue with her theatrical antecedents: most notably with Sophocles (*Antigona Furiosa*, 1988), Chekhov (*Penas sin importancia*, 1990), and Shakespeare (*La Señora Macbeth*, 2002).

Her erudition is not intellectual pyrotechnics, however. Rather, her readings become internal furniture which are integrated into her craft. Perhaps it is from the far corner of Argentina that Gambaro is liberated to claim these cornerstones of European drama as her own, seeing them, as she does, sometimes with irreverence but always reading into their depths with a penetrating gaze.

Here Gambaro takes on Ibsen in her reimagining of *A Doll's House*. This play might be personal in tone, as one critic suggests in the title of his review 'Querido Ibsen: soy Griselda'; this is Gambaro herself in dialogue with Ibsen through her own creation of Nora. In the UK, *A Doll's House* continues to be made into new 'versions' on the English-speaking stage. Modern playwrights 'update' the play by using past translations from the Norwegian to create a new play which speaks to our times where elements of the 'original' are either suppressed or made more contemporary. In Gambaro's reimagining, events unfold very much as they do in Ibsen's play. The central scandal is that Nora has taken a loan unbeknown to her husband, and has forged her father's signature as her guarantor. All this is in order to pay for a trip abroad to cure her husband's illness. Nora's dilemma is how to tell the truth, and for her choices and actions to be understood in the circumstances they were made. Gambaro is perhaps more explicit in her way of addressing the aspects of the play which don't 'work' for her by conjuring an Ibsen of her imagination onstage with whom the character of Nora can negotiate her own fate, becoming author of her own identity. Nora comes to Torvald (and to her creator, Ibsen) as Elena comes to Mario in *Asking Too Much*: no longer willing to go along with false storylines and determined to be true to herself, and thus to those around her.

Nora's increasingly mobilised imagination is beginning to conceive of a different world where things do not need to go on as they have been, nor, indeed, as they are. Ibsen, however, seeks to keep her in her place:

Henrik   No, no. Now you will be docile, you will laugh a lot.

Nora   No.

Henrik   You will laugh so that they'll believe you're a sweet, enchanting creature . . . a little girlish.

Nora   That's not how I am!

Henrik   (*he puts a finger to his lips*)   Sshh!

Nora   You're the one who makes me laugh. Too much. Oh how happy I am all the time! Like a moron.

Henrik   Sshh!

Dear Ibsen, I Am Nora depicts the movements involved in the act of writing, the sense of characters in construction and the dramaturgical considerations made which go towards crafting a piece of theatre. As in Ibsen's play, the character of Nora's husband, Torvald, is shown by Gambaro as doubly limited in his understanding of his situation, and of his wife. Nora points this out to Ibsen at one point, and pulls him up on the discrepancy between the constant tweaking and adjustments she undergoes as a character, while Torvald is left wholly untouched, to which Ibsen responds, perhaps somewhat defeatist (or content with the status quo), that with some characters it simply isn't possible:

Nora   I have to silence myself, don't I? You never amend Torvald's plan.

Henrik   With some characters it's not possible. They need to suffer more blows.

Nora   And where will they come from? From whom? From me, correct? (**Henrik** *is silent.*) Why don't you answer me?

Henrik   I don't know yet.

This 'not yet knowing' feels true to the act of writing, that writers describe how, at its best, during the process, the story begins to tell itself, characters begin to write themselves and the work takes on a life of its own. Here the suggestion also seems to be that there is something akin to a collective consciousness, that the imagination is not only reserved for the *auteur*, Ibsen, but to us all. And yet Ibsen deludes himself that he is in control of Nora and of her character *development*.

Henrik   When I made you suffer, it was to make you realise. You could finally decide what you wanted, couldn't you? If I contrived painful circumstances, those circumstances led to you being a different woman.

Nora   I always was. Not so different either. Simply a woman like many who drowned obeying her father, her husband, some rules dictated by others. Remember? The restlessness.

Henrik   Without me, you wouldn't have spoken, Nora. Without me, you would not have known how to face adversity.

Nora   Do you really believe that? Before, long before you tried to speak for me, Mr Henrik, I was already writing myself. You just copied me in your own way. (*She is about to leave. She comes back.*) Thank you, thank you anyway. (*Embraces him lightly.*) Goodbye.

Henrik   Goodbye. (*After a moment he smiles.*) Good luck.

Curtain.

Ibsen's smile at the end is ambiguous. Perhaps he too is liberated by Nora's (Griselda's) boldness. This is a deeply affecting play about a woman finding her voice. It will speak to many women and their struggle to have agency and to be in command of their own destinies, despite the scripts which draw them, however insidiously, into false and unwanted roles. It resonates with the dissonance felt between the woman inside and the woman who must negotiate her life, resisting being authored by patriarchal societies.[7]

The Gift (2015)

Finally, this collection concludes with *The Gift*. This is Griselda Gambaro's most recent play to date and the work has an economy and charge which shows her at the height of

---

[7] Silvio Lang notes that the figure of the woman ventriloquist in Gambaro's theatre as a central and enduring theme: 'Gambaro assumes that historically women have been spoken by male voices. The woman-ventriloquist became an obsession of hers'. ['Gambaro assume que históricamente las mujeres han sido habladas por voces masculinas. La mujer-ventrílocuo se convirte en una obsesión de su dramaturgía.'] (Gambaro 2011: prologue).

her creative powers. It is spare, elemental and characteristically unforgiving in the impact it delivers.

In an unnamed seaside town, Márgara is a woman with the gift of prophecy. Like Cassandra, people do not believe her, even though what she predicts is the hope of the world. All we need to save ourselves, she presages, is for humanity to hear and understand that goodness brings profit. Márgara has come to live with her daughter, Sonia, and Sonia's husband Efraín, who is the owner of fishing boats which go out to sea. His men risk their lives from which he profits. Efraín is not happy about his mother-in-law coming to stay because of the cost of maintaining her and the irritations she causes. Renata, a neighbour, visits Márgara, having heard of her powers of prediction, and wanting a prophecy about her husband who is gravely ill. Márgara tells her, without compassion, that she foresees him under the ground. Renata is horrified and implies that she would have preferred to be lied to. Later Renata will say with candid simplicity that she wants to be the one who dies first: an all too human sentiment. When Renata leaves, incredulous at Márgara's unforgiving vision of her husband's future, Efraín is insensed that Márgara has forgone a potentially lucrative income stream of fortune telling. Sonia tries to placate and to pacify Efraín until, later, she herself is no longer able to withstand his tyrrany. As a result, Efraín throws her out along with her mother. He will not tolerate these green shoots of her potential liberation.

At the end of the play, the crowds which Márgara prophesised to (either real or imagined) are gone and mother and daughter are alone on the beach facing destitution. They trace back to the early communications between mother and child, both what Márgara remembers (or invents/imagines) of those between herself and her own mother and those between Márgara and Sonia; the simple and familiar notion of 'kiss it better' between mother and young child, who believes the mother to have the powers of healing with her kiss. Sonia asks who is left for them to turn to and it is a moment of great and unexpected comic relief when Márgara proposes, of all people, Renata. And yet it is an exquisite and poetic moment at the end of the play when Renata appears on stage after Sonia and Márgara have accepted the hopelessness of their situation, almost to show Márgara's suggestion of Renata being their saviour, which at first seemed ridiculous, as a final prophecy of humanity's capacity to be good.

> *Overwhelmed, she slides onto* **Márgara***'s lap, closes her eyes.* **Márgara** *strokes her head. After a moment, without them noticing,* **Renata** *reveals herself.* **Renata** *takes a few steps forward, stops and looks at them. Slowly she raises her arm, slowly she opens her hand towards them as the light dies out.*

Perhaps we can trace a movement through Gambaro's work, and in particular in this selection of plays, which is a transition towards emancipation: from object to subject, from puppet to agent. In the end, Sonia does leave Efraín where Ignacio could not cut the cord which kept him bound to Lorenzo.

It is of course Griselda Gambaro herself who possesses the gift; who is a remarkably *gifted* writer. Might she be looking back on her work in this latter stage of her career and asking what she has done with her gift? As Diana Taylor noted early on, Gambaro's power to observe the world around her and to predict the consequences of histories and events shows an imagination which is not only incisive but uncannily prophetic. Might she have experienced her powers of prophecy as harrowing at times? 'If I know what's coming, what power does my art have to prevent what I foresee?' If this is her question, *The Gift* will not offer up any simple answers. Then again, might Gambaro also be ironising this view of herself as omnipotent, all-knowing? Does she seek to distance her work from this grandiose view, and to remind us that her true gift is not in prophecy but in her commitment to paying attention?

Griselda Gambaro's theatre reacquaints us with painful feelings and thoughts, often the ones we repress because they are too much to bear. Nevertheless, the audience enters into a pact with the dramatist, willing to go through the experience, and to be marked by it, because we trust in the profound humanity which is at the heart of all her work. Gambaro's conviction is that the human imagination has the power to keep dreaming of and fighting for a better world. And then, of course, there is her irresistible black humour which ultimately resists analysis, and is perhaps her most powerful form of subversion, liberating us to think in ways we haven't thought before.

Bibliography

Boyle, Catherine (1990). 'Griselda Gambaro and the female dramatist: The audacious trespasser' in Susan Bassnett, ed., *Knives and Angels: Women Writers in Latin America*. London: Bloomsbury.
Gambaro, Griselda (2014). *El Teatro Vulnerable*. Buenos Aires: Alfaguara.
Garfield, Evelyn Picon (1985). *Women's Voices from Latin America*. Detroit, MI: Wayne State University Press.
Information for Foreigners: Three Plays by Griselda Gambaro, translated by Marguerite Feitlowitz, Northwestern University Press, 1991.
Kaiser-Lenoir, Claudia (1977). *El grotesco criollo estilo teatral de una época*. Havana: Casa de las Américas.
Pellettieri, Osvaldo (2008). *El sainete y el grotesco criollo: del autor al actor*. Buenos Aires: Galerna.
Pérez, Irene, ed. (1986). *El grotesco criollo: Discépolo-Cossa*. Buenos Aires: Colihue.
Lang, Silvio (2011). 'Prólogo' in Griselda Gambaro, *Obra Reunida*. Buenos Aires: Ediciones de la Flor.
Richardson, Ruth (1975). *Florencio Sánchez and the Argentine Theatre*. New York: Gordon Press.
Sarlo, Beatriz (1998). *La máquina cultural*. Buenos Aires: Ariel.
Taylor, Diana (1991). *Theatre of Crisis: Drama and Politics in Latin America*. Lexington, KY: University Press of Kentucky.
Viñas, David (1973). *Grotesco, inmigración y fracaso*. Buenos Aires: Corregidor.

Siamese Twins (1967)

The premiere of *Siamese Twins* was performed on 25 August 1967 in the Centre for Audiovisual Experimentation at the Torcuato Di Tella Institute in Buenos Aires, with the following cast:

Lorenzo	Jorge Petraglia
Ignacio	Roberto Villanueva
Smiley Man	Jorge Fiszon
Nasal Man	Carlos Marchi
Old Man	Alberto Busaid/Miguel Ángel Castro
Young Man	Enrique Arimán

Set Design and Costume: Juan Carlos Distéfano

Staging and Direction: Jorge Petraglia

Characters

Lorenzo
Ignacio
Smiley Man
Nasal Man
Old Man
Young Man

Act One

Scene One

Interior of a furnished room with a small pine table, a stool, three chairs, a rickety old wardrobe and two single beds with the mattresses showing, no sheets, just a couple of ordinary blankets at the foot of the beds. A bottle of water with two glasses on the table. In the corner, on the floor, an extremely tall pile of old newspapers. A door which opens onto the street. Some distance away from this door, but also looking onto the street, a high window, closed without curtains. Another door with a worn-out canvas drape leads to an inside courtyard.

When the curtain goes up, the stage appears empty for some moments. Then the blundering footsteps of **Lorenzo** *running can be heard.* **Lorenzo** *enters and immediately locks the door, as if someone was following him. With immense relief, he leans against the wall and starts shrieking with laughter. He has obviously escaped danger and he's celebrating. Being out of breath cuts his laughter short and, while it comes back spasmodically, little by little he stops laughing. A pause.*

Lorenzo (*breathing excitedly*)   I got away! I can run better alone . . . than . . . with someone. (*Pats himself on the back affectionately.*) What a race! (*Bending over he pats and slaps his calves.*) The muscles of a runner! Yes, indeed, the muscles of a runner, strong, robust. Why did I never devote my life to sport? My name in the papers. The great . . . great . . . great . . . (*He starts sliding down the door until he ends up sitting on the floor, exhausted.*) I could have gone on . . . running . . . until . . . until . . . (*Abruptly remembers something which he finds funny and bursts out laughing.*) Ignacio! Poor old Ignacio with his rubber legs! (*Without being able to stop, he laughs, wheezing with fatigue. He's only interrupted when someone moves the door handle and knocks at the door. The faltering and distressed voice of* **Ignacio** *can be heard.*)

Voice of Ignacio   Let me in, Lorenzo! Why have you locked me out? Let me in! (**Lorenzo** *listens with a certain air of polite consideration and does not answer.*) Let me in, he's getting closer! Don't be stupid! Open the door!

Lorenzo (*without moving*)   Coming! (*Softly, almost sorrowful.*) He's screwed.

Voice of Ignacio (*with growing urgency*)   Let me in right now! Why have you locked me out? Damn you! (*Desperate.*) He's coming straight for me! Open up!

Lorenzo (*in a soothing tone, but without actually moving*)   I'll let you in! Are you alone?

Voice of Ignacio   Let me in!

Lorenzo   Right away! But the thing is, I've caught my nail.

Voice of Ignacio   Why did you shut me out?

Lorenzo   Don't you believe me? It got caught on my . . . trouser leg. Fancy that!

Voice of Ignacio   Open the door!

Lorenzo   Are you alone?

Voice of Ignacio   He's come round the corner! (*Almost weeping with desperation.*) Please, let me in, please, let me in! (*Bangs the door and rattles the door handle.*)

Lorenzo (*annoyed*)   Don't break the door down! Are you alone? That's what I'm asking you (*He raises his voice. Meaning well.*) Do you hear me? Shall I pass you a little piece of paper under the door? (*He gets up, takes a piece of paper from the table drawer and writes something down, first standing, then he gets a chair and sits down. He writes slowly, with difficulty and with meticulous attention.* **Ignacio** *goes on banging the door.*)

Voice of Ignacio   Why won't you let me in? (*Desperate.*) I'll . . . I'll . . . I'll find you a girl. He's caught up with me! Don't be a cretin! Lorenzo! Lorenzo!

Lorenzo (*raises his eyes from the paper, sits up and leans on the table. Calmly he asks*)   Is he close? You hear me? I'm asking you if he's close! In case he jumps on top of me if I open the door. I don't want any surprises.

Is he near? You hear? (*He listens for a moment, but only* **Ignacio***'s desperate cries of 'Let me in! Let me in!' and his banging on the door can be heard.* **Lorenzo**, *contemptuous.*) No, you hear nothing. Your fear won't let you hear a thing. (*He sits down again.*) Better that I write this down as well. (*He spells out the words as he slowly writes them down.*) Dear Ignacio: I ask if he is close by . . . (*He lifts his head and scratches his chin uncertainly. Suddenly a shriek from* **Ignacio** *can be heard and the beating of a body which has been violently flung against the door.* **Lorenzo**, *absorbed in thought.*) Shall I put in the bit about fear or not? No, he's going to take offence. So many things to be tactful about! (*He cocks his head and listens. Serenely sorrowful.*) They're going to break the door down. (*Gets up and passes the little bit of paper under the door.*) Hang on, I'll pass you the pencil. (*He does.*) Answer me in writing! I want to know if you are alone! (*He listens with the same air of politeness to the punches and the beatings. The shrieks of* **Ignacio** *have turned into groans which diminish and then stop altogether.* **Lorenzo** *pins his ear to the door. Silence. He raps the door with his knuckles. Calls softly.*) Ignacio? (*A pause.*) Ignacio! (*A grunt in reply.*) Can't you speak? Are there people there? (*Silence.*) Did you get my note? (*He moves away, annoyed.*) He's gone quiet, he's gone quiet! How on earth are we going to understand each other? (*He gets closer to the door again, low voice.*) Are you alone? Has he gone? (*An affirmative grunt in reply.* **Lorenzo**, *almost sadly.*) Why didn't you go to the other side? Closed doors are closed doors. (*A chuckle.*) Open doors are open doors, from the start. You can see it in children. Me, ever since I was a boy, I gave away toys, I wanted to make myself kind. (*Suddenly discovering it for himself, happy.*) You don't see it in children, I'm nothing like the boy that I was, I don't give anything, I close doors. (*Laughs.*) I was a patricidal boy. And you, Ignacio? We were born together and I don't remember how you were before. (*A silence.*) Can't you answer with something, a line? It's boring to talk alone. (*He bends down and spies through the keyhole.*) What's that there? Your head? Everything looks black; what is it? Stand back a bit. Shall I write to him? (*Hesitates.*) No, it's useless. He's practically illiterate. (*He looks again and laughs.*) You're on the floor! (*He sees something which strikes him and stops laughing. He turns, leaning against the door and closes his eyes. With distressed amazement.*) Oh! What a state he's left you in! What a shame! Ignacio! Ignacio! Do you hear me? Did you pass out? (*He clutches his side with both hands as if an intense pain is suddenly attacking him.*) Ow! (*He drops to his knees and drags himself to the table, takes some pills out of a box and swallows some with a glass of water. He goes back to the door on his hands and knees. Pained.*) Ignacio, get up, I need you. (*He remains leaning against the door, rocking himself with cries of pain.*)

Voice of Ignacio (*distant and weak*)   Lorenzo . . .

Lorenzo (*alert*) Yes!

Voice of Ignacio   Open the door.

Lorenzo (*hesitates, bites his lips*)   Has he gone?

Voice of Ignacio   Yes. He's gone.

Lorenzo (*mistrustful*)   Are you sure? What if he comes back?

Voice of Ignacio (*weakened*)   No. (*A pause.*) No. He's not going to come back.

Lorenzo   How do you know? He'll beat the two of us. If he sees me, he'll remember that we were together and he'll start punching again.

Voice of Ignacio   No.

Lorenzo   And he won't just hit me. One punch for me, another for you. You'll get another share. And what for? You won't be able to take it. Have patience, eh? Sleep. Why don't you sleep a little? The blows will heal themselves while you sleep. Get some rest.

Voice of Ignacio   Give me water.

Lorenzo (*wilful*)   Yes, yes I'll give you water. Why not! As much as you want. (*He gets up agilely, without showing any sign of pain now, and he fills a glass of water. He walks purposefully towards the door, sees it's closed and, unperturbed, he bends over and tips the water underneath the door. He sweeps it with a broom. Affectionate.*) Can you do it? (*He looks through the keyhole.*) Slowly . . . Slowly . . . Don't choke. What's that you're spitting out? (*Offended.*) My water? (*He looks. He laughs, amused.*) A tooth! The one right in the middle! Your beauty . . . (*Laughs.*) Where did it go? Now you can work in a circus! (*He interrupts himself. Sincere.*) I'm sorry. I didn't mean to hurt you.

Voice of Ignacio (*lifeless*)   Lorenzo. Lo . . . ren . . . zo.

Lorenzo (*sorrowful*)   Don't call for me. What's wrong? I can't open the door. If he comes back, he'll beat the both of us. He's a strong guy, a real brute. He won't make distinctions. He won't say: I've already hit this guy so now I'll leave him in peace, poor thing. I'll set to work on this one (*Pointing to himself.*), on me. He won't say that. He'll beat you again, poor Ignacio. On the other hand, if he sees you on the floor, all bloody with a missing tooth . . . The man's an animal, but no one beats a guy who's already down. I suppose . . . and if you were a corpse, you'd be even safer still.

Voice of Ignacio Lorenzo . . .

Lorenzo (*very irritated*) Lorenzo, Lorenzo! I'm not opening the door! Leave me in peace!

Voice of Ignacio Everything hurts . . . my body . . .

Lorenzo (*compassionate*) Do you want more water? You know what I'm going to do? I'm going to lie down here, on the floor. Are you in agreement with that? I don't want you to feel alone, Ignacio. Does that help you at all, does it comfort you? (*He lies down along the length of the door. He yawns.*) I'm so sleepy! (**Ignacio** *scratches the door. Annoyed.*) Why are you scratching? It's impossible to close my eyes if you're making noise. (*The noise stops. He yawns.*) I'm tired, after the running . . . Aren't you? (*A pause.*) Would you answer me! (*He gets up and spies through the keyhole. Resentful.*) He's gone to sleep. He can sleep like a log. (*He lies down and crosses his arms behind his head.*) How uncomfortable! (*He props himself up on his elbow and looks anxiously at the beds. He gets up and grabs a pillow.*) I'll sleep on the floor, I promised him I would. But my head's got nothing to do with my promises. Anyway, the head is the most delicate part of the body. It's not a question of taking a physical risk. (*Knocks on the door with his knuckles.*) Ignacio, do you agree? (*A silence.*) Thanks, I knew you'd understand. (*Lies down.*) Yes, I'm more comfortable. (*Crosses his legs and waves one in the air. He asks himself, capriciously.*) Was it my fault, was it his fault, who threw the stone? (*Sings softly.*) Who puts the bell on the collar of the cat? (*Sincere.*) I suspect that . . . it was me who threw the stone. But who is capable of differentiating between the two of us? I can't. We're the same. This is our misfortune. We are so much the same that our actions get confused. (*Amused.*) In a nutshell: the hand which threw the stone could have been anyone's. Poor Ignacio! What a beating! (*He gets up and looks through the keyhole. Spiteful.*) Look how he sleeps! He's snoring. He's all soiled with blood. How can he sleep like that? How filthy! He's not dead, is he? (*Spies for a moment in silence. Hisses.*) Ignacio! Ignacio! (*A pause.*) No. He's breathing (*Laughs shakily.*) He wouldn't have been missed much. But I'm still not cured, I need him. He leaves quite a lot to be desired as a nurse. He's so negligent with my pills! (*Takes another look through the keyhole.*) Poor thing! His face has changed. Now no one will get us confused. (*Lies down.*) How uncomfortable this is! I'm not used to it, my bones hurt. He's snoring. And I can't sleep. It's unfair. (*A pause.*) My bones are hurting so much, I've got no time for repentance. And even so, I still have to repent. (*He looks at the bed. He gets up and throws the mattress off. He drags it to the door. He's going to lie down, looks at the mattress on* **Ignacio**'*s bed, takes that as well and climbs on top of them both with evident satisfaction. He lies down.*) Now that's more like it. (*He bounces.*) So comfortable! I can think. Now I'm repentant again. I have to do something to make it up to him for the beating. Is it enough to sleep on the floor? Yes, yes, enough is enough. (*He holds onto his knees with his hands and waves his legs in the air as if he was running. Amused.*) Running along with his rubber legs! (*He yawns. Grabs a corner of one of the blankets and pulls it towards him. He covers himself. Sings softly.*) Pa-pa-pa-pa! (*Without conviction.*) Poor Ignacio . . . ! If I had my girl on the mattress . . . (*Slavers lustfully.*)

Voice of Ignacio (*distant and weak*) Lorenzo . . . Lo . . . ren . . . zo . . . (*He scrapes the door.* **Lorenzo** *turns over and burrows further under the blanket. He laughs between dreams. Only the sound of the scratching of the door can be heard until it stops completely.*)

Scene Two

The same room, the following morning. The mattresses have disappeared. **Lorenzo** *appears with his ear against the door. He's freshly groomed and is wearing a coat. He listens. Silence.*

Lorenzo Ignacio! Ignacio! How are you? What? I can't hear you! Speak up. Ignacio, I want to come out. (*A silence.*) Stop holding the door, please.

Voice of Ignacio Let me in.

Lorenzo Again? Why don't you get out of the way? I have to come out.

Voice of Ignacio Let me in!

Lorenzo (*annoyed*) I said no! Go away. I don't know you.

Voice of Ignacio Alright: you don't know me. I don't know you. But let me in!

Lorenzo How can I open the door if I don't know you? (*Laughs.*) That's very risky, darling. Are you selling something? (*Furious and unintelligible whispering from* **Ignacio**. **Lorenzo** *understands because he exclaims, offended.*) What? No, I don't need it! Let me come out!

Voice of Ignacio And let me come in! Open the door!

Lorenzo (*changing his tone of voice*) Did the rain do you good last night? It must have refreshed your face. (*He spies through the keyhole.*) I can't see a thing. (*Laughs.*) That's better. You've got your shirt undone and I can see your bellybutton. They tied the knot badly. (*Extremely violent blows on the door. He steps back.*) Hey! Calm down. I should be the impatient one. I've been wanting to come out for three hours. Three hours! Why don't you go away? Walk round the corner and hop on a bus. That way we won't see each other. You have to be able to take a break from people. Sleep rough for a few days. Nothing will happen to you. You'll make yourself into more of a man. (*Giggles.*) You could do with that! (*Spies through the keyhole again.*) Ignacio? (*Silence.*) Ignacio! (*With utmost caution, half opens the door, but* **Ignacio**, *who has been keeping hidden, jams his foot in the door and pushes it so violently that* **Lorenzo** *ends up on the floor. Offended.*) What good manners you have! (**Ignacio** *enters. He doesn't look anything like* **Lorenzo**. *His middle tooth is missing and his face is bruised black and blue. He dabs his mouth with a blood soaked handkerchief and leaves it on the table.* **Lorenzo** *quickly gets up. Disgusted.*) Don't be disgusting! (*Flings the handkerchief to the floor; with the same expression of disgust, he kicks it into a corner.* **Ignacio** *plonks himself down on a chair, looks at the beds with the intention of lying down.*)

Ignacio   Where are the mattresses?

Lorenzo   Outside, on the patio.

Ignacio (*very tired*)   Bring them in.

Lorenzo   No. I just carried them out there.

Ignacio   I want to go to bed.

Lorenzo   Sleep at night. They need to be aired out. If not, they're a breeding ground for bedbugs. I don't want filth in the room.

Ignacio   Why didn't you open the door?

Lorenzo (*making time to think*)   Why didn't I open the door to you? (*Brief silence.*) I explained that to you in writing. You didn't answer me. (*Turns towards the door, opens it, looks for something on the ground; comes back with a torn and scrunched up piece of paper.*) You got it completely soaked with the water. You can't read a word. Why did I bother?

Ignacio (*exhausted*)   Bring in the mattresses.

Lorenzo (*shaking his head*)   They're being aired out. (**Ignacio** *gets to his feet.*) And don't you go to get them either. I tied them up with wire. I don't want bedbugs. (**Ignacio** *turns towards one of the beds and lies down on top of the elastic mesh.* **Lorenzo** *looks at him, takes off his jacket, hangs it on the back of a chair and lies down next to* **Ignacio**.)

Ignacio (*upset*)   What are you doing? Don't you have your own bed?

Lorenzo   I like to have company. It's horrible sleeping on the floor, like a dog. Sleeping no, suffering insomnia.

Ignacio   You should have opened the door, you cretin! Push off back to your own bed! (**Lorenzo** *snores gently.*) Lorenzo, are you sleeping? (*Carefully, he starts to push him to the edge of the bed. But* **Lorenzo** *isn't sleeping. When he's just about to fall off the bed, he grabs* **Ignacio**'s *hand and sends him flying to the floor.*)

Lorenzo   Did you want to throw me off?

Ignacio   No.

Lorenzo   What did you say? Have you got a spud in your mouth? I can't understand a thing.

Ignacio   Can't you see that he kicked me in the teeth?

Lorenzo   No, I didn't see that. How could I from this side of the door. (*Sits down on the bed.*) I had a bad night. I slept on the floor. You knew that, didn't you?

Ignacio   Yes.

Lorenzo   I'm not used to it. I heard you snoring.

Ignacio (*apologetically*)   I sleep easily.

Lorenzo   I don't. Help me to do the exercise.

Ignacio   Now? I don't feel like it, Lorenzo.

Lorenzo   Well, I do. They beat you, but you snored. Smile.

(**Ignacio** *looks at him, seriously.* **Lorenzo***, with a sincere, moving wish to see him smile.*) Smile. (**Ignacio** *smiles. His smile is laboured and ungenuine, a little ridiculous due to the absence of the tooth.* **Lorenzo** *can't help making the most out of it.*) You smiled: you're in agreement. (*The two begin to walk around the room. They stick to each other, side to side, stepping in unison.*)

Ignacio   Lorenzo . . .

Lorenzo   What?

Ignacio   I would like to, I would like to . . . cut the cord.

Lorenzo   What cord?

Ignacio   Why don't you leave?

Lorenzo (*he looks at him, still walking, and laughs*)   Now that's a great idea! What's brought that on?

Ignacio   Find yourself another friend. A miserable wretch.

Lorenzo (*obliging*)   Are you a miserable wretch?

Ignacio   You take advantage.

Lorenzo   Me? Of whom? Ignacio, Ignacio don't be unfair. You torment me. Where am I supposed to go? Or rather, not where am I to go, but how?

Ignacio   How? You can go to a hotel.

Lorenzo (*laughing*)   I'm not a millionaire!

Ignacio   To a guest house. You could live . . . in a guest house, couldn't you?

Lorenzo   Yes, yes, I could. But don't you understand? How can I? What shall I do with you? Will you come with me?

Ignacio   No. I'll stay here. It's my house. The home of my parents.

Lorenzo   Your parents were my parents.

Ignacio   No. My parents were *mine* and not yours.

Lorenzo   They were ashamed of me. Everybody is ashamed of me. Even my parents.

Ignacio   What did you say?

Lorenzo   Anyway, we won't be able to separate ourselves. We're stuck together, we eat together, we breathe together. You see? We walk and we walk, and we're stuck.

Ignacio I think we can. We can separate ourselves. (*He stands.*)

Lorenzo (*aggressive*) Keep on walking around! I need at least one hundred laps daily to be able to start my day well. If not, it's a waste of time.

Ignacio (*faltering*) I'm not doing any more.

Lorenzo (*he digs him in the ribs. Hard*) Get up! Stand up straight! (*They walk in silence for a few seconds. Then* **Lorenzo** *bursts out laughing.*) The way you ran yesterday! What a pair of legs! Show me them.

Ignacio Why should I?

Lorenzo Pull your trousers down. (**Ignacio** *takes down his trousers.* **Lorenzo** *looks at his legs and bursts out laughing.*) Didn't I tell you? (He pinches him hard. **Ignacio** *cries out.*) Rubber, rubber foam. How can you run with these legs? All bandy. (*Mortified,* **Ignacio** *pulls up his trousers.* **Lorenzo** *sits down and commands like a lord.*) Pass me the newspaper.

Ignacio How comfortable you are!

Lorenzo I was brought up this way. I've explained to you a thousand times. I'm not comfortable out of choice.

Ignacio (*he goes towards the mountain of old newspapers and selects one at random*) There you go. (*He gives it to him and lies down on the bed.*)

Lorenzo (*he settles down to read, making himself comfortable on the chair. He bursts out, distressed*) Christ! Kennedy's been killed! (**Ignacio** *doesn't hear him.* **Lorenzo** *gets up and shakes him frenetically, dumbstruck.*) Did you hear? Kennedy's been killed!

Ignacio (*calm*) A while ago.

Lorenzo Yesterday! It says here yesterday!

Ignacio It's an old paper.

Lorenzo Damn you! Here it says yesterday. Why did you give me this newspaper? You did it on purpose! (*He sits down and rests his head on the table.*)

Ignacio (*looks at him, gets up slowly. Leans towards* **Lorenzo** *and tries to console him*) Why should it matter to you? It happened a long time ago.

Lorenzo (*lifts his head, dumbstruck*) But . . . but, my dear brother, if this can happen to Kennedy, what wouldn't they do to us? He had bodyguards. I don't have anything! I have nothing!

Ignacio Why would you have a bodyguard? What for?

Lorenzo To look after me! This grew up but I'm still the same, alone, without protection. Look at my skin, Ignacio. It doesn't protect me, you scratch me and I bleed.

Ignacio Don't be afraid. (*Almost remorsefully.*) I'm . . . I'm here.

Lorenzo (*with eyes lowered*)   Give me my pills. (**Ignacio** *goes towards the drawer on the table, takes the pills and administers them to* **Lorenzo** *as any normal pills are administered.* **Lorenzo***, furious.*) Not like this! You take them with water!

Ignacio   They're mints!

Lorenzo   It doesn't matter! They do me good, that's why I take them. (**Ignacio** *gently removes the newspaper which he has resting on his knees without* **Lorenzo** *seeming to notice and replaces it with another. He brings water and* **Lorenzo** *takes the pills.*) Stay here.

Ignacio   I'm going to get a chair.

Lorenzo (*grabbing him by his clothes*)   No! Stay here. (**Ignacio** *squats down next to* **Lorenzo***'s chair.* **Lorenzo** *takes the newspaper again and opens it up. He reads and smiles.*) Ignacio! Here it doesn't say anything about Kennedy. Doesn't even mention him.

Ignacio   Good.

Lorenzo   Did it happen a long time ago?

Ignacio (*dozing off*)   What?

Lorenzo   About Kennedy.

Ignacio   Yes, you were very little. (*A pause.*) Just a few months old.

Lorenzo   Were we stuck together then? (*Before* **Ignacio** *can answer.*) Of course. We were nearer to our birth. And this, being stuck together, is from our birth. (**Ignacio***, who little by little has been getting more and more slumped so that he is nearly sitting on the floor, snorts with annoyance.* **Lorenzo** *notices both things and kicks him in the shins.*) If you go any lower, you'll pull me down with you. Do you think I'm made of iron? (*Thoughtful.*) The operation was a failure.

Ignacio (*to shut him up*)   Yes, yes. (*Abruptly.*) I have never set foot in a hospital.

Lorenzo (*aggressive*)   Well, I have!

Ignacio (*hypocritical*)   Okay then. These kinds of operations are always a failure.

Lorenzo (*happy*)   You should know! (*A pause.*) But we are disentangled, separate. What happens in these operations is that it's not possible to save both, one is left ruined. For one to be left in perfect condition, the other has to be ruined. That's just the way it is. What did we have in common? What are you missing? (*Tries to touch him.*)

Ignacio (*pushing his hands away*)   Nothing!

Lorenzo   You must be lacking something! I'm complete. One of the two will die young. And I know who that will be! (*Gives a meaningful look to* **Ignacio** *and laughs smugly. Someone knocks at the door.* **Lorenzo** *stops laughing. Suspiciously:*) Are you expecting anyone?

Ignacio No.

Lorenzo (*idem*) You haven't invited a girl over? It wouldn't be the first time.

Ignacio (*surprised*) Me?

Lorenzo Yes.

Ignacio When? I always try to make sure that you don't realise, that you're far away.

Lorenzo (*laughs*) Do you take me for a fool? I hide behind the curtain. I've done that many times. I see everything. I listen. Listening is worse than seeing. It's something repulsive.

Ignacio (*furious*) I'm delighted! (*Gets up, agitated.*) You were here, you saw everything? You degenerate!

Lorenzo (*almost humbly*) No, I'm not a degenerate. I needed to know. It's not possible that I always get it wrong.

Ignacio Why did you hide? Looking at other people won't make you any better.

Lorenzo (*peacefully*) Goodness knows! I didn't hide for the sake of it: you might have got inhibited. All the same, I didn't learn a thing.

Ignacio I'm glad! You pervert!

Lorenzo Why? Are you bitter? (*Thoughtful.*) Yes, yes everything you do is completely elementary. But if you had known that I was spying on you, you would have made more of an effort, wouldn't you? (*Laughs.*) I'll warn you. Ah ha! I didn't know that you had those particular preferences!

Ignacio I will not allow you to do this! (*Choking with indignation.*) That . . . that I have . . .! (*Once again, someone knocks on the door, but as if beating out the rhythm of a song.*)

Lorenzo They're a patient lot, eh?

Harsh Voice Would you mind opening the door?

Lorenzo (*to the door*) Who is it? (*Loud nasal sounds.*) A dog. (*Abruptly.*) They've come looking for you for throwing the stone.

Ignacio (*surprised*) For me?

Lorenzo Give me a coin!

Ignacio What for?

Lorenzo Give me a coin, I said! Quick! I've got an idea!

Ignacio *digs in his pockets and gives him a coin.* **Lorenzo** *holds it in his hand while he takes out a sponge for wetting stamps, some stamps and a receipt book of telegrams from the drawer on the table. He tears out a form and writes something quickly, hiding it from* **Ignacio**'s *sight. Searches among the stamps, chooses one, stamps the form and folds it. His gestures are rapid and precise.*

Ignacio Where did you get that stamp? Did you steal it?

Lorenzo (*aggressive*) What does it matter to you? Prevention is better that cure. (*Keeps everything, except the telegram, inside the drawer.*) If they're looking for you for the stoning, I don't know you. Just to warn you so you don't get offended. Open the door. (**Ignacio** *goes towards the door and opens it. Out of the emptiness, two police officers appear:* **Smiley Man** *and* **Nasal Man**. *They are dressed in plain clothes.* **Smiley Man**, *despite his outbursts of anger or annoyance, speaks always with a wide and open toothy grin.* **Nasal Man** *has a very white face and a dozy expression; he only speaks occasionally but when he does, he opens his mouth wide, exaggeratedly pronouncing the syllables, and everything is said through his nose.*)

Smiley Man Good afternoon. May we come in?

Ignacio (*turning to* **Lorenzo**) It's for you.

Lorenzo For me? Are you sure, sir?

Ignacio Why are you calling me sir?

The two policemen come into the room. **Nasal Man** *goes straight to a chair and plonks himself down on it, murmuring something unintelligible.*

Nasal Man (*mouthing a great deal, but without emitting any sound*) You could have had an armchair!

Lorenzo (*terrified*) What did he say?

Nasal Man *as before.*

Lorenzo (*idem*) What? What did he say?

Smiley Man (*annoyed*) You could have had an armchair! That's what he said!

Lorenzo (*smiling subserviently*) We didn't think about it. It didn't occur to us to buy an armchair. Sometimes, one lets oneself go and doesn't even think about buying the most essential thing. If we had known . . . that the gentleman . . . wanted . . . an armchair . . . We would have . . . an armchair . . . (*Smiles unendingly until the smile freezes his face. A painful silence.*)

Nasal Man Who is the owner of the house?

Ignacio (*while* **Lorenzo**, *anxious, draws nearer to him*) What is it he's saying? Why doesn't he write it down?

Smiley Man (*annoyed*) What would he write? Are you trying to tell me he's mute? (*Abruptly.*) Are you . . . are you both deaf?

Lorenzo (*pulls away from* **Ignacio** *believing he can interpret* **Smiley Man**'s *question. He signals to* **Ignacio**, *garrulous*) This gentleman threw the stone, if that's what you wanted to know. Yes, for fun. There was a boy in the street and he threw a stone at him. Purely to amuse himself. (**Ignacio** *looks at him stupefied.* **Lorenzo**, *with less and less conviction, trying to make a joke out of it.*) But then he was hit on the head with a stone. So, a stone for a stone . . . and . . . a stoning . . . for a . . . ston . . . ing.

Ignacio   Are you nuts? Why are you laying the blame on me?

Lorenzo   Are you trying to tell me you're not covered in bruises? They must have beaten you up for a reason.

Nasal Man   Who is the owner of the house?

Lorenzo (*desperate*)   What?

Nasal Man (*exasperated*)   The landlord, who is it?

Lorenzo and Ignacio (*with different levels of desperation*)   What did he say?

Nasal Man, *signalling to* **Lorenzo** *to come closer, says something quickly through his nose.*

Lorenzo (*wringing his hands in desperation*)   I don't understand. I don't understand! (*Passionately, pointing towards* **Ignacio**.) It wasn't me. The bad guy . . . is him. What a mean person! To hit a child with a stone! He split his head open!

Ignacio   What?

Smiley Man (*with annoyance, while* **Lorenzo** *smiles relieved*)   Get lost! Who asked you? Neither of the two understands what he's saying. What language does he speak? Chinese?

Lorenzo (*starts scratching himself as if he has fleas. He doesn't understand a word. Suddenly, his face lights up. He draws near to* **Smiley Man** *in a complicit and affable way*)

Lorenzo   Listen, the gentleman is deaf. (*Points to* **Ignacio**.) Completely deaf. You were right, sir. He's as deaf as a ditch.

Ignacio (*automatically correcting him*)   As a doorpost.

Lorenzo   You see? He says it himself. He's as deaf as a doorpost. And on top of that, he's got selective hearing.

Smiley Man (*laughs*)   I had thought that one of the two of you seemed hard of hearing. Selective hearing, eh? I hate duplicity. (*Raises his voice as if talking to deaf people and looks at* **Ignacio** *suspiciously*.) The owner of the house, who is it?

Lorenzo (*quickly*)   Not me. The property's in his name. I only came round to deliver this telegram.

Nasal Man, *having drifted off on the chair, lifts his head and murmurs something, the 'g' of the telegram, a 'ggggg' sound rolling around the back of his throat.*

Lorenzo (*picks up the telegram on the table*)   Ok then. It's crystal clear what it says! Here's the telegram. The postage stamp is intact. It hasn't been opened yet. He's not terribly interested in his affairs, it has to be said. Or he pretends not to be. Would you like to read it, gentlemen?

Ignacio (*laughs good-humouredly and condescendingly*)   Lorenzo, how are they going to buy that story? (**Smiley Man** *opens the telegram, reads it and, excited, tries to rouse* **Nasal Man** *who has dropped off to sleep again.*)

Lorenzo (*moves away from* **Ignacio** *and laughs in a fake way*)   Don't play the innocent, Ignacio. (*Corrects himself.*) Don't play the innocent, sir. (*To the policemen.*) Gentlemen, have you read the telegram? Doesn't it say so? 'Congratulations on the strike, Ignacio.' Signed: 'the boss'.

Smiley Man (*amazed*)   Yes. Exactly! You guessed. How did you do it?

Lorenzo (*modest*)   I can read through the paper.

Smiley Man (*idem*)   Marvellous!

Ignacio (*to* **Lorenzo**)   Shut up. What are you talking about? Do you think they're foolish enough to buy that?

Lorenzo (*dryly*)   Don't bring me into it. You're the fool.

Angry, **Ignacio** *opens the drawer and tips out everything: stamp sponge, stamps, forms, on top of the table. Triumphant, he observes the policemen. They all, including* **Lorenzo**, *look without taking any notice. They look as if they had seen nothing.*

Smiley Man (*shaking the telegram*)   Who is the boss?

Ignacio   Who? He's made it up. Look at this. (*He pushes the props towards the policemen, but they look on indifferently. A minute of waiting. He pushes the props towards the policemen again, looking at them, until they fall on the floor.*)

Smiley Man (*kicks the props under the table. To* **Lorenzo**)   Who is the boss? (*Pointing to* **Ignacio**.) This guy's not going to spill the beans.

Lorenzo   I don't know. I only brought the telegram. It must be his boss, the brain behind it all.

Yawning, **Nasal Man** *wakes up, and directs a question to* **Lorenzo**, *who doesn't understand. Scared, he backs towards* **Ignacio** *and, without turning around, he reaches his hand out behind him and gropes around in search of him.* **Nasal Man** *repeats the question, speaking through his nose hysterically, frenetically.*

Lorenzo (*comes closer to* **Ignacio**, *voice dropped*)   Ignacio, darling, what did he say? He asked me something. I don't understand a thing. Why doesn't he speak more clearly? What's he saying?

Ignacio (*pulls away from him*)   I don't know. You're frightened. I should smash your face.

Lorenzo (*amazed*)   Mine?

Nasal Man *speaks loudly and hysterically through his nose.* **Lorenzo** *clings tighter to* **Ignacio**, *his lips trembling.*

Smiley Man (*advances towards them, his face flushed, hysterical*)   I urge you to listen! (**Lorenzo** *clings further still to* **Ignacio** *and buries his face in his shoulder.* **Smiley Man** *reaches them, looks at them and gives* **Ignacio** *an extremely violent slap.*) Shake your head!

Lorenzo *pulls away, touching himself. He plonks himself down on a chair. He laughs convulsively and sincerely with relief.*

Lorenzo Oh, now I understand! What a good idea! Like when you get water in your ears. A good shake and they get unblocked. Shake your head, Ignacio! (*The policemen start laughing with him, calm, good-natured.* **Lorenzo**, *to* **Smiley Man**:) The gentleman had asked . . .?

Smiley Man . . . Who are you, sir?

Lorenzo (*at ease*) Come on, what have I got to do with it. Nothing at all, sir, nothing. I'm the post office's messenger. This gentleman Ignacio held me up with his conversation. I couldn't extract myself from it. I trust I can free myself now, thanks to you both.

Ignacio (*exploding with indignation*) Cut the cord! Cut the cord, Lorenzo!

Smiley Man (*with suspicion*) What cord?

Lorenzo Now you see. He is full of mysteries. Beware. That's how I was when he was talking to me. Beware, I said to myself. Why would a guy talk to a post-office messenger about his girlfriend? What for? Does he want me to steal her? Speaking of stealing, the girlfriend shoplifts. He gave me a tip. It can't be said that he's magnanimous . . . (*Keeping his fist closed, he draws near to the policemen. They put their heads together and wait until he opens his hand and shows them the coin. Then they nod and observe admiringly.*)

Ignacio (*indignant*) You asked me for a coin, Lorenzo!

Lorenzo Because if I didn't I would've still been waiting for it.

Smiley Man (*takes out a handkerchief and picks up the coin with meticulous caution. Pointing to* **Ignacio**) There we have it. It must have his fingerprints. (*Puts the handkerchief in his pocket.*)

Lorenzo Can I go? I have other telegrams to deliver. (*With rapid movements, he takes out new props from the drawer, writes two telegrams, closes and seals them.*)

Ignacio Don't you see! He's writing them himself.

Lorenzo (*dignified*) Someone's got to. I'm going.

Ignacio What a complete mess you've created. How are you going to leave? We're stuck together.

Lorenzo (*acrimoniously*) What a cheek! Where? (*Sweeps the air at his side with an open hand.*) When it suits you. I'm free. Take it easy. (*Begins to walk towards the exit, but* **Ignacio** *is stuck to him. Furious.*) Why did you take it out on me?

Ignacio You didn't want to leave because we were stuck together!

Lorenzo (*digs him in the ribs*) Leave me in peace, idiot! (*Observes the policemen who are looking at him, intrigued. Through gritted teeth.*) Stay in your place! Don't follow me!

Smiley Man Wait. (*A pause.*) Have you known him long?

Lorenzo (*pushing* **Ignacio** *furiously to one side, but keeping up appearances on the other, while speaking to the policemen*) Him? I know him from the area, from delivering telegrams. They're all the same style.

Smiley Man (*very pleasant*)   Sit down for a few minutes, then. (**Lorenzo** *returns to the middle of the room and sits down.* **Ignacio** *continues to be stuck to him and squats down next to him.* **Smiley Man**, *intrigued:*) What's going on?

Lorenzo (*forced smile*)   Nothing. Obsessions.

Smiley Man (*takes out his handkerchief and blows his nose. He watches the coin roll away with indifference. Then his takes out a bundle of cigarettes and offers one to* **Lorenzo**. *Affable*)   Help yourself. Tell us, my dear man, everything he chatted about. When they let their tongue go, they're lost. Vanity is their downfall. I speak from experience.

Lorenzo (*smokes badly, thinks, doesn't know what to invent*)   He talked . . . nineteen to the dozen. (*He looks at his elbows and smiles, distracted. Looks at* **Ignacio** *and punches him again.*) Pest!

Smiley Man   Who is the boss. Did you find out?

Lorenzo (*his face lights up*)   Yes, yes. I did find out. He chatted a lot. The boss is him. He robbed a bank. They've done loads of jobs. Let me see. (*Gets up, kicking* **Ignacio** *who follows him, docile, obstinately, and begins to turn the pile of old newspapers upside down. He pulls some out flinging them into the air. He finds the newspaper that he's looking for and spreads it open to the side of* **Smiley Man**, *continually slapping* **Ignacio** *away.*) Read. It proves he committed this robbery. Four million. (*Admiringly to* **Ignacio**, *as if he sincerely believed it*.) You robbed four million?

Ignacio (*incredulous, in pain*)   They're not such imbeciles as to believe you! You're getting yourself mixed up in things!

Lorenzo (*fiercely happy*) No! And get away from me!

Ignacio   I can't . . . I want to feel near to somebody . . .

Lorenzo   So go to bed with your grandmother!

Ignacio   No, no . . . Lorenzo, I'm scared.

Lorenzo   You should have behaved honestly! Have you read the newspaper, sir?

Smiley Man (*has opened the newspaper, leafs through it. Comments laughing*)   Look at those curves! (*He reluctantly turns away from photo and wakes* **Nasal Man**.) Fat catch! (**Nasal Man** *throws a disinterested glance, smiles peacefully and dozes off again.* **Smiley Man**, *raising four fingers.*) Here it says: four assailants.

Lorenzo (*without batting an eyelid*)   Yes, alibis. Quadruple splitting of the personality. He's an expert at that. He's skilful. (*Tries to move away from* **Ignacio** *by kicking him, but* **Ignacio** *clings to him tenaciously.* **Lorenzo** *furious.*) Leave me in peace! (*Walks towards the door, but* **Ignacio** *follows him. Mutters.*) What a lack of tact! How inappropriate! Stay in your place. What kind of obsession is this sticking yourself to me? Leech! (*Smiles a toothy grin outwardly towards the policemen, while ferociously shoving* **Ignacio**.) Don't be a miserguts! Wretch!

Ignacio (*in a quiet voice*)   Please, Lorenzo. Make it clear that it's all lies. They could believe them. You never know. Set them straight.

Lorenzo   I'm not setting anything straight! I want to live in peace. Set me free!

Ignacio (*trapping* **Lorenzo** *and turning him towards the policemen. Feverish, while* **Lorenzo** *attempts to free himself*)   I will explain everything. Lorenzo had the idea of throwing stones at a can. And then he saw a little boy and he threw a stone at his head. He almost missed cutting his head open. He didn't do it maliciously. He didn't . . . mean to. That's . . . the way he is. (**Lorenzo** *kicks him.* **Ignacio** *furious*.) He did it on purpose! And then he closed the door on me . . . and a man who saw us together . . . smashed my face in. He smashed *my* face in! (*To* **Lorenzo**.) There we go! I've told them everything! Why can't you keep your lies to yourself? Impotent devil! You ruin everything because you can't think about anything else!

Lorenzo (*angry*)   What do you mean I don't think about anything else? I've got loads of women! Scum! Who did they beat the crap out of? Innocent people get left in peace! Look at your face! It looks like a squashed tomato.

Smiley Man (*gets up and puts his hand on* **Lorenzo**'s *shoulder. Soothing.*)   Don't worry. They always try to pass on the blame. (*Pointing to the newspaper and the telegram.*) Luckily, we have the evidence.

Lorenzo (*smiles*)   Thank you, sir. I'm glad that you are witnesses of this scene: an honourable man is never as violent as this. He's worse than a dog. (*To* **Ignacio**, *shouting.*) Why don't you leave me in peace!

Ignacio (*frightened*)   No, no.

Lorenzo (*still trapped, twists his neck towards* **Smiley Man**. *Worldly.*)   Would you be so kind as . . . to help me?

Smiley Man (*idem*)   Of course!

Lorenzo (*worldly*)   Push him back. I'll throw myself forward. (**Smiley Man** *nods repeatedly, takes off his jacket and deposits it carefully on the back of the chair. Takes* **Ignacio** *by the waist and forces him backwards.* **Nasal Man** *wakes up; coming to with a gargling sound, gets up and joins the group.* **Ignacio** *falls to the floor, but without breaking free of* **Lorenzo** *who falls down with him.* **Smiley Man** *flings himself on top of them and tries to separate them, while* **Nasal Man** *takes* **Ignacio** *by the legs and pushes in every direction.* **Ignacio** *lets out a shriek.*)

Lorenzo (*shouting*)   Damned idiot! Leave me alone! Leave me alone! (*Manages to separate himself while* **Ignacio** *rolls around on the floor under the policemen who are punching him.* **Smiley Man**'s *smile gets more exasperated as his enthusiasm rises.* **Nasal Man** *makes nasal sounds more and more frenetically. At the same time,* **Ignacio**'s *screams can be heard.* **Lorenzo** *flings himself towards the door, opens it and reaches his arms out with an exclamation of delight.*) Ah, what wonderful fresh air, what wonderful fresh air!

Act Two

Scene One

The same room, one or several days afterwards. A ladder against the wall, next to a brush with a long handle. The daylight comes in through the window. **Lorenzo** *is in the room, hammering the leg of a chair. Whistles, very happy. Finishes hammering, rests the chair on the floor. The chair wobbles and falls over.*

Lorenzo (*happy*)   Excellent! What skill! (As *the chair falls over, he rests it against the wall. Straightaway he takes some newspapers and a big jar of glue and sticks newspapers over the windows. Light is blocked out little by little.* **Lorenzo**, *disconcerted.*) You can't see anything . . . (*Stumbles down the ladder, finds the electric light.*) Anyway, I hate light. I'm fine on my own . . . I feel . . . fine! Perhaps I'm a healthy man and he makes me ill. But if he comes back . . . (*Laughs.*) I've got an idea, a magnificent idea! He's not the brightest spark, but he'll understand. Clear as day. (*He pulls out an old dirty cardboard suitcase from under the bed. He opens it on top of the bed. Disgusted.*) How filthy! Just as something to lend to him. It smells of schnitzel. (*Looks through the room, lifts up a mattress and pulls out a pair of socks which he puts in the suitcase. He shakes a shoe until some more socks fall out, very dusty, tied in a knot, which he also puts into the suitcase. He does the same with a t-shirt full of holes which he takes out of a drawer.*) What else has he got? A pair of trousers. Two pairs of trousers, he's wearing one pair. (*Looks in the drawers.*) Where can they have got to? (*With an exclamation of delight, he discovers them on the floor, under a scrubbing brush. He shakes them.*) They're damp. (*He folds them, puts them inside the suitcase.*) I'll put the suitcase in the hallway; if he comes back, he'll get the message. I don't want to get involved. Someone who gets into trouble with the police is not good to have too close. Or I could put the suitcase on the doorstep. If somebody steals it, too bad. (*Closes the suitcase, strains to lift it, but the suitcase doesn't weigh a thing and the effort he puts into lifting it is excessive. Disconcerted.*) It doesn't weigh a thing . . .! I'll fill it with newspapers. He'll see that I don't wish him any ill. My things and your things. Good will starts from here. Too bad if yours doesn't exist. Ignacio bought the newspapers. He can take them with him. (*Fills the suitcase with the old newspapers, presses them down and closes it. Picks up the suitcase and sets it on the floor.*) Now it's heavy. (*A silence.*) I feel fine! (*Breathes in and out deeply.*) Two mattresses. I'll join them together and . . . (*Resolute.*) I'll start to look at women. (*Gets up on the stool and opens the window. Leans half his body outside, takes a comb out of his pocket and starts combing his hair.*) I'll try my luck with the first one who comes along. Fat or thin, old or young. If I'm going to give it a go, I can't be too choosy. (*Giggling.*) As long as she's got all the essential bits! (*Looks. Disgusted:*) What about this one? Where did she come from? She's a dried-up old thing! It's fine to let yourself go, but she's got nothing going for her! (*Turns back into the room, saying.*) You see, what's that all about Ignacio? (*He stops short, furious.*) It's easier with two mattresses, he was cramping my style. (*Looks out again.*) What about this one? She's a cow! If I pick her up, I'll suffocate. And all caked in make-up! Gross! Imagine what her face would look like when she woke up in the morning! You'd be better off sleeping with a bogeyman! (*Leans half his body outside the window; now he looks in the other direction and shouts.*) Hey! You think you can get away with anything just because you've got nice tits? Fatso! (*Laughs, but interrupts himself abruptly and closes the window, frightened.*) Did she hear me? (*Gets off the stool, goes towards the front door and locks it.*) What bad luck! She was standing on the corner, to kiss that face . . . He was an ox! . . . (*Laughing involuntarily.*) Of course, the oxen with the cow! Ha ha! I've got time. Today someone's going to fall into my arms. Patience. Now I'm alone. The house is mine, the mattresses are mine. I'll rent out this room and live off the rent. Women are gold diggers. (*Opens a small gap in the window and spies. Relaxes and opens it completely, propping up his elbows on the window sill.*) What a scarcity of women! Where are they all? But I've got all the ti . . . (*Sees something and falls silent.*) How is it possible? (*Dumbstruck.*) There is no such thing as security, you can't trust anyone! (*Closes the window in a hurry. Takes a few steps into the room, wringing his hands in a strange way, as if he was applauding, very nervous. Sees the suitcase, picks it up.*) I'll put the suitcase in the street, that way he'll get the message . . . As clear as day. (*Opens the door decisively.* **Ignacio** *is in the doorway, the same look as before, only that he seems even more beaten up.* **Lorenzo** *blushing, stammering.*) Hi . . .

Ignacio (*with a croaking voice*)   Are you leaving?

Lorenzo (*stammering*)   No . . . I was just carrying your . . . your . . . suitcase . . .

Ignacio   Where to?

Lorenzo   Where to? . . . I thought you were still . . . in the . . . (*Retches.*) I feel . . . bad . . . (**Ignacio** *meets* **Lorenzo***'s surprise by walking past him without looking at him, crosses the room and lies down on the bed.* **Lorenzo** *also goes inside, sits on a chair next to the table. A silence. Worldly.*) What do you want me to talk to you about? (*A silence. Loses his surety.*) I feel . . . out of . . . sort . . . (*Starts to tremble violently, it's not put on, but he exaggerates. A silence. Suddenly.*) Why is your voice like that?

Ignacio   I caught a cold. It gave me a croaky voice.

Lorenzo   How are you?

Ignacio   Bad.

Lorenzo (*surprised*)   Bad? Why? (*Suspiciously.*) I don't recognise your voice. Are you Ignacio or did you send something else in your place? I wouldn't put it past you.

(*He sits up in his chair and looks at him. Sociable.*) How did they treat you?

Ignacio   They replaced my tooth.

Lorenzo   Did they? How nice of them! They were kind. They seemed very agreeable to me. And to you? Of course, throwing stones at a little boy doesn't produce a good response in anybody, especially in those who have to look after them . . .

Ignacio It wasn't about the stone.

Lorenzo (*enlivened by the conversation*)   No? Oh, for the robbery of four million? (*Smiles.*) Did they believe it? It was a joke! The forms, the stamps, it was all already on the table.

Ignacio It wasn't about that either. I struck them as . . . suspicious. (*Sad and wounded.*) Lorenzo, why did you do this to me?

Lorenzo (*making excuses for himself like a child*)   What did I do to you? I didn't do anything to you. You struck them as suspicious. That is to say . . . you didn't come over friendly. All the same they could have . . . (*Doesn't want to laugh, but can't contain himself.*) That's it! That's what you're saying! I seemed like the nice guy! That really cheers me up . . . to turn out to be nice! Me, the nice guy! (*Laughs wildly while* **Ignacio** *looks at him. He stops, little by little, diverting his gaze, conscious of* **Ignacio** *looking at him, rests his elbows on the table and starts to scratch his head. A painful silence.*)

Ignacio   Lorenzo . . .

Lorenzo (*obliging*)   Yes, yes, darling, at your service.

Ignacio   Some day . . . I'm . . . I'm going to get you.

Lorenzo (*goes pale, wraps his hands around his sides*)   Ignacio . . . I feel bad. I . . . I need you.

Ignacio   Go to hell!

Lorenzo (*rests his face on the table and starts to cry*)   I didn't want to . . . do you damage . . . I was just thinking . . . about the house. I like . . . this house. I like . . . (*Lifts his head.*) the way you laugh. That's why I play dirty tricks on you, so that you laugh as little as possible.

Ignacio   What do you get out of it?

Lorenzo   Not losing. Every time . . . you laugh it takes something away from me, what isn't mine. And why? Why don't I laugh like that? (*Smiles with a grimace, laughs with a rasping breath.*) I don't like it! (*Dejected.*) I crave the way you laugh . . . and . . . and there is nothing to be done about it. I don't get it, Ignacio . . . (**Ignacio** *is silent.*) I didn't mean for them to hurt you. We're brothers, we were born together. If you die, everything will be left to me, the beds . . . and . . . and the chairs . . . and . . . but I don't want you to die. I don't want, I don't want to do you any harm, Ignacio! (*Crying.*) I'm a cretin, a cretin! (**Ignacio** *gets up and looks at him.* **Lorenzo** *is crying, but less sincerely now; he looks out through the corner of his eye at the effect of his crying, exaggerating slightly.*)

Ignacio (*placated*)   Lorenzo, Lorenzo . . . (**Lorenzo** *shows a clownish and triumphant smile to one side, then he turns back to* **Ignacio** *and shows him his pained expressions, remorseful.*)

Scene Two

The same room. **Lorenzo** *is at the table putting on some rubber gloves as if he were a surgeon. He has a contented and busy air about him. On the table, paper, ink, a book. From the door which leads out onto the patio,* **Ignacio** *throws a plastic aeroplane which hits* **Lorenzo** *on the head.*

Lorenzo (*turns furious*)   What are you doing? You're really making progress with that. If every time you make a toy, you end up playing with it yourself, you're really going to make progress. And then you complain that we don't have any money.

Ignacio (*picks up the plane*)   Why don't you give me a bit of help?

Lorenzo   Me? I only work for pleasure. And I also get bored for pleasure.

Ignacio   Why have you put those gloves on?

Lorenzo (*very proud*)   We weren't talking about me. But I will answer your question. I don't want to get my hands dirty. Have you finished your job?

Ignacio   No.

Lorenzo   Hurry up. You know I'm useless at earning a living.

Ignacio (*he turns towards the courtyard*)   I'll finish it today. (*Returns straightaway with a hessian sack full of toys, empties them onto the floor, sits down and starts to put them together.*)

Lorenzo (*starts to write carefully. Then he puts the paper in the envelope*)   Please, don't go to the bakery again. The bread's as hard as stone.

Ignacio (*excusing himself*)   I asked for old bread, so they didn't charge us too much.

Lorenzo   What an idiot! (*A pause.*) Then again, everything they've got is a load of rubbish.

Ignacio (*impassioned*)   No, no!

Lorenzo   I'm telling you it is! The patio is overflowing with old bread. We'll get rats.

Ignacio (*happy*)   The more bread I buy, the more I can talk to her.

Lorenzo   You've got strange taste! Each to their own. That woman's a troll.

Ignacio   She's pretty. (*Shyly.*) I'd like to get married, live here.

Lorenzo (*indifferent*)   Who's stopping you?

Ignacio   But three people living in a room . . .

Lorenzo   And I'm one too many, aren't I?

Ignacio   No.

Lorenzo   Sometimes, you can be unspeakably vile. I realise that I'm the extra one. It's ok. Get married. Cain.

Ignacio No, no. We will go on seeing each other, you can be Inés's friend too.

Lorenzo Oh, so she's called Inés?

Ignacio Yes.

Lorenzo What are you going to do about the father?

Ignacio Who?

Lorenzo With the father. He doesn't let her out of his sight.

Ignacio I'll talk to him.

Lorenzo He'll smash your teeth in. He's a very jumpy foreigner. He takes good care of that hideous girl!

Ignacio There are lots of creeps. They all show up at the bakery. When they grab the bread, they stretch out their arm further and touch her.

Lorenzo She must like it. And the father, what does he do?

Ignacio He shoves them out of the shop. He glares at me with evil eyes. Yesterday he shoved me.

Lorenzo You too! Why don't you wait until the girl grows up?

Ignacio She's fifteen.

Lorenzo But she's a troll all the same.

Ignacio Don't you like her? Are you being serious?

Lorenzo Hmmm. She'd be alright, if it weren't for her face. She's got wonky legs, average hands and, from head to toe, she's all one piece: no waist. She'll do, but she's not my type.

Ignacio (*gets up and goes near the table.* **Lorenzo** *hides everything with his hands*)   What are you writing?

Lorenzo Letters. I'm writing myself letters.

Ignacio Why have you got out *The Erotic Memoirs of a Russian Princess*?

Lorenzo I'm looking for inspiration. No one sends me letters. It's sad.

Ignacio I'll write to you.

Lorenzo About time! I used your paper. Why didn't you print your name on it?

Ignacio What for?

Lorenzo How stupid! So everyone knows it's yours! It's all grubby. You could wash your hands once in a while.

Ignacio It's true. Inés is very clean. She doesn't even have dirt under her nails. Lorenzo, would it really bother you to live on your own? You could come over whenever you wanted. This house would be your house too. (*Smiles.*) Besides, I'm not safe.

Lorenzo (*genuinely surprised*)   With whom? With me?

Ignacio   Yes. You've played lots of dirty tricks on me.

Lorenzo   Me? Yes, yes, I played lots of tricks on you. But do you know why? I'm unhappy. I hiss at them, and hiss at them, and it's as if it was raining.

Ignacio   Keep trying.

Lorenzo   And if one of them flirts with me, what would happen then? They could stay on the mattress for years.

Ignacio   Keep trying. Women are strange, some of them even like to wait. Don't give up because of that. Keep trying but don't hiss at them. They don't like it, they're not dogs.

Lorenzo (*annoyed*)   We all have our own way of doing things!

Ignacio   But your way doesn't get you anywhere!

Lorenzo   Scum! (*Contains himself, hypocritical.*) You're going to be very comfortable here, when I'm gone. (*Smiles strangely.*)

Ignacio   Why are you smiling like that? What are you up to?

Lorenzo   Nothing! I'm very happy for you.

Ignacio (*looks at him in silence, then, moved*)   Have you changed?

Lorenzo (*sincere*)   Yes, yes. I've changed.

Ignacio (*laughs*)   Who can say, Lorenzo . . . I'll tell her to get lost!

Lorenzo (*idem*)   No, no! Because of me, no!

Ignacio   Well, no. I couldn't. But I can see her out of the house. Convince her father. Here is a brother, a friend.

Lorenzo (*looks at him honestly*)   Me. I could be . . . (*Happy,* **Ignacio** *takes out a piece of bread from his pocket and starts to eat it.* **Lorenzo** *is lost in thought for a moment, sighs, amused, and gets up. He picks up the letters.*) I'm going to post these letters. (*Takes off his rubber gloves and puts on some thick woollen mittens. It's obvious that he's trying not to touch the letters with his bare hands.*)

Ignacio (*when he sees the mittens*)   What are you doing? They're going to think you're crazy.

Lorenzo   No they won't. (*Puts the letters in his pockets.*) Why are you talking with your mouth full? You can see the food. You're gross.

Ignacio (*swallows*)   It's hot.

Lorenzo   Exactly. It's hot and I'm sweating. The wool absorbs the sweat. In summer I'm going to dress myself in wool from head to toe. (*Laughs.*) If you're going to deliver the toys, pass by the bakery. Pass by there every day from today onwards. Have you won Inés over? You'll win over her father.

Ignacio (*comes forward, punches him affectionately with his fist*)   Lorenzo!

Lorenzo (*smiling and friendly*)   I'm going to post this, maybe by hand or by post. We could go for a little walk beforehand.

Ignacio   By hand? But who did you write to?

Lorenzo   Myself. Don't ask me the same questions. Don't you fancy a walk? I feel fine, but I would appreciate having one last memory of these strolls. At the end of the day, I'm pretty sentimental. (*Laughs. They walk around, their arms mutually resting on each other's shoulders. They step in unison.*)

Ignacio (*also laughing*)   One last memory?

Lorenzo (*very smiley*)   Did I say one last memory? Of course, if you get married! (*After a moment, he laughs again. Without knowing what he is laughing at,* **Ignacio** *joins him, happy. They keep walking.*)

Scene Three

The same room, days afterwards. There is only one bed now. The table is covered in bread and packages from the bakery wrapped in white paper and tied up with ribbon. **Lorenzo** *is up on the stool, leaning out of the window, with half his body outside, hissing at women.*

Lorenzo (*excited*)   My God, what a beauty! (*Anxious.*) What shall I say to her? Quick! Ignacio, can't you think of anything? (*Turns, glancing round looking for him.*) Where can he have got to? (*Hisses outside again.*) My little love. My litt . . . le . . . love . . . What a pair of eyes! (*He's obviously rebuffed, because he stays there motionless, perplexed; then he leans out of the window again and shouts, furious.*) You piece of crap! (*A silence.*) Who are they kidding? I'm telling them lies. They've got tiny beady bird's eyes, legs with the muscles of a boxer, all bandy. (*He clutches his side, calls.*) Ignacio! (*Furious.*) Ignacio! (**Ignacio** *comes in through the door which leads out onto the patio; he has lost his happy expression.*) I'm hurting.

Ignacio (*dryly*)   Lie down if you're hurting.

Lorenzo   You know that lying down does nothing for me. (**Ignacio** *whistles indifferently.* **Lorenzo**, *upset.*) You're still holding a grudge? What are you accusing me of now? I haven't done anything to you.

Ignacio   I don't know if you haven't done anything to me.

Lorenzo   Oh, fine! You don't know but you accuse me all the same! What's up with you? You're going to catch pneumonia sleeping out of the patio. Why don't you leave straightaway?

Ignacio   Yes, I'm going.

Lorenzo   Yes, I'm going. But then you come back. It's your house.

Ignacio   Keep it! (*With enraged grief.*) I can't look at your face anymore. I can't look at anyone's face anymore!

Lorenzo (*focused on what interests him*) You'll give me the house, but without the deeds. Any day you can come back and say to me: get lost.

Ignacio (*incensed*) What do you want me to do? Put your name in the deeds?

Lorenzo No. But you could write a will.

Ignacio (*getting more and more enraged*) I don't have anybody! Nobody is going to claim it from you.

Lorenzo You never know.

Ignacio I'm giving you the house! But first I'll kill you.

Grabs him by the shirt and pushes him.

Lorenzo (*steps back terrified, sincerely saddened*) Ignacio, Ignacio, my little brother . . .

Ignacio (*lets go of him. Ashamed*) Why did the foreigner hit me, Lorenzo? I have to get my own back for it. Why did he hit me?

Lorenzo God knows!

Ignacio Just for looking at her!

Lorenzo People are like this: crazy!

Ignacio He beat me and said: you can write filth to your mother! To my mother!

Lorenzo You don't have one!

Ignacio Write . . . (*Suspects something, looks at **Lorenzo** who maintains an innocent expression.*) What were you writing the other day? To whom?

Lorenzo To myself. Tomorrow I'll receive the letters. But I won't let you read them.

Ignacio You know how to immitate my handwriting, you know how to copy . . .

Lorenzo I was never able to fake your handwriting perfectly. You're practically illiterate.

Ignacio But once you faked bank notes.

Lorenzo I still have them. (*A pause. Sincere:*) Ignacio, how could I have done that to you? Write filthy things to a fifteen-year-old girl? In your name!

Ignacio Yes. (*Looks at him. A pause.*) You're innocent. Innocent.

Lorenzo (*excited*) Yes, do you see? My innocence is the worst thing about me. (*A pause. Smiling.*) Did you take things too far with the daughter?

Ignacio No. He hit me just for looking at her.

Lorenzo And he didn't call the police?

Ignacio Why would he call them?

Lorenzo (*aside, pensive*)   So many precautions, and for what? I was boiling hot in those woollen gloves. Idiot! Foreign idiot! But it's not inventiveness which I'm lacking. (*Goes near the table and cuts off a piece of bread.*)

Ignacio   Why is there so much bread? Who gave it to you?

Lorenzo   Money gave it to me.

Ignacio   You're a real miser. Why did you go and buy so much bread? And pastries? . . .

Lorenzo (*draws near, empties out the parcel of pastries. Shuffles them around disrespectfully, ends up not choosing one, throwing the rejects on the floor*)   What a load of crap! (*Cuts another piece of bread. Chewing, ordinarily, triumphant.*) Think what you like. I have my odd jobs.

Ignacio   Where?

Lorenzo   In bakeries. Women seek me out.

Ignacio   Which women? (**Lorenzo** *responds with a tut tut, satisfied.*) I'm off. This time I'm really going.

Lorenzo (*instantaneous, takes out the suitcase from under the bed*)   Here's your suitcase. (*Sweeps the bread and pastries onto the floor and opens the suitcase on the table.*)

Ignacio (*comes near*)   Why have you lined it with paper?

Lorenzo   You can thank me for the trouble, can't you? The bottom was caked in grease. What did you have inside it? Food?

Ignacio   I lent it to you for a picnic and the parcel of schnitzels broke open.

Lorenzo   Ah, but that was a while ago, wasn't it? The grease dried out.

Ignacio (*gently*)   I'm very careless. (*Starts to look around.*) Where are my clothes?

Lorenzo   You don't have any. (**Ignacio** *puts a shirt inside the suitcase, takes out his trousers from underneath the scrubbing brush, shakes them out and puts them in.*) You can take my toothbrush.

Ignacio   I don't want to.

Lorenzo   So proud!

Ignacio (*looks inside the wardrobe which is full of suits*)   Where did you get so many clothes?

Lorenzo   My darling, I have my odd jobs. I don't need women. What did you think? I'm not useless.

Ignacio   Did you use the fake bank notes? (*A pause.*) Then . . . the bread . . .

Lorenzo   I bought it! In another bakery. (*Laughs through his nose, as if he were blowing out a candle.*)

Ignacio (*smiles, then laughs, incredibly relieved. The two sit down and pull their chairs closer together. They pat each other's knees*) And all these clothes . . .

Lorenzo Are for both of us.

Ignacio (*laughing*) You're not such a brute!

Lorenzo No, no, I'm not!

Ignacio I've supported you all these years . . .

Lorenzo And I've been hard-working and thrifty! (*The two laugh. Without knocking, the two policemen enter:* **Smiley Man** *and* **Nasal Man**. **Ignacio** *stops laughing, surprised.* **Lorenzo** *continues to laugh through his nose, as if he were blowing out a candle, calmly.* **Nasal Man** *comes near the suitcase and shakes the contents in the air. He says something unintelligible through his nose.*)

Smiley Man (*translates, smiley*) The bird has flown!

Ignacio (*like* **Nasal Man**, *continues shaking the suitcase*) It's empty! (*The two policemen look at each other, smiling.* **Nasal Man**, *highly amused, moves his lips without a word being heard.* **Ignacio**, *smiling disconcerted.*) I don't understand!

Smiley Man (*while* **Nasal Man** *starts to shake the suitcase again; very smiley*) No, it's not empty! (*With evident pleasure,* **Nasal Man** *starts to pull out the paper. A shower of false banknotes.*)

Lorenzo (*stops blowing through his nose. Half-heartedly surprised*) Fake banknotes! Oh, what a pig! (*Blows through his nose again until it gets blocked up and he has to let his laughter explode like a gush of water, violently, in guffaws.*)

Scene Four

In the foreground is the prison's pavement. The prison, behind, is a simple painted curtain. An **Old Man** *is sitting on the curb, moving his feet around in a strange way. He never takes his eyes off his own feet. After a moment,* **Lorenzo** *comes in. He has dressed as a Jew, with a long black overcoat down to his ankles, a round-brimmed hat from which the curls of a wig escape. He speaks normally. He casts a thinly veiled look towards the prison and approaches the* **Old Man** *who doesn't stop moving his feet and therefore never looks at him.*

Lorenzo (*polite*) Have you been here for long, sir?

Old Man I sit here every afternoon, to have some fresh air. In my home there are no chairs, no air: I'm gasping.

Lorenzo I'm looking for a short little man, very dark, pockmarked, with his teeth sticking out and glasses. Do you know him?

Old Man No.

Lorenzo It's my son. A man with an unhappy look on his face punched him. He had a tooth missing, here, in the middle . . . (*Points, stops.*) Can't you see?

Old Man No.

Lorenzo It doesn't matter. They've already given him another one. Do you know him? Have you seen him around here?

Old Man No.

Lorenzo It doesn't matter. (*A pause.*) He's called . . . Horacio . . . or Ignacio. I only ask if you've seen him because I want to smash his face in. He hit my son.

Old Man I don't see anyone. I try not to get my feet wet. The drain's blocked. The water doesn't run away and it spills over. If I get wet I'm ready. At my age, it's serious. A cold can send you to the grave.

Voice of Ignacio (*from faraway*) Lorenzo! Lo . . . ren . . . zo!

Old Man Are they calling you?

Lorenzo Are you crazy? Have you ever heard of a Jew called Lorenzo? (*Suspicious.*) Aren't you called Lorenzo?

Old Man No. I've been coming here for ages, I never see anyone, no one ever calls for me.

Ignacio's *voice is heard again, distant, calling. In response,* **Lorenzo** *folds his arms in an expressive gesture and leaves, furious.*

Old Man (*pensive*) If I get a stick, I will be able to unblock the drain. Then the water will run away and I will be able to look at people from time to time. I couldn't answer the gentleman as I should have done. Fresh air is lovely, but at the end of the day, not being able to see anyone ends up being boring. Life should be enjoyable, because if not, one thinks too much about death, (*Laughs.*) and ends up wishing for it. With a stick, I can slide all the muck to one side and the water will drain away. I'll be happy. (*While he's talking,* **Lorenzo** *enters dressed as a blind man. He's wearing the same black overcoat, but has changed his wig, and wears one with hair down to his shoulders. He's wearing some black glasses and a walking stick which he uses to feel out the edge of the pavement. When he gets to the* **Old Man**, *he whacks him maliciously, but as if he hadn't noticed his presence.*)

Lorenzo (*striking*) What have we here? What's this?

Old Man (*without stopping moving his feet, shielding himself with his arms*) Hey! Hey, brother, I'm here! An old man.

Lorenzo An old man? Forgive me. Have I hurt you?

Old Man No.

Lorenzo Could you spare me a bit of change?

Old Man Why?

Lorenzo I'm blind.

Old Man Blind? What terrible misfortune! I don't have any.

Lorenzo Old men are always stingy. What for? There'll only be room for their bones in the coffin. How tall are you? One metre, seventy? Leave everything else outside, scrooge. They'll have it made smaller.

Old Man (*genuinely frightened*) Smaller? You think so? I've always liked to be comfortable. I'm not stingy. (*He turns out his pockets, gropes around and brings out a small bit of change which* **Lorenzo** *picks up greedily.*) Take it, I don't have any more. Careful of the water.

Lorenzo There's water?

Old Man Yes, overflowing the drain. The day I find a stick, I'll unblock it. But it's difficult to find a stick.

Lorenzo Ah, that's why my feet are wet!

Old Man Do you come here often? You see, I've never seen you before. I like blind people, they can't see.

Lorenzo I come every day. You know why? It's the optimum spot for begging. (*Points to the prison.*) The people inside there are good. The staff, of course. There was one prisoner who screwed me around. Have you ever seen him?

Old Man No.

Lorenzo I haven't heard him for a long time. Have they set him free? Did you, sir, see if they set him free?

Old Man I never see anyone. It's also possible that he's died.

Lorenzo (*happy*) You think so?

Old Man Yes. All the better for you. It's horrible to be screwed around by somebody. (*Accidentally, he touches* **Lorenzo**'s *walking stick.*) Have you got a stick?

Lorenzo It's a walking stick.

Old Man A walking stick will do. Will you lend it to me?

Lorenzo Do you want me to kill myself? Without the walking stick, I'll fall.

Old Man Sit down here. Careful not to get your feet wet. With the walking stick, I can unblock the drain. Give it to me! (*Groping, he stretches out his hand.*)

Lorenzo (*whacks him with the walking stick*) Keep still! (*Puts the walking stick under his arm.*) If he's dead, I won't come anymore. But who's going to pay any attention to this old man? He's talking nonsense. (*Grumbles furiously as he goes out.*) What a waste of time!

Old Man Why did you hit me? You're an old man too. And blind, to top it all off. (*Feels around with his hand, first cautiously, then more freely.*) Where are you? Lend me your stick. Nobody's going to step in front of you. I'll look after you. I like looking after blind people. Lend me your stick. (*Waits.*) No answer? Have you gone? (*After a pause.*) Answer me, have you gone? (*A pause, sighs.*) Yes, he's gone. What a character! I don't like blind people: they don't see anything, they don't want other people to see. The walking stick would have been ideal. I would have been able to scrape away all the muck, to do it with my hand makes me feel sick. So I get fresh air, but I don't enjoy it. How selfish! What would it have cost him? (**Lorenzo** *comes in dragging a little cart full of bits of junk. When he passes in front of the* **Old Man** *a broom handle falls out. The* **Old Man** *eagerly scoops it up and without getting up, moving his feet, so as to avoid the water, he crawls to one side, where he begins to scrape the drain, very happy, almost feverishly.* **Lorenzo** *has shaved his head, he is wearing a striped suit and a speckled handkerchief around his neck. He is reminiscent of a concentration camp prisoner, although his appearance is much healthier. He stops and looks anxiously towards the prison.*)

Lorenzo (*very quietly*)   Ignacio . . .! (*He bends down to get one of his feet into his plimsole and calls out, with his gaze fixed to the ground, and in a thin thread of a voice.*) Ignacio . . .! (*Brief pause.*) But don't go and call me by my name, idiot. Don't get me involved. I'm only asking after your health. Don't get me involved: misery loves company.

Old Man (*happy, without stopping moving his feet*)   I've unblocked it! The water's draining away. There was a bad smell. But I can't stop moving my feet. I'm so used to it!

Lorenzo (*bitter*)   Are you selling something?

Old Man   No!

Lorenzo   Then stop bending my ear! (*Shouts.*) I'll buy bottles, old beds, old Ignacio rags, old newpapers!

Smiley Man *comes out. He looks at both sides of the street and calls to* **Lorenzo**, *without recognising him.*

Smiley Man   Come here!

Lorenzo (*terrified, turns to the* **Old Man**)   He's calling you!

Old Man (*slowly sitting up*)   No, no, he's calling you.

Smiley Man   Come here!

Lorenzo (*conscientiously, he goes towards the* **Old Man** *and shoves him towards* **Smiley Man**)   Go on!

Smiley Man (*to* **Lorenzo**)   Thank you.

Lorenzo *hurries to take hold of the cart and pushes it towards the exit. But there he bumps into* **Nasal Man**, *who is joined by a* **Young Man**. **Nasal Man** *opens his arms and also pushes* **Lorenzo** *back.*

Nasal Man   What's the rush? (*To* **Smiley Man**.)   Will they do?

Lorenzo (*dumbstruck*)   Do you speak?

Nasal Man (*who speaks normally and who also doesn't recognise him. Surprised*)   Yes. Always. Why?

Lorenzo   No, no. I was just saying. I . . . I was mute for a long time. Then I got over it, with a fright. Now I talk ten to the dozen. When I was little I didn't speak either. I didn't know who to speak to.

Smiley Man   Who's asking you?

Lorenzo (*compliant*)   No one! Fortunately, no one's asking me anything. It's a free world. (*Gets muddled.*) No one asks . . . no one answers. When we talk it's . . . when . . .

Nasal Man (*affable*)   Well, yes. Stop, my dear. Your face . . . seems familiar.

Lorenzo   My face? Of course. There are millions like it! It's revoltingly common. Look, look at my profile. It's cheap!

Smiley Man   He's holding us up!

Nasal Man   This old man and this idiot.

Lorenzo (*insulted; quietly*)   Idiot? Me, an idiot?

Nasal Man   . . . Will they do for the job?

Smiley Man   Yes. You, empty the cart.

Lorenzo (*compliant*)   Yes, yes. Of course! At your service. (*Diligently hurls the cart's load onto the ground: bottles, floor sweepings, a rusty dishpan.*)

Smiley Man   Don't worry. If it's too small, we'll fold it in half.

Young Man   We'll fold what?

Lorenzo   He spoke!

Smiley Man   The cargo! In single file, please. (*They all get into line.* **Lorenzo** *rushes to be first in line. Signalling for them to wait, the policemen leave and return immediately with a body,* **Ignacio***'s, wrapped up in a thin cloth. They load him onto the cart. They have difficulty in getting him to fit. The head remains hidden, but an arm falls out, a leg, and this repeats several times. Between the dead body which refuses to lie still and the policemen who are intent on making it comply, there is an obstinate struggle, with violent overtones. Finally the policemen opt for folding the head forward onto the legs. From inside the prison, someone chucks a spade. It falls straight onto* **Lorenzo** *who cries out in pain.*)

Smiley Man   We're going to the countryside. Fresh air, the sun's out. We'll walk slowly. We won't treat this like a chore.

Lorenzo   I wouldn't treat it as a chore. It isn't!

Old Man   You're taking me for a stroll!

Nasal Man   That's exactly it, a stroll.

Smiley Man   Everybody happy?

Lorenzo and the Old Man   Yes, everybody happy!

Smiley Man   Then, off to the country we go! (**Lorenzo** *violently seizes the cart's handle which the* **Old Man** *attempted to grab hold of and heads the line, pushing and panting heavily. They exit.*)

Scene Five

A bare expanse of land. The two policemen are seated on the grass with their legs crossed. Alternately, they breathe deeply, taking pleasure. **Nasal Man** *relishes smelling a flower. The* **Old Man** *and the* **Young Man** *are behind them, standing up.* **Lorenzo** *grabs the spade and starts digging. The cart is at the edge of the stage. Silence.*

Old Man (*timidly*)   There was a cow on the road. Did you see it? (*No one pays attention. Another silence. Goes up to* **Lorenzo**, *pokes his shoulder.* **Lorenzo** *turns round. The* **Old Man**, *pointing to the spade. Timidly.*) May I? I would like to . . . do a few shovelfuls. To do a bit of exercise. (*Anxious.*) It's a good opportunity, you see?

Lorenzo (*looks at him sullenly*)   They threw the spade at me. I'm the most able, the strongest. I'm sorry. (*Turns his back on him and continues digging. The* **Old Man** *is motionless, anxious, without wholly believing in his failure.*)

Young Man   Let him be. He can deal with it on his own.

Lorenzo   Yes! I can deal with it on my own!

Old Man   On the road, there was a cow. I've never seen a cow, so close up. (*Stroking the back of his hand against his cheek.*) I would have liked . . . to touch her. They have silky skin, warm. And she seemed good . . . A good cow she seemed like . . . (*A silence.*)

Lorenzo   What do I care? Let me get on with my work!

Old Man (*calls* **Lorenzo** *again, timid and anxiously*)   Let me . . . (*He puts out his hand and* **Lorenzo**, *begrudgingly, drops the spade. The* **Old Man**, *with a smile on his face, picks it up and has hardly done two clumsy shovelfuls when* **Lorenzo** *wrenches it out of his hands.*)

Lorenzo   You don't know how to.

Old Man (*mortified*)   Give it to me! (*In response,* **Lorenzo**, *panting, attempts to whistle.*) And to top it off, I didn't dare touch her . . . The cow. I was left wanting to. (*Hopeless.*) Why did I unblock the drain? At my age . . . to be left yearning. With two . . .

Lorenzo (*stops digging*)   It's done.

Smiley Man   It's done? Excellent!

The two policemen go up to the cart and whip off the cloth. **Ignacio** *falls to the ground.* **Lorenzo** *quickly goes near. He looks and is dumbfounded.*

Lorenzo   My God!

Young Man (*more quietly*)   My God!

Lorenzo   Ignacio, my little brother!

Smiley Man   What's wrong?

Lorenzo (*touching* **Ignacio** *with his foot*)   Who is this? I don't know him. (*Hurriedly.*) Nor do I care who he is. Everyone gets the fate they deserve. This . . . this guy must have done his fair share of stupid things.

Young Man   Shut up.

Lorenzo   He's telling me to shut up!

Nasal Man (*dark*)   Don't tell him to shut up.

Lorenzo   Thank you! Why's he getting involved?

Smiley Man (*affable*)   Guys! Don't argue! Finish up quickly. It's getting dark. I want to see my kids before they go to bed.

Lorenzo (*laughing tremulously*)   As do I! (*The* **Old Man** *rushes to push* **Ignacio** *into the hole, snatches the spade, making the most of* **Lorenzo** *being distracted and, very happily, continues to do a few more shovelfuls, but* **Lorenzo** *sees him, trips him up and flings him to the ground. He grabs the spade and quickly takes charge of it. Pats the earth down hard with the back of the shovel. The* **Old Man** *steps away, vexed.* **Lorenzo**, *to the policemen, with a servile smile.*) That's it. Job done. It was a pleasure. (*Sees the cloth on the floor, folds it in four and hands it back to the policemen.*)

Nasal Man and Smiley Man   Thanks, everyone!

Lorenzo (*disappointed*)   What do you mean thanks, everyone? It was me who did all the hard work. They're witnesses.

Nasal Man and Smiley Man (*without hearing him*)   See you soon, guys! It'll happen again. Thanks again! See you soon! (*They exit, taking the spade and the cart with them. Silence.*)

Lorenzo   Bastards! They stole my cart!

Old Man (*sorrowful and hard done by*)   I just wanted to do a bit of exercise. Why didn't you let me?

Lorenzo   Go away! You're no good to anyone.

Old Man   And to add insult to injury I saw the cow, but never touched her. I'll never get another chance.

Yound Man   You'll find her again.

Old Man   No . . . She will have gone to sleep. And she was good . . . she seemed like a good cow . . . And you . . .

Lorenzo (*barking*)   Me, what?

Old Man   Your father! Tell your father what you've done to me! You'll see. Insulting an old man like that . . . (*Goes to exit and stops.*) Just for two shovels . . . (*Leaves.*)

Lorenzo (*furious*)   Shut it, you wretch! I don't have a father. You should be pushing up daisies by now. Go and die! (*He turns towards the* **Young Man** *who has his back turned and is standing next to the grave. Angry.*) And you. What are you doing? Why don't you go?

Young Man   Did you know him?

Lorenzo   Who?

Young Man (*pointing to the grave*)   Him.

Lorenzo (*aggressive*)   No. I don't know your grandmother either.

Young Man   I thought . . . that you knew him. His eyes were open, they were grey.

Lorenzo   He should have closed them. (*Laughs anxiously.*) They'll be full of soil now.

Young Man (*turns his back again*)   Be quiet . . .

Lorenzo   Be quiet yourself! Busybody! Scum! Why don't you get lost! (*Linking his two hands together, he jumps on top of the* **Young Man** *and starts hammering him violently between the shoulders.*) Go away, go away, I tell you! (*The man moves away bent over, with his head sunk between his shoulders to protect himself from the blows, and he leaves, staggering.*) The cheek to talk to me like that! Who knows him? How the hell should I know if he had grey eyes? Go and compromise your . . . your . . . (*For want of a better word. Bursts out.*) your grandmother! (*Turns and sits at the side of the grave. Still furious.*) Did you hear that, Ignacio? He wanted to compromise me! (*Silence. Calls, disbelieving, checking.*) Ignacio . . . Ignacio! (*Waits.*) Don't be frightened, I won't call you anymore. I was just checking. I wanted to be sure. You've given me worse surprises than that in my time. And now, from the grave, you're playing tricks on me! You couldn't wait to be dead could you? Eh? Why? So you could play tricks on me! (*Without moving.*) I'm off. It's a twenty-block walk home, to 'my' home. It's all left for me, the walls, the doors. It's all mine, even the thing which annoyed me most, your smile. (*Humbly.*) I wanted your smile, Ignacio. And I wanted . . . your patience . . . What stamina! Is it true, that we were born together, that you were my brother? (*Laughs, but stops immediately.*) It also bothered me . . . what you used to think. (*Annoyed.*) Why did you think that I was your brother? You didn't stop thinking that for a minute, I realised. We couldn't live in the same room, share anything. I didn't want to share anything, idiot! (*A silence. Without moving.*) I'm going. To see if I have your smile. (*Smiles with a horrible smile, fake, just teeth.*) Yes, yes. It's yours, I feel it. I'm going. (*A silence. Goes on sitting, motionless, little by little his smile disappears. He hunches over.*) It's so cold. I'm going, now I am, I'm going. (*Stays still, a silence. Timid, desolately.*) Ignacio, Ignacio . . . (*He bows his head onto his knees in a similar pose to* **Ignacio** *in the cart. A long silence.*)

Curtain.

Mother by Trade (1999)

The premiere of *Mother by Trade* was performed in 1999 at the Teatro del Pueblo in Buenos Aires with the following cast:

Matilde	María Rosa Gallo
Eugenia	Catalina Speroni
Leticia	Alicia Zanca

Set Design and Costume: Graciela Galán

Sound: Claudio Koremblit

Assistant Direction: Oscar Álvarez Monet

Staging and Direction: Laura Yusem

Characters

Matilde
Eugenia
Leticia

A sofa and a chair are the only pieces of furniture, the doors the only form of scenery.

Matilde *and* **Eugenia** *are sitting on the sofa, holding hands.*

Eugenia   I would tell her.

Matilde   I wouldn't.

Eugenia   If we don't, it'll be difficult to live together. There can't be secrets between people who live together.

Matilde   I'm the mother. And I think differently. Anyway, it'll just be a visit. She's not going to turn up and move in.

Eugenia   So why buy a new bedspread?

Matilde   Out of courtesy. She'll spend a night. Or two. A week. A month, a year. Forever. Who knows?

Eugenia   A short visit.

Matilde   If it bothers you . . . I'll take the new bedspread off the bed.

Eugenia   No. You've already put it on. Why should it bother me? I want to meet her. (*Pause. Obstinate.*) I'd tell her.

Matilde   No.

Eugenia   If she was a baby, we'd tell her.

Matilde   With a baby there's no need for words. A baby knows nothing about the world. It puts out its hand, sees a face . . . accepts it. Like ducks.

Eugenia   She's not a duck.

Matilde   She'll come with expectations.

Eugenia   How old is she?

Matilde   She must be thirty-ish . . .

Eugenia   You don't know?

Matilde   Forty-five.

Eugenia   She's big for a baby.

Matilde   I wrote to her . . . to say I wanted to meet her. That I had a family here.

Eugenia (*resentful*)   I suppose you didn't go into details. You saved the fine details. I always knew I fell into that category.

Matilde   Don't be a pain! I'm nervous.

Eugenia   I don't see the point.

Matilde   Oh . . .! (*She contains herself.*) She should be here by now.

Eugenia   The train could be delayed. Or the taxi.

Matilde   I don't know why we have to complicate things for ourselves.

Eugenia   It was your idea. What's missing from our lives? Complications. (*Apologetic, she kisses her hand.*) Don't worry. Complications are part of life.

Matilde (*sighs*)   Life is simple. Good health and you're away.

Eugenia   Until a rock trips you up. And we've tripped up on her. Are you sure your daughter won't be . . .? (*A gesture.*)

Matilde   You spurred me on.

Eugenia   You were sad. But I don't know if I did it to make you happy.

Matilde   What's wrong now? We're mother and daughter. We'll know each other straight away. I'll touch her hair, look into her eyes. A flurry of caresses, kisses, hugs . . .

Eugenia (*doubtful*)   Knowing you . . .

Matilde   Look at me. I'm trembling. I can't control myself. I've lost my voice. Pure emotion. She's late! She's sat twiddling her thumbs somewhere.

Eugenia   Does she know the city? I'm guessing she doesn't. Girls get distracted. They see the lights, the shop windows . . .

Matilde   What lights? It's the afternoon.

Leticia *comes in. She's carrying a handbag and a small suitcase.*

Leticia   Hi.

Eugenia (*effusive, goes to meet her*)   Hi! Come in. We were waiting for you. We were getting worried.

Leticia   I was window shopping.

Eugenia (*to* **Matilde**, *triumphant*)   What did I tell you? (*To* **Leticia**.) Those windows are a magnet to me. Did you have a good journey?

Leticia   Long. Tiring.

Eugenia   Sit down. I'll make you a cup of tea. (*To* **Matilde**.) So pretty!

Leticia (*looks at* **Eugenia**)   This is how I imagined you.

Matilde   I . . . I'm Matilde. I am! Not her. Me! I'm your . . . (*The word doesn't come out.*) In the flesh.

Eugenia   She is.

Leticia   Oh . . .

Matilde   It's me. (*She waits for a reaction. There isn't one. She smiles, uncomfortable.*) What a surprise, eh? (*Nervous and garrulous.*) I feel completely ridiculous. Out of focus. There's a certain . . . implausibility about this situation that gives me the giggles. Ha! Sends shivers down my spine.

Eugenia (*warning her*) Matilde.

Matilde It's true! How can I say: I am your mother! But I am. I'll say it like this, without accentuating it, neutral. At the most a surprised tone. I am profoundly sorry for not having brought you up. Your father . . . your father . . . took you. One morning you were in your cradle and the next morning you weren't. I couldn't find you. Days went by. I worked a lot. Day after day, one day after another. He moved house a lot.

Leticia (*ironic*) Day after day.

Matilde Yes. You see, I couldn't find you. This country is enormous.

Eugenia It's easy to get lost.

Matilde Would you like tea?

Leticia No.

Matilde A coffee? You look worn out.

Eugenia You have a room here. You can rest here. I put a magnolia flower on a little saucer on the bedside table. I stole it from the street.

Leticia (*looks at her*) I don't know your name.

Eugenia (*smiles warmly*) Eugenia.

Leticia Pleased to meet you, Eugenia. (*She gives her her hand.*)

Eugenia A kiss. (*She kisses her.*)

Matilde What an awkward situation, eh? It's got me. What should one feel? It's a mystery to me. Did you imagine me like this?

Leticia No.

Matilde How?

Leticia Blonde.

Matilde (*crestfallen*) That's nice.

Leticia Taller.

Matilde Really?

Leticia More round.

Matilde Fat?

Leticia (*gently*) No, no.

Matilde You mean healthier.

Leticia (*idem*) No. You look okay.

Matilde (*irritated*) What do you mean I look ok? How do I compare to how you imagined me?

Leticia   Actually, (*pointing to* **Eugenia**) she fits better.

Eugenia (*smiling from ear to ear*)   Really? How lovely. You see, Matilde? Sometimes the voice of blood is silent. Or sings someone else's song. (*She laughs.*)

Matilde   Well, what can we do? Can't please everyone.

Eugenia   Yes, and some can't please anyone. (*Distancing herself from* **Matilde**'*s murderous look, turns towards* **Leticia**. *Politely*.) Tell us a bit about your life.

Leticia   There's not much to tell.

Matilde   Start with the essentials.

Leticia   I got married, I got divorced.

Matilde   Children?

Leticia   No.

Matilde   It's better that way. I know from experience. Children are a burd . . . (*Falls silent. Bursts out abruptly*.) I am your mother, your mummy! You turn up all calm. Incredible! I wouldn't have believed it if they'd told me. It doesn't happen every day. Or maybe it does to you?

Leticia (*coldly*)   It's the first time.

Matilde   Act like it then!

Eugenia   Matilde.

Matilde (*aggravated and furious*)   You took her for me! So calm. You should have felt an insane emotion, an unbearable churning, sick with nerves, with . . .! But no. Serene, impervious. It's outrageous! I can't bear it!

Leticia (*smiling cynically*)   I'm sorry.

Matilde (*laughs*)   She's sorry!

Eugenia (*accommodating*)   Better than nothing. (*To* **Leticia**.) She doesn't mean to offend . . .

Matilde (*interrupting her, ferocious*)   Sshhh! (*To* **Leticia**.) Am I a stranger?

Leticia   Yes.

Matilde   No! No I'm not a stranger! I'm your mother. I gave you life. I searched for you.

Leticia   After . . . how many years? Forty?

Matilde   I was . . . very busy.

Leticia   I understand. You wrote to tell me you had a family. Where is he? Or your children, for that matter.

Matilde   It's not him. It's her.

Leticia   Her?

Eugenia   Me.

Matilde   She is my family.

Leticia   Since when?

Matilde   Since forever.

Leticia   Not since forever. After me.

Matilde   Of course it was after you. A lot happened.

Eugenia   She was a singer.

Leticia   I didn't know.

Matilde   But I stopped a while ago. (*She points towards her throat.*) A problem. You have to protect your throat. From the cold most of all. I didn't and . . .

Leticia   You fell mute.

Matilde   Not as such.

Leticia   What a shame.

Matilde   That I didn't . . .? (*A gesture.*)

Leticia (*with an unkind smile*)   You can talk. (*Uncomfortable pause.*)

Matilde   But I had success.

Eugenia   Briefly.

Matilde (*gives her a murderous glance*)   It wasn't that brief.

Eugenia   A flash.

Matilde   You think so? I bought this apartment thanks to that *brief* moment of success. A flash that lasted a long time.

Eugenia   We bought it together, Matilde. Stop putting on airs. That habit of yours drives me round the bend.

Matilde   Me? Me putting on airs? You never allow me the slightest allusion to my . . . to my career. You were always a bit envious, weren't you?

Eugenia   Of what?

Matilde   You were just a housewife.

Eugenia   Better to be a talented housewife than a talentless singer.

Leticia (*they have completely forgotten her*)   I have to go.

Matilde   You just arrived.

Eugenia   Out of the question. What are you thinking? I'll make tea. We'll drink it like ladies, conversing round the table.

Leticia (*to* **Matilde**)   A pleasure to meet you. Thanks for paying for the trip. I am grateful to you. As soon as I got to the station I realised that me coming was a mistake. Now it seems all the more so.

Matilde   What are you doing? I've got a room ready for you. There's no hurry. Feelings don't gush out like water from a spring. You have to care for them, let them grow. So . . . Can't you . . . give me your hand like you gave it to her? You gave her your hand.

Eugenia   And a kiss!

Leticia (*to* **Matilde**, *coldly*)   How do you do? (*She gives her her hand.*)

Matilde (*not letting her go, looks into her face*)   You're fair. Your father was dark.

Leticia   I know. I lived with him.

Matilde   You look like me.

Leticia   No. I don't look like you. I look like myself. With defects, yes. (*Pulls her hand away.*)

Matilde   This girl, this girl drives me mad!

Leticia   Goodbye, Eugenia. Goodbye, señora. (*Picks up her suitcase and leaves.*)

Matilde   Why did she go?

Eugenia   I don't think she liked our family. Besides, you weren't that tender.

Matilde   Me? She didn't offer me her hand.

Eugenia   She shook your hand.

Matilde   Barely, if you call brushing me with her fingers shaking hands.

Eugenia   You weren't tender.

Matilde   She's a block of ice. How can you be tender towards a block of ice?

Eugenia   You didn't explain the situation well. It was bad taste to argue in front of her.

Matilde   I got carried away.

Eugenia   I'm not saying that you had a magnificent voice but you sang reasonably well. It was pleasant to listen to you.

Matilde   She didn't show the slightest bit of interest. In my voice, in anything. I thought . . . I thought . . . that I would open the door and she would throw herself into my arms. That she would cry in my arms . . .

Eugenia   Yes, you did. But she imagined you differently. Forty years of imagining you differently. How to reconcile after that? She had to pluck out your blonde hair and replace it with black hair, make your nose bigger, add wrinkles, take out your teeth . . .

Matilde And what else? You missed out this age spot, the fur on my upper lip, the attacks of rheumatism, colitis . . .

Eugenia Yes, reality hits you hard.

Leticia (*enters*) I forgot my handbag.

Matilde (*quickly looks for it. Gives it to her*) Take it, take it, darling. Off you go. It was a pleasure to meet you. We were just going to have a cup of tea. We don't want it to get cold. It tastes bad cold. Besides, the traffic's heavy, you could miss your train, your taxi, I don't know how you came . . . But don't waste time. Have you got your handbag, your suitcase? You haven't forgotten anything? Because if we're in the middle of drinking tea and you come by again . . .

Eugenia She's happy to see you.

Leticia Goodbye.

Matilde Leticia! How dare you? Do you realise what you're doing? Who gave you the right?

Leticia To do what?

Matilde To leave! Did I pay for your ticket, for this? For you to come, give me the once over and say: I don't like you, I imagined you blonde, with more teeth and fewer wrinkles, and leave like this, just like this. Insolent brat! . . . Heartless child!

Leticia (*calm, to* **Eugenia**) What's got into her?

Eugenia She's a bit impulsive.

Matilde I too imagined you differently! I imagined a gentle child, beside herself with tears, and instead I get this . . . this superior and indifferent being. Go then! No one's stopping you! The door's open! To come in, to go out, to break it down! (*To* **Eugenia**.) She's a block of ice! Didn't I tell you she's a block of ice?

Eugenia She doesn't mean that.

Matilde Yes, yes, I do mean that!

Leticia (*puts her bag down*) I'd have a coffee.

Matilde She'd have a coffee! There isn't any coffee!

Eugenia There is coffee. I'll bring it.

Matilde You won't bring anything! This isn't a restaurant! (*Laughs.*) What a cheek! I never cry, so I was worried. My daughter will come and I should cry with emotion, but how can I?, I thought. I went out of my mind. Sleepless nights! But I don't need to. The last thing I need to do is cry! When your father took you, I danced around the table. The first thing I did was to throw out your cot. Isn't that right, Eugenia, what did I do?

Eugenia I don't know. I didn't know you then.

Matilde You can imagine! Did I complain? Did I talk to you about her?

Eugenia Never.

Matilde Do you know what a void never talking about it made in me?

Eugenia Until recently. Suddenly she started talking. She got all nostalgic! (*Laughs.*) Sorry. You started to feel . . .

Matilde Yes?

Eugenia That this void left you feeling empty.

Matilde Yes.

Eugenia That the only thing you could feel was guilt.

Matilde So much so . . . (**Eugenia** *tries to caress her.* **Matilde** *immediately pushes her away.*) No! Nobody touches me to console me!

Leticia Console you, about what?

Matilde Console me? Eugenia, did I say that word?

Eugenia Yes. Don't say that you didn't.

Matilde A slip of the tongue. It happens sometimes. You want to say . . . I don't know . . . that it's a cloudy day and you get confused. It's raining and you say: it's sunny.

Leticia It's *very* cloudy.

Matilde It's very late isn't it?

Leticia (*hard*) It's very late.

Matilde (*she puts out her hand in search of* **Eugenia**'s *who takes it and squeezes it in her own. Quietly, to* **Eugenia**) If I could cry, would that move her?

Leticia No, it wouldn't move me.

Matilde (*retracts her hand. Sourly*) So why did you come?

Leticia Out of curiosity.

Eugenia Well, at least that's something. Everything begins with curiosity.

Leticia I've got my own life.

Matilde And there's no room for me?

Leticia To bring someone into a life already made, they have to be really loved.

Matilde (*indignant*) You hear that? Did you hear what I did?

Eugenia I hear it differently from where I'm standing.

Leticia From any standpoint, there's no room for her. I don't need her anymore. You're two mature women, almost old ladies, soon you'll have a whole host of ailments. I don't see myself looking after you. It's too late. (*She picks up her handbag and suitcase. Exits.*)

Eugenia (*after a silence*)   Shall we have a cup of tea?

Matilde   She meant you as well. Two mature women, she said, almost old ladies . . .

Eugenia   I understand. She addressed us both to be polite. It would have been pretty brutal to just refer to you.

Matilde   It must be nice to be so accommodating.

Eugenia   Are you talking about me? But, Matilde, it's staring you in the face. I'm just the spare part in this situation. Thank goodness.

Matilde   She feels hatred towards me.

Eugenia   Tons! When a cord is cut, it's cut. And I think you got it wrong.

Matilde   I was so young. I looked for her for a while. Then life went on. I met you.

Eugenia   You weren't tender. You should have . . . spoken to her in a different way. In a more . . . maternal way.

Matilde   Maternal? How? I don't know. I never knew how. Not even when she was born.

Eugenia (*surprised*)   What about instinct?

Matilde   It was dormant, dead. When she cried in the cot, I would have thrown myself out the window. I'd pick her up and she'd carry on crying, I would have thrown myself out of the window with her! Such exhaustion! I was so tired that all I wanted was to sleep.

Eugenia   You never knew that being a mother means taking on such responsibility.

Matilde   I always knew it! But I couldn't take it on. I was nineteen.

Eugenia   Nineteen, twenty-nine, it's the same.

Matilde (*looks at her coldly*)   Sometimes I don't know why I confide in you. You don't understand anything!

Eugenia   Yes, I do. I don't excuse you but I do understand you. People who love you, love you, *despite* understanding you.

Matilde   Despite understanding what?

Eugenia   You don't think much about other people. You put yourself first, being exhausted, being cold, wanting to sleep, being nineteen.

Matilde   He took her far away.

Eugenia   He moved around.

Matilde   I lost track of him. (**Leticia** *comes in.*) What have you forgotten now?

Leticia   Nothing.

Matilde   So?

Leticia There isn't another train until early tomorrow morning. I walked around for a while and said to myself: seeing as I've already made the journey . . . Let's see.

Eugenia (*smiles*) Welcome. We're delighted. A long conversation and the misunderstandings fade away. (*Digging* **Matilde** *in the shoulder*.) Make conversation! Talk!

Matilde (*after a silence*) I wasn't nice.

Leticia No.

Matilde I was selfish.

Leticia Yes.

Matilde I looked for you.

Leticia But not enough.

Eugenia Even so . . . I can vouch . . .

Leticia (*cutting*) You, say nothing.

Eugenia (*wounded*) I'll be quiet.

Matilde I threw out the cot.

Leticia (*ironic*) You were suffering.

Matilde A little. You grew up far away from me.

Leticia I had another mother. I loved her.

Matilde (*acidic*) Congratulations. You've lifted a weight from my shoulders.

Eugenia Even so . . . (*Remembers and is quiet*.)

Leticia Between you and me is a territory that nobody knows. And there's no path between one place and the other.

Matilde Cross-country.

Leticia What?

Matilde Cross-country. I started to walk cross-country.

Leticia But you don't get anywhere. You lose the way. (**Matilde** *looks at* **Eugenia**. *Asking for help*.)

Eugenia She doesn't want me to speak.

Leticia Forgive me.

Eugenia (*enthused*) She loses her way, what does it matter? She retraces her steps. So what if she got lost in the woods or stuck in the undergrowth.

Leticia She's too old for so much walking.

Matilde (*to* **Eugenia**) You see. You see how she responds!

Eugenia She's trying again. But don't trip her up.

Leticia How?

Eugenia By changing your position.

Leticia (*she stands*) It's too late.

Matilde (*aggressively*) I can see that! So why did you come back? Shouldn't you have gone? Are you trying to humiliate me? I'm too old for that as well. Do you want me to get down on my knees? Ask for your forgiveness?

Eugenia That's not necessary. It's never too late if you gi . . .

Matilde Save your clichés. This matter is between her and me.

Leticia Why did you write to me?

Matilde I had a craving to.

Leticia After so many years.

Matilde Yes! A craving, a whim. Suddenly I remembered you. What can have happened to that darling baby girl, I said to myself.

Leticia (*acidic*) What must have happened to that darling mummy, I said to myself.

Matilde We're on the same page. I looked for you, now I have more money, more means. It was easy. Don't think I made sacrifices to find you. That I got into debt, and was desperate. No. I looked calmly, without surprises. If I found you, fine. It I didn't find you, it was all the same to me. At my age you save yourself the suffering.

Leticia You saved yourself at every age. They say . . . that you keep in better shape if you don't suffer, if egoism swaddles us so we live in a land where there's no one else. Pain makes things fall apart. On the other hand, stoicism conserves our elegance, hardly marking our face, our body shrinks less. (*Looks at her. Fixedly.*) But that's not always the case, right? Some, no matter how much they protect themselves, end up in a terrible state.

Eugenia (*looks at* **Matilde**, *worried*) I wouldn't go that far . . . I remember . . . When my father died, after so much crying my eyes became more . . . more moist!

Matilde (*doesn't hear her*) We, being *old ladies*, are very stuck in our ways. We like to have supper in peace and go to bed early. Any alteration, a strange presence for example, bothers us, makes us unhinged, drives us mad!

Eugenia Speak for yourself! (*To* **Leticia**.) I'm very happy you're here.

Matilde I'm not talking about her. (*To* **Leticia**.) You missed your train. Are you going to wait until tomorrow? There's a coach service.

Leticia (*picking up her suitcase*) Yes. I'll take the coach.

Eugenia (*taking it out of her hands*) No, no. (*Wants to make her sit down.*) Leticia, Leticia. Look at her.

Leticia (*resisting. Stands*) I see her.

Matilde I am not in the habit of wailing. It seems repulsive to me. Blackmail. I can't stand people who cry either.

Eugenia She's crying . . . On the inside.

Matilde Don't translate me! And badly at that.

Eugenia She says that there wasn't a single day that went by that she didn't remember you.

Matilde How trite!

Leticia *sits down abruptly and hides her face in her lap.*

Matilde (*terrified*) What's wrong with her?

Eugenia She came to find her mother and she found an old harpy! Go to her, stroke her head.

Matilde No. I can't! As far as I'm concerned, she is fallen from Mars. Who is she? A stranger. I don't feel anything. No remorse, no guilt, no love. Nothing. I want her to get out of my sight, I don't want her to annoy me anymore, upset me. Twenty years with me . . .

Eugenia Twenty-five.

Matilde Twenty years and you weren't able to warn me, to leave the past in peace, you can't change what it was. What's she doing? Is she crying? This girl's incoherent! I can't stand seeing anybody cry. If she doesn't go, I will!

Leticia (*furiously, she dries her face. She stands up*) Don't trouble yourself. I'm going.

Matilde Safe journey.

Eugenia I don't understand her. Twenty, twenty-five years, and I don't understand her!

Leticia *goes to leave. Before she does, she turns and looks at* **Matilde.**

Matilde (*with a sweetened tone of voice*) What are you doing?

Eugenia My darling baby girl.

Matilde My darling baby girl, what are you doing?

Leticia I'm going. It's not worth getting upset just for this. My husband told me it was stupid to come.

Matilde Didn't you say you were divorced?

Leticia No. I have two kids.

Eugenia You're a grandmother!

Matilde Shut up. We can do without your input. Two kids?

Leticia Yes.

Matilde Do they want to meet me?

Leticia No.

Matilde Of course they don't. The way they've been brought up . . .! You must have talked to them about me. But why would you talk to them about me, right?

Leticia (*furiously, she hurls her suitcase to the floor*) What are you saying, you crazy old woman! I'm full of rage. I think that's why I came. Out of rage. And to know what my mother was like. And now I know. You could only expect such neglect from someone like you.

Matilde Have you finished?

Leticia No. Actually, I came to confirm what I already knew. My father told me what you were like.

Matilde That man.

Leticia That you liked to go out, go dancing. I was a nuisance. I don't even believe that you looked for me when he took me away.

Eugenia I'm the witness that . . . (*A furious look from* **Leticia** *strikes her dumb.*)

Matilde Yes, yes. I did! I moved heaven and earth. That's for sure. (*She interrupts herself. Abruptly.*) I hardly looked for you at all! (*Laughs.*) A pretence of looking for you, a pretence of being troubled.

Eugenia Shut up! This mania of yours for going on talking! You're hard. Better that nobody asks you to explain. If I had asked you to . . .

Matilde (*under her breath*) Weren't you happy with me?

Eugenia I was. But then, so much abandonment, so many shameful secrets!

Matilde I was never ashamed of . . .

Eugenia Better not to go into explanations. The truth is what you feel now.

Matilde Which is what?

Eugenia What moved you to look for her . . . Now.

Leticia Because before she didn't have time.

Matilde You're right! I didn't look for you much. I felt cheated. And when he took you, I cried, but what a relief! I was young again, carefree again. Why is it that I miss you now? I don't know.

Leticia (*comes near. Hard*) I do. You're going to die and old people want their children to hold their hand.

Eugenia (*distressed*) I can . . .

Leticia You might die first. Having children is safer. And they think that something of themselves will live on in the world. A son, a daughter. Dreams.

Matilde That's not the reason.

Eugenia (*helpless*) And so what if it was? It's a natural feeling. If I had a daughter I too would like . . .

Matilde (*looks at* **Leticia** *for a long time. Then*) We don't have anything to say to each other.

Leticia No.

Eugenia Quite the contrary. I think you have a lot to chat about. Without having a go at each other! To get to know each other, to . . . My darling baby girl.

Matilde Give me time. Give me time for the words I never said. They're new, but mouldy. Give me time.

Leticia It's getting late señora.

Eugenia But if we try hard . . . if we sit around the table . . . and have a cup of tea.

Matilde Would you like a cup of tea?

Leticia (*after a pause*) It's cold. Why not?

Matilde And . . . and you tell me how I can get fat . . . What diet is the best to get fat with. There must be thousands. I don't use creams, but . . . there are good anti-wrinkle creams . . .

Eugenia They can work miracles.

Matilde (*to* **Eugenia**) Young people know a lot about diets and . . . and beauty. (*To* **Leticia**.) How would blonde hair suit me? I was blonde when I was young. Dyed, of course. With good creams, hair dye, maybe all of a sudden I can . . . ask for your forgiveness.

Leticia I'll never forgive you.

Matilde (*puffs, irritated*) Casting pearls before swine! Pearls before swine!

Eugenia No! Do you think it's so easy? She hates you. You hate her, don't you?

Leticia Yes.

Matilde You see? Didn't I tell you? She wants me to get down on my knees!

Leticia Yes. (**Matilde**, *enraged, goes down on her knees.* **Leticia** *picks her up brutally by her arm.*) Not like this! That you get down on your knees at every corner, that you earn the past and build it up again. I'm a little girl in my cot, and I'm two years old, and then I'm six and you pick me up from school. I'm ill and you don't leave my side even to drink a glass of water. Every day you're with me, every morning I wake up and see you, I go to sleep and I see you . . . Create that past! No, what am I saying? No one can change it and I'm full of rage for you. But rage is tiring.

Matilde *falls silent. Slowly she goes towards her chair and sits down. With her head hung, she looks at her hands.*

Leticia (*hurting*)   You've got so many age spots on your hands! They show your age. A lot.

Matilde (*hides them*)   They're sun spots.

Leticia (*contemplates her. A silence*)   I know quite a bit about creams. I sold them at one time, from door to door.

Matilde (*with a thin thread of a voice*)   Hard work.

Eugenia   Do you think she needs them? She's not that wrinkly.

Matilde   Yes, I'm full of wrinkles. And bags under my eyes. I have a pain in my leg . . . Maybe you can recommend something to me . . . I'm healthy! Apart from that pain . . .

Leticia (*laughs*)   A young mother is a delight. But to meet her as an old woman, full of aches and pains . . . You've grown some long fur, here. Curly. (*She points at her own chin.*) Old women never realise when they start growing these little hairs. They don't see well, they don't pull them out. Pathetic.

Matilde   Only that pain . . .

Leticia   I'll never forgive you. The little girl that I was will never forgive you. Don't expect that. I won't hold your hand when you die. I'll live far away and I won't know about it. Intuition only exists if we love each other. And sometimes not even then. Perhaps you'll be dying one day and that same day I'll be happy, laughing at my kids making a joke. Who knows?

Eugenia   You don't have the right . . .

Leticia   I have every right! (*To* **Matilde**.) I'll never forgive you. But, please . . . (*Quietly and intensely.*) do what you can so that I can love you, so that I can love you . . .

Matilde (*looks at her. Then, at* **Eugenia**)   How? (**Eugenia** *doesn't know. She shrugs her shoulders.* **Matilde** *draws near to* **Leticia**, *reaches out her hand, hesitantly, towards her face.* **Leticia** *pulls back and turns her face away.* **Matilde** *lets her hand fall. To* **Eugenia**, *defeated.*) Will you bring us some tea?

Eugenia   I'll bring it. (*Leaves.*)

Leticia *and* **Matilde** *look at each other,* **Leticia** *with hardness. A long pause.*

Leticia   Mummy.

Curtain.

As the Dream Dictates (2002)

The premiere of *As the Dream Dictates* was in August 2002 in the Sala Cascuberta in the Teatro General San Martín in Buenos Aires, with the following cast:

Ana	Alicia Zanca
Old Man (and Butler)	Jorge Suárez
Director	Horacio Peña
Julia	Julia Calvo
Manuel	Luis Machín

Set and Costume Design: Graciela Galán

Music: Carmen Baliero

Assistant Direction: Libertad Alzogaray and Rubén Pinta

Staging and Direction: Laura Yusem

Characters

Ana
Old Man (and Butler)
Director
Julia
Manuel

Scene One	*Perfect dream*
Scene Two	*Something blends*
Scene Three	*In another era*
Scene Four	*Impossible recomposition*
Scene Five	*The dreamed one's rebellion*
Scene Six	*As the dream dictates*

Scene One: Perfect Dream

A large room in which there are only two white metal beds and a metal chair. Two doors and a large window at the back. **Ana** *is onstage. She's young with graceful movements, she's wearing a pale dress and has shoulder-length hair. A woman's voice can be heard in the distance from an open space calling 'Manuel! Manuel!'*

Ana   Manuel. I'm calling you. Don't hide. Manuel, Manuel.

Manuel *enters. He's wearing a cap and is dressed in elegant nautical clothes.*

Manuel   I'm not hiding. Here I am.

Ana   Manuel! (*She runs to embrace him.*)

Manuel   Little sister.

Ana   When did you arrive?

Manuel   A moment ago.

Ana   I wasn't expecting you. Actually, not a minute went by without me waiting for you. Despite knowing you were far away at sea or in a port, distracted with other things, with other people.

Manuel   Not any more. I missed you a lot, little sister.

Ana   I missed you. I felt like I was in a well, I needed you like air.

Manuel   And now? (*She laughs joyfully*.) And now?

Ana   To see you, to hear your voice – la la la la la la – you've brought me to the surface.

Manuel   And?

Ana   Everything is light. I can breathe, so happy!

Manuel   I'm more than happy: delighted. I couldn't imagine the time I'd embrace you. (*He puts his hands round her waist and spins.*) Even the sea bored me. I brought a present. For whom?

Ana   For me!

Manuel   Where is it? (*He puts his arms out so that she can look in his pockets.*)

Ana (*she searches*)   Not here . . . Or here. Here! (*She takes out a jewellery box from one of his pockets.*) What is it?

Manuel   Open it.

Ana (*she opens it. She finds a gold chain*)   Oh, how beautiful!

Manuel   For you. (*He fastens it on her.*) Gold over your golden heart, beauty for your beauty. Your radiance could make the gold seem tarnished in comparison but it's generous and it won't.

Ana (*she covers it with her hand*) I'll never take it off.

Manuel That's what I want. Ana, I'll go to sea again. Will you come with me?

Ana Now? So soon?

Manuel Will you come with me?

Ana (*she laughs*) The sea makes me seasick!

Manuel Liar. You never got seasick.

Ana No?

Manuel Not even in the worst hurricane.

Ana (*she begins to go along with this*) Not even in the worst . . . It's true! I didn't get seasick.

Manuel Everyone was lying down, vomiting, and you were the only calm one.

Ana Yes, as if the deck were the floor of this room.

Manuel So, how could I not want you with me? You'll be my helmsman.

Ana (*smiles*) And your cabin boy.

Manuel Close your eyes. (*He takes her to the window. He opens it. Some masts can be seen, a sail, barely moving in the afternoon light.*) Look. What do you think? The most beautiful of all the sailing boats.

Ana (*with an exclamation of wonderment*) It's another one! Bigger.

Manuel Bigger. It never rocks too much.

Ana I don't mind if it rocks. (*She laughs.*) I don't get seasick even in the worst hurricane! Or when it floods and the wind goes crazy.

Manuel And though the darkness surrounds us, the boat continues being a safe home for you. I'm almost superfluous.

Ana (*charmed*) No . . .!

Manuel No coasts in sight, only the horizon. We'll sail the open sea.

Ana The seagulls will change their course and follow us. The trees will follow us. I'll steer the rudder as you tell me to, to the East, to the West . . . , and the boat will obey my hand.

Manuel Yes, the open sea. And one morning, at dawn, we'll find an island just for us. We'll discover it, beyond maps, deserted, with forest and a fresh water lake. In the ocean – seaweed, lobsters, fish . . .

Ana Paradise. No one will be able to punish us for so much happiness.

Manuel No one. Not even God.

Ana Oh, Manuel! (*She embraces him.*) I want to set sail.

Manuel So do I. At once. The sailing boat's already prepared.

Ana I'm going to get changed. Can I bring Mum's furniture, her rocking chair, her bed, her crochet bedspread . . .?

Manuel There's space.

Ana And my high-heeled shoes? Some perfume? The little dog?

Manuel Whatever you want.

Ana Give me one moment. (*She turns back before leaving.*) What's the sailing boat called?

Manuel What else could it be called? Your name. Ana. Ana!

She laughs happily. She goes out. **Manuel** *changes his expression, turning from benevolent joy to indifference. He remains motionless. Through the open window, slowly, the masts of the sailing boat get further and further away.*

Scene Two: Something Blends

The same space, two beds and a chair. The window's closed. The sound of the sea can be heard. In one of the beds is an **Old Man** *lying down dressed in a thick white night shirt. After a moment, he sits up with difficultly then lies back down again, his back against the bars.*

Ana, *dressed in a blue maid's uniform with apron and cap, is leaning on a mop, rocking gently with a sleepy face, her eyes closed, a happy half smile. She appears older. When the* **Old Man** *says 'pssst' trying to get her attention,* **Ana**, *without opening her eyes, brings her hand to her chest, she leaves it where the little chain hangs. The* **Old Man** *keeps trying to say something. Then, with a sigh,* **Ana** *opens her eyes, looks at the* **Old Man** *as if he's woken her up. Then she begins to clean the floor with a rag that she soaks in a bucket.*

Old Man There's a flood. I can hear the sound of water.

Ana It's the sea.

Old Man Yes, the Riochuelo.

Ana No. It's the sea crashing against the quay.

Old Man What are you talking about? They're dirty waters.

Ana The crystal clear sea.

Old Man Has the river gone? Now I can see myself floating on a bed in that muck.

Ana The sea.

Old Man Feet soaked.

Ana I was in a sailing boat with three masts. I was onboard, did you know that? A long journey.

Old Man Yes, even the house opposite. Check to see if water's got into the corridor.

Ana It's the tide. As it rises, it beats against the quay. (*The sound of the sea stops.*)

Old Man I don't hear anything. The wind's changed. It's hit somewhere else!

Ana The tides have fixed times. They follow the moon.

Old Man The wind's changed from the South, I'm telling you! The flood's stopped! (**Ana** *smiles, shakes her head as if before a childish absurdity. The* **Old Man**, *aggrieved.*) Why are you shaking your head with that stupid smile? (*He looks at her with hostility.*) I don't know you.

Ana (*cleaning*) I'm new. I started work today.

Old Man No doubt the minister recommended you.

Ana (*she stops, surprised*) Yes. My brother. My brother is the minister.

Old Man Prize job he gave you.

Ana He's very generous. He wanted to give me another position.

Old Man In the embassy.

Ana In the sailing . . . How did you know?

Old Man You didn't want it.

Ana No. What would I do in the embassy? Everyone speaking other languages. In this job I can . . . serve.

Old Man Are you really the sister of a minister?

Ana Not quite. But he's got an important job. He's the secretary of a minister.

Old Man Now I get it. You're in cloud cuckoo land. You're not lowering yourself from the heights of the ministerial offices.

Ana (*this doesn't register. She smiles*) Have you been here long?

Old Man Since I began to get in the way.

Ana Don't say that. You're well looked after.

Old Man Before, old people would die in their own bed.

Ana Don't talk about dying. You'll get better soon, grandpa.

Old Man (*jumps, chokes*) S . . . sorry? What? Hold your tongue!

Ana What happened?

Old Man Grandpa! Keep your 'grandpas' to yourself.

Ana I said it affectionately. Don't get annoyed.

Old Man   I certainly will! Not only do I have to deal with the curse of having a family, but I have strangers as relatives.

Ana   Forgive me.

Old Man (*calms down, looks at her speculatively*)   Do you smoke?

Ana   Never!

Old Man   Lucky you! Can't you find me a cigarette?

Ana   It's no smoking in here.

Old Man   Go to the shop and buy me one.

Ana   It's no smoking. I sing well. Would you like . . . ?

Old Man   Don't even think about it!

Ana   Why? I sing rock, pop, punk, the most current stuff. (*She looks at him doubtfully. Then she sings defiantly.*) Hushaby baby . . . And if that rocking bird don't sing . . .

Old Man   Shut up! I'm an old man, not a baby. You can never get anything right!

The **Director** *of the old people's home enters.*

Director (*with professional exuberance, to the* **Old Man**)   How are you? How do you feel? Good, right? I can tell by your fresh face. Why aren't you watching television with the other old folk? (*Changes his tone of voice. To* **Ana**.) And you, what are you doing?

Ana   I'm cleaning.

Director   Clean the corridors, they're more visible.

Ana   I was going to bring him a little water. He feels like drinking water. (*To the* **Old Man**.) Cold or hot?

Director   Don't get involved with the old people! They don't exist for you. Concentrate on the corridors! (**Ana** *picks up the bucket and quickly leaves.*) How are you? Are you comfortable? This is not a dream. At last your worries are over. Free from thoughts like a lion in the jungle. Free! Happy, eh? You'll be able to go out on Sundays.

Old Man   You make me sick! (*He turns his back to the* **Director**.)

Director   Have they already given you breakfast?

Old Man (*turns his head. Hatefully*)   They gave me tea. I drink *mate*.

Director   You'll get used to it.

Old Man   Why? Why do I need to get used to it? I like *mate*! I've drunk *mate* my whole life!

Director   Okay, okay . . .

Old Man   Okay, okay! You talk like an idiot!

Director (*impassive, takes out a prescription book from his pocket, writes*)   We're going to prescribe you . . . so that you'll be calm . . .

Old Man   I won't swallow a thing!

Director   You won't swallow a thing . . . Okay, okay . . . You're very upset . . . (*Exits writing.*)

Old Man   Bastard! Go calm your grandmother! I won't swallow a thing! You won't be able to open my mouth, not even with pliers! (*Acting it out.*) You're very upset . . . Well, yes! I am upset! (*He gets up, begins to throw off the sheets, pulls them, rolls them up.*) I'm off! I'm going to sleep under bridges! My trousers! Where did they hide my trousers! (*He looks for them under the mattress, kicks the sheets.*) Bastards!

Ana (*leaning in*)   Has he gone? Here. (*She gives him a cigarette.*) Don't smoke it now. The director's around. Smoking's bad for you.

Old Man (*puts the cigarette in his mouth, anxiously takes in one puff after another. Takes it out of his mouth, shouts*)   Fire!

Ana   Oh my God! Where? (*Irritated, the* **Old Man** *points at the cigarette.* **Ana** *laughs.*) You scared me! I don't have a lighter.

Old Man   You don't have one! You bring me an unlit cigarette, pointless! Stupid woman! Block head! (*Furious, he breaks the cigarette, shreds it, desolate.*) What have I done? (*Tries to piece together the shreds.*)

Ana   Cheer up. Cigarettes are detrimental to your health.

Old Man   Are you a halfwit? Other things are worse. (*Out of breath, he sits down on the other bed.*) I have to eat the rubbish they give me, nothing salty, nothing spicy, no meat. Tea with milk.

Ana   You're ill, grandp . . . sir.

Old Man   With old age! It's a terrible illness when others decide it for you. Will you show me your tits?

Ana (*laughs*)   How did you think of that? (*She sees the unmade bed.*) What's happened here? Was it you? They're going to tell you off. (*She makes the bed.*)

Old Man   There were little crumbs. (*He looks at her breasts.*) They're not very big.

Ana   You don't think so?

Old Man   No. I like big tits. But I'll make do.

Ana   No.

Old Man   It wouldn't cost you anything? I still have eyes. I'll finish off the rest myself.

Ana   What do you mean by 'the rest'?

Old Man (*lascivious*)   Can't you imagine? (*Gets depressed.*) But sometimes I find it difficult.

Scene Two: Something Blends

Ana I can help you.

Old Man (*brightens*) Really? You'd do that?

Ana Of course I would! (*The* **Old Man** *immediately throws himself on the bed.*) Not today, in time.

Old Man When we trust each other! In time I'll have gone senile. From being here!

Ana No. Today is my first day's work. Wait a little. Today is Tuesday, let's say . . . Thursday.

Old Man I'll take your word for it. The works. Strip off and . . .

Ana I promise. (*She puts her finger to her lips, goes to the door and spies.*) He's gone. (*She points to the bed.*)

Old Man Is it today?

Ana No. I just want to sit down. I have a lovely surprise in store for you. Of another kind. Do you like the sea?

Old Man (*grumpy*) I don't.

Ana To sail on a boat. I can take you with me. You can sunbathe on the deck.

Old Man I can't stand the sun. I come out in blotches.

Ana You'll be in the shade. All you'll hear is the silence and the rustling of the sails . . .

Old Man I want biscuits.

Ana At sea you can also have biscuits . . . .

Old Man No, I want them on dry land!

Ana (*smiles*) You'll have them. Don't close your eyes.

Old Man I never close my eyes! I hate missing something.

Ana Keep calm.

Old Man (*very agitated*) Yes.

Ana Relax.

Old Man Such a build-up!

Ana Your hands like this. (*She uncurls and lays them out over the blanket.*)

Old Man (*very anxious*) A surprise, you said? I close my eyes?

Ana No. Keep them open. (*She closes her own eyes, smiles.*)

Old Man And? Is that it? A smile?

Ana Shhhh . . . Wait . . . (*She brings his hand to her chest, where the little chain falls. She remains still, a half smile, as if invoking something happy that's about to take place.*

The **Old Man**, *attentive, turns his head with the movements of a curious bird. The* **Director** *leans in. The* **Old Man**, *frightened, tries to catch* **Ana**'s *attention. Although the* **Director**'s *face denotes kindness and interest, his actions suggest otherwise.*)

Director (*comes near, cordially*)   How do you find yourself, my friend?

Old Man (*surprised*)   Me? Your friend?

Director   All the residents are like parents to me. Parents and friends.

Old Man (*flattered*)   Really!

Director (*draws up a chair to the bed, sits down*)   It's hard to be here, I know. A brutal change. Your children have brought you here without wanting to. They suffer more than you do.

Old Man   They suffer?

Director   What did you think?

Old Man (*without conviction*)   It was necessary.

Director   Yes. Otherwise, you would never . . .

Old Man (*thinks about it*)   Oh, good! Never! Did you hear that, miss? (**Ana** *opens her eyes, nods. The* **Old Man**, *happy*.) Otherwise, never! I would have died next to them, with them losing sleep holding my hand, drowning in tears . . . me dying and them suffering without relief . . . (*Abruptly*.) How do you find me?

Director (*smiles*)   A young man in the flower of his youth. Twenty years old.

Old Man   Aren't you exaggerating? Let's say . . . thirty.

Director   Twenty. Ana, darling, I'm not exaggerating am I?

Ana   Absolutely not.

Old Man (*at the height of pleasure*)   Okay . . . I'll have to believe you!

Director   For you. (*He gives him a packet of cigarettes.*)

Old Man   Cigarettes! (*With growing suspicion.*) What about matches?

Director   Here they are. (*He adds a little box.*)

Old Man   Can I . . . smoke them?

Director   Of course! If you don't overdo it. We'll let him, won't we Ana?

Ana   Five a day.

Old Man (*amazed*)   Five!

Director   Alternate with these. (*He gives him a little bag of sweets.*)

Old Man   Sweets!

Director   One more gift and then we're done. Two tickets to a concert at the Colón Theatre. Enjoy them.

Old Man Two? I can invite someone! How . . . how did you know that I like music?

Director Oh, I've noticed you're so intelligent, sensitive!

Old Man Yes?

Ana No one hums the Viennese waltz like him.

Old Man The tango!

Director I can imagine. He must be an expert.

Old Man I am! Music is the only thing which calms me down. It doesn't nag at me, or criticise me . . .

Director Now I'll bring you your clothes and you'll be able to go down to have breakfast.

Old Man Tea!

Director We know you prefer *mate*.

Old Man *mate*?

Director With croissants and biscuits.

Old Man My dream! I . . . I . . . if I'm honest, I thought they didn't exist anymore.

Director They exist. (*To* **Ana**, *reassuring*.) Do it! He doesn't dare ask for it, but before every woman he sees, it's his wish.

Ana And every woman obliges. Happy like the Virgin nursing Jesus. (*She opens her blouse, reveals a breast*.)

Old Man You're showing me your tits! They're not so tiny!

Director And later you'll be able to go for a walk in the park.

Old Man Ah! There's a park?

Director A park, trees. A forest of pines. Which tree do you like?

Old Man (*looks at the breast. Occasionally takes his eyes off it to be able to respond*) All of them! But . . . Floss silk trees. In flower. Those pink flowers blow my mind. I like them so much!

Director Did I say pine trees? There are only floss silk trees in the park. And, what a coincidence, all flowering in pink.

Old Man What a feast for the eyes! It must be . . . wonderful!

Director It is. Do you wish for anything else?

Old Man Me . . . me wish? Can I wish like this, without anyone cutting me off, yapping at my heels?

Director (*pats him on the back affectionately*) You can wish for whatever you want. All the time. (*Goes to leave. Turns back. To* **Ana**, *with a smile*.) Whatever he wants, you give him. (*Exits*.)

Old Man   Oh, oh, lady, miss . . .! I can't take all this happiness. What are you doing with your tits on show?

Ana   Shall I button up my blouse?

Old Man   Yes, that's enough for today. Can you see how he changed. He seemed like someone else.

Ana (*with a little laugh*)   Yes.

Old Man   He gave me tickets to a concert at the Colón theatre! And cigarettes! (*He goes to open the packet.*) No, I'll smoke them later. I have to get up. He wants me to go and have breakfast in the dining room. And then to go to the park . . . the floss silk trees . . . I thought that the tits were going to drive me crazy, but no. I like the floss silk trees more, the seedlings, perhaps . . . geraniums . . .

Ana (*she plumps the pillow*)   Well, now rest. (*She kisses him on the forehead.*)

Old Man   Yes. Twenty years he said! I'll rest a little so that I can . . . get up . . . with all my strength . . . The park! How kind he was! I can . . . I can . . . wish no matter what . . .

Ana   Rest. (*She goes to kiss him again.*)

Old Man (*pushes her away*)   Who told you to kiss me, stupid woman? (*Wounded, she backs away startled. The* **Director** *leans into the room. He's lost his affable air.* **Ana** *steadies herself on the mop and cleans. Waving his arms, with a wide smile, the* **Old Man** *greets the* **Director** *cheerfully.*) Hello! Hello!

Director (*doesn't register. To* **Ana**)   The corridor! It's filthy, you stupid woman! I won't tell you again: clean it or get lost! On the streets! (*To the* **Old Man**.) And you, why aren't you sleeping?

Frightened, the **Old Man** *hides under the sheets.*

Scene Three: In Another Era

In the same space, with the big window in the background and the two doors, the house. A sofa, two armchairs. **Ana** *is sitting on one of the armchairs, her eyes closed, her hand on her chest. She's dressed in her uniform, but without her cap and apron. Her face is absorbed and sweetened, she hums in an imprecise way. Little by little her voice becomes in tune and rises in volume. Dressed in the fashion of 1800, the* **Director** *of the old people's home,* **Manuel** *and* **Julia** *come in.* **Manuel** *is cleaning his teeth with a toothpick.*

Manuel   The custom of men drinking coffee and cognac alone after dinner doesn't agree with me. I never understood it. After eating well, for the women to leave during the after-dinner conversation seems like sacrilege. At precisely the pleasing moment to listen to them, to delight in looking at them. (*He goes towards* **Ana**, *brushes his hand against her cheek, picks her up and squeezes her against his chest.*) How's it going, lonely girl?

Julia Ah, Manuel! The gift of the gab. That's why I fell in love with you.

Director You don't need a reason. You and Ana are the best storyline.

Manuel But they allow us to smoke, right, Ana?

Ana Yes, Manuel.

Manuel (*takes out Havana cigars, offers them to the* **Director**. *They sit down*) And now, tell us, how's the hospital going?

Director Thanks to your support, we don't have any problems. The children are well fed, recover easily. And Ana blesses us with invaluable help.

Julia (*laughs*) She's blushing!

Ana No. I don't deserve . . .

Director Everything! You put your hand on a feverish forehead and the fever subsides, the sobbing subsides. Every day when I pop my head around the door, the children, even the ones in the most serious conditions, lift their heads and smile. And the smiles are the most beautiful I have ever seen. (**Ana**, *shaking her head embarrassed, hides her face.*) And the geriatric ward wait for her, you can't imagine how much! She's warm for the cold, shelter from the elements, sleep for insomnia. I prescribe medications to no avail, she is the best cure.

Julia (*goes towards* **Ana**, *lovingly uncovers her face*) Come on, Ana, Anushka, don't be shy, don't be modest. Our friend is telling the truth. I am so sorry not to have your character.

Ana It's easy for me. I love children. Old people. Some begin to live and others cease to, but people find one another in their defencelessness. And I think that if I help them, they'll gain strength, the children will start their lives happily and the old people will end them . . . curious, about what it is, death . . .

Julia It sounds so simple from your lips. But I lack your energy, your generosity. Everyone loves you for it.

Director Everyone.

Ana (*looks at him*) You too?

Director (*looking back at her*) Me too. More than anyone.

Manuel (*after a moment*) Ana, you owe me something. A little song, right?

Ana Oh, no!

Julia Please, Ana!

Manuel No excuses. Your brother is asking you.

Director I'm asking you to. Sincerely.

Ana (*looks at the* **Director**) For you, then.

Manuel For us both, right?

Ana (*smiles*) For everyone! (*She sings, and she sings well.*)

Director Delicious!

Manuel (*embracing her*) You sing wonderfully. But you're greedy about letting yourself be heard.

Ana No. Your ear is more generous than my voice. (*He kisses her on the forehead.*)

Julia I've given the order that we all wake up early tomorrow.

Ana (*with cheerful surprise*) Why? What for?

Julia An excursion to the river.

Ana Beautiful! You must have thought of that for me. But I can't . . .

Manuel Of course. For you. You like water.

Julia To sit on the grass and eat.

Manuel The two of us had the idea.

Ana (*draws near to* **Julia**, *impulsively kisses her on the cheek*) You're so good to me.

Manuel Hush. How would we not be good to you?

Ana But I can't tomorrow because the hospital . . .

Director Tomorrow is Sunday. And you'll rest. That's an order. And then, I'll join the party.

Ana You . . . (*The* **Butler** *enters. He's the* **Old Man** *from the old people's home, but he's wearing a uniform and is standing up very straight.*)

Butler Forgive me for interrupting. (*To* **Manuel**.) You are so kind that I didn't want to take advantage.

Manuel My friend, you well know that you never bother me.

Butler (*leans towards him*) My profound gratitude. Some tenants have requested you, sir.

Ana Let them come in.

Manuel (*lovingly*) How can we let them in, silly? I'll attend to them at the door.

Ana No, Manuel. In the study.

Manuel At the door or in the study, they won't notice the difference. And if they do notice, the study will intimidate them.

Ana It's cold.

Manuel I will also suffer it, the cold. (*The* **Butler** *drapes a coat over his shoulders.*)

Ana Don't be mean.

Manuel (*joking*) What? A moment ago I was good and now I'm mean?

Ana Good to me. Mean to others.

Manuel I'm never mean to anyone. (*Exits with the* **Butler**.)

Director What is it that they want?

Julia What they'll always want.

Ana Mercy. And Manuel will grant it.

Director No, no! Shut up, little baby!

Julia You don't have experience of the world. These people do hardly any work and expect great earnings. You have to sweat from dawn till dusk to acquire the comforts in life. Do you remember how much we sweated at harvest time? Manuel is a softy, a jelly.

Director Better that he hardens up a little.

Ana And yet . . . What harvest?

The **Director** *tuts at* **Ana** *affectionately.*

Julia Manuel is easily taken in. They tell him about some woe and he gets emotional. He starts crying and blesses them. How many times have I heard him say: may God go with you.

Ana They're hungry. They come to the hospital very thin.

Director Ana darling, don't listen to the sirens' song. Hunger, hunger, hunger, how boring!

Julia They're alive. They must eat something.

Ana They come to the hospital . . .

Julia It's impatience which sends them to the hospital, not hunger. They want to be happy, to be cared for. And these people (*She points to the door.*) I'll deal with them. Don't worry. They won't leave empty handed. Manuel is a softy, so I'll only need to apply a little pressure.

Ana (*she throws her arms around Julia's neck*) I knew it, I knew it! (**Julia** *gently pulls away.*) And . . .? You're not leaving?

Julia Later. There's no better place to get your own way with a man than in bed. You caress them and they lose their mind. I wonder when you'll get married. We're happy to have you with us. It's not that you're a nuisance, but . . . You should create your own family. How long will you go on turning away suitors?

The **Director** *nods warmly.*

Ana Only for a time. I attend to so many little ones in the hospital that . . .

Julia (*changes her tone of voice*) Don't talk to me about that hospital. It stinks.

The **Director** *cocks his head, disbelieving.*

Ana It stinks? We don't have many things to occupy them with, but . . . It's clean.

Julia (*hard*) Floor-mopping slave!

Ana Julia! Yes, I mop floors, what does it matter? The doctor says that I'm . . .

Julia An idiot! You could at least bring home enough money!

Ana I bring home everything. (*Anguished, she fleetingly closes her eyes, brings her hand to her chest as if she were searching for the little chain.*)

Julia Big deal! We feel sorry for you. (*Politely.*) Tell me, doctor, what can one do other than to feel sorry for her?

Director (*false and exaggerated*) Oh, no!

Ana Only just now you were . . . so kind.

Julia I am!

Ana Speak to me with affection.

Julia Affection dries up. Mine dried up a moment ago.

Director (*walks around wringing his hands*) What a categorical assertion!

Ana When I was singing, you had the face . . . of a little girl.

Julia (*flattered*) Me?

Ana You used not to let me fall into this darkness.

Julia (*she sits down. Abruptly, she smiles*) Forgive me. I lost my temper. I'm not saying what I think. I'm a hysterical woman. I'd cut off both my hands before hurting you.

Ana I was scared. I . . . I'm not worthy of pity, am I?

Julia Please! Would we have thought of the outing to the river, would Manuel have paid you so much attention? He even prefers talking with you to talking with me.

Ana Really?

Julia Yes.

Manuel *enters.*

Manuel (*smiles*) Where's my little sister? I missed her.

Julia What did they want?

Manuel Benefits, extensions. They live on hope. They expect rain when it's convenient and sun when it suits. With the first rain of the season, it'll reach up to here. (*Points to his forehead.*) Do they think I was born yesterday?

Ana You granted them another term.

Manuel Yes.

Ana Manuel, darling!

Manuel (*coldly*) Another term until they're old, until their body crumbles and they die. Is that what you want?

Julia We sacrificed so much for our fortune! How we sweated in the harvest!

Manuel Others are already waiting who would work at least twice as much.

Ana And what will happen with . . .?

Manuel With whom? They've gone. A puff of smoke! Did they exist? Not to me. Julia? To you, doctor?

Julia *and the* **Director** *shake their heads with a jokey demeanour, they shrug their shoulders.*

Ana I don't understand.

Julia *and the* **Director** *laugh affectionately.*

Manuel This little head doesn't understand much about anything. What's to be done?

Ana Not this situation. But I do understand. I understand!

Manuel Nothing about finances. Nothing about anything. You walk with your right foot and you trip up with your left. (*Acts this out grotesquely.*)

Julia Manuel, don't torment her.

Manuel I don't mean to, but she drives me round the bend.

Ana Manuel, I'm your younger sister. I was always your favourite.

Manuel (*laughs*) I didn't have any other sisters to choose from.

Director Now, now! This discussion's got heavy.

Ana You gave me this gold chain, do you remember? (*She fumbles at her chest.*) You took me in your sailing boat. We went to the isl . . .

Manuel (*as if he begins to remember, without wanting to*) Oh, yes. The island. It was a lovely voyage.

Ana Just the two of us.

Manuel (*more enthusiastic*) Of course. We swam in the freshwater lake and the crystal clear sea . . .

Ana We can do it again whenever you want to . . .

Manuel I don't know if I want to.

Ana Did you get bored?

Manuel No! (*Unsure.*) And yet . . .

Julia (*interrupts*)   And yet, nothing. (*Points to the* **Director**.) We're the bored ones. (*Does a few steps of a dance.*) I'd like to stretch my legs. Doctor?

Director   I'm hopeless. I'll watch.

Manuel   I'll dance with my wife. Forgive me, chicken. I've been neglecting you.

Julia (*sweetly*)   Just a little bit!

Ana   Yes, yes, dance with Julia. It'll be a party!

Manuel   You've a weak heart. You think of nothing more than having fun. You've forgotten about the poor people already. (*Voice hoarse with emotion.*) They made me cry.

Ana   I didn't forget. I wanted to make you happy. You were so annoyed . . .

Manuel   Me annoyed? Annoyed with my favourite little sister? I was cruel, I know. (*He trips up his left foot with his right.*) Julia, if it won't make you jealous, I'll dance with Ana.

Ana (*lighting up*)   With me?

Manuel   She follows me better than you do.

Julia   I don't take offence or get jealous. There's no better choice. You two dance. I never get tired of watching you.

Manuel *seems as though he's about to walk towards* **Ana**, *who waits for him with a smile. He smiles as well but with an ambiguous smile, then walks in the opposite direction and puts his arms around* **Julia**. *They remain motionless.*

Director   Ana . . . (*She turns her head towards him, smiles helpless.*) I don't know how to dance, but I'd like to embrace you. I love you, you knew that, didn't you?

Ana   The old man in the old people's home . . .

Director   Who?

Ana   The grumpy one. Can I ask something of you?

Director   Anything you want. The more difficult it is, the happier you'll make me.

Ana   He wants *mate*. And . . . if possible . . . biscuits.

Director (*darkens*)   I'm not in control of everything. You know that I can't be in control of everything.

Ana   You love me?

Director   Yes. I've done nothing but love you my whole life. In silence, like someone who doesn't have the faintest hope of it being reciprocated. But now the hope is there, I only dream of . . .

Ana   What?

Director (*brings his face near as if to kiss her. Suddenly cracks up, can't keep a straight face*)   Bop! Bop! With that face! (*Bends over double, laughing.*) How could you think . . . ?

Ana (*half closes her eyes*)   You have to kiss me! You have to kiss me! (*He kneels on the floor, takes her hand, repeatedly kisses it. She gasps for breath, like a little girl after a fright.*)

Scene Four: Impossible Recomposition

The room in the old people's home. The **Old Man** *is sitting on the floor, a short chain around his ankle attaches him to the foot of the bed. He searches for a comfortable position, but he's unable to find one and he remains still. He has an anguished expression, but when* **Ana** *comes in with the mop and bucket, he tries to take on his usual air. She stops still when she sees him.*

Ana   The director will come and scream blue murder.

Old Man   I went to the concert at the Colón Theatre. No, no I didn't go.

Ana   And he'll say: what do you mean you haven't been to the concert at the Colón Theatre? (*Distressed, she goes towards the door, spies.*) No . . . no he still hasn't come. But when he gets here . . .

Old Man (*acidic*)   He'll exclaim: poor old man!

Ana   Yes. There's a padlock. (*She yanks at the chain.*) Whose idea was this? How . . . ? When did it happen?

Old Man   God asks fewer questions and still he forgives.

Ana   I'm asking you . . . because I don't need to forgive you.

Old Man   I wanted to get changed to go to the concert. He gave me two tickets as a gift.

Ana   You have cold feet.

Old Man   Yes. I'm freezing. Don't touch me!

Ana   I'll talk to the Director. He can't be in control of everything. That's why . . .

Old Man   No! Don't talk to that man! It's him who put me here.

Ana   Impossible.

Old Man   I should know!

Ana   What for?

Old Man   I made a scene. I wanted to go to the concert. Why give me two tickets if I couldn't go?

Ana   I'll bring you a chair. (*She looks at him. Forgets about her offer.*) Would you like . . . would you like me to show you? (*She lifts her hand to her cleavage.*)

Old Man   I'm not in the mood today. I have other things to think about.

Ana You've eaten.

Old Man Tea.

Ana He didn't give you . . . biscuits?

Old Man They kicked me out of the dining room. Biscuits! Ha, ha!

Ana But he said . . . He didn't give you cigarettes?

Old Man Yes!

Ana And sweets?

Old Man Yes! And then he took everything away from me, because of lung cancer and diabetes, and everything else under the sun!

Director (*comes in. To* **Ana**) What are you doing here?

Ana I was conversing with the gentleman.

Old Man (*tries to stand up straight*) Me!

Ana He has to get dressed to go to the park.

Director You're crazy. Don't interfere with the residents. I told you that. You sweep, clean, empty the chamber pots. Dead for the rest.

Ana He's . . . chained.

Director I ordered him to be. I had no other choice. He made a racket all night long.

Old Man My children will come and you'll see.

Director Shhhhh! Be quiet!

Old Man They'll come.

Director Your son pays the bill and runs away. The youngest, that is. Because the others . . .

Old Man They cried. What are you saying to me . . . to me!

Ana Your son is kind, a good heart.

Old Man Not so good . . .

Ana And the others suffer more because they don't have the money to pay for your pension.

Director He pays and runs away. He doesn't ask questions, he doesn't want to know about anything. And the others . . . they were born under a cabbage leaf: if I've seen you before, I don't remember.

Ana (*quietly*) They love, they love you.

Director In the afternoon I'll take off the chains, I'll give you six tranquillisers, but be sensible! Don't go and make a scene! (*To* **Ana**.) And you, get to cleaning the corridors! (*Exits*.)

Ana Yes, right away. (*She picks up the mop and bucket.*)

Old Man Don't go! You said you would bring me a chair. (**Ana** *looks for the metal chair, helps him to sit down, twisted at an angle, because the chain won't allow for more.*) Ah, I'm more comfortable. Don't you want to have a conversation?

Ana The Director ordered me to clean the . . .

Old Man He was lovely the other day. Couldn't you make him come back . . . kinder and . . . take these off me . . . and bring me . . .

Ana Yes.

Old Man I'm calm, my hands placed here. (*Contorted, he stretches them out on his thighs,* **Ana** *looks at him, serious.*) But before you were smiling. (**Ana** *attempts a smile.*) Not like that. It was a better smile. Everything changed. That smile gives me the creeps. I'm tired of not moving.

Ana (*tries to smile*) Oh God, I'm so sorry! (*She cries.*)

Old Man (*horrified*) Why are you crying? How disgusting! I haven't seen that for years! I don't want to see crying! (*Buries his head in his hands.*)

Ana (*looks at the* **Old Man**. *Contains her crying, wipes away her tears. She touches him gently*) Grandp . . . Mr Pérez . . . Forgive me. I had a stomach ache.

Old Man (*lifts his head, looks at her*) You're feeling delicate.

Ana Yes.

Old Man Is it hurting you now?

Ana No. Not anymore. A cramp. It came and went.

Old Man Well then? I'm getting ready. You gave me a fright. (*He makes himself comfortable on the chair.*) Ready. My old hands . . . (*He carefully lays them out on his thighs. He looks at* **Ana**, *anxiously waits.*) Smile! (*She smiles without being happy.*) Well, what's wrong? (*Looks around him.*) Nothing's wrong!

Ana Don't be impatient.

Old Man I'm sorry, I was confused. How should I sit?

Ana Like that is fine.

Old Man How can I be fine! Twisted on this chair, dying of cold. But you'd be able to. Couldn't you?

Ana Yes. He'll come . . . the Director and he'll say: how could they have put Mr Pérez in these conditions?

Old Man (*enthusiastically agrees*) Yes.

Ana He'll get upset. He'll . . . he'll take you to the park . . .

Old Man With the floss silk trees!

Ana   He himself. With his arm around your shoulders.

Old Man   He'll give me sweets. And I'll eat them all in one go so that later they don't take them away. (*He pauses.*) Well, I'm waiting! (*Anxious and desperate.*) Please, please! The other day was so lovely! I could wish for any old thing . . .!

Ana (*with a half smile, her eyes closed*)   It was lovely.

Director (*comes in, cheerfully greeting them*)   How I like to see you two together! How satisfying!

Old Man (*happy*)   She thought she had to clean the corridors! She's a slave in here. (*Points to his head.*) But she has to look after me. Doesn't she have to look after me?

Director   Constantly.

Old Man   Look. I'm chained. It's not a good therapy.

Director   My friend, it's me who decides about therapy.

Old Man (*briefly disconcerted*)   Miss . . . How should I understand him? (**Ana** *opens her eyes, her expression is sad. The* **Old Man** *to the* **Director**.) Of course! You would never decide to do something . . . stupid!

Director (*to* **Ana**)   Always here, twiddling your thumbs. And the corridors? Filthy!

Ana   I cleaned them.

Director   They're . . . Gleaming!

Old Man   Seeing as you're here, the chains . . . They put me in chains . . . ha, ha. The staff have lost their mind. You're not in control of everything, right?

Director   It was my instruction. So you wouldn't go astray.

Old Man   Don't you think it's a little excessive? How will I be able to go to the park . . . to . . . to the concert. How do I seem to you? A young man of . . .

Director   Decrepid.

Old Man   Decrepid?

Director   Ready for the hole in the ground.

Old Man   What did you say? Me . . . me ready for the hole in the ground? (*To* **Ana**.) It's your fault! You could change everything! And now? Why do you have to humiliate me?

Ana   I'll take you with me.

Old Man   Promise me nothing! Hopeless! Look! (*Rattles the chain.*)

Ana   I'll take you on a sailing boat. You'll like the sea. You'll see the seagulls which trail us, the water lapping the hull and the horizon so open . . .

Director   The only water she knows is that. (*Points to the bucket.*)

Old Man   She's mocking! She's mocking us! (*To* **Ana**.) Whore! You're making fun out me! I'll knock your teeth out! (*He tries to attack her, but he only manages to fall off the chair.*)

Director   Calm yourself. It's not worth it. (*To* **Ana**.) Disappear. Go and clean the corridors. Go! (**Ana** *picks up the mop and bucket and leaves*.)

Old Man   Good, now we're alone without that stupid girl. I would have to sit on the chair and put my hands like this . . . (*The* **Director** *goes towards him and helps him to sit*.) And so you . . . Why don't you fire her?

Director   I can't. Her brother recommended her.

Old Man   I can't stand her. So much prefacing with that shitty smile of hers!

Director   What was she doing? Because she was doing something, right? No sooner do I turn my back than I suspect the dumb girl's laughing at me.

Old Man   Her? She wasn't doing anything. She puts on airs and graces! She put my hands like this and closed her eyes and smiled . . . With that shitty smile!

Director   And?

Old Man   And you, do you remember? You came and gave me tickets to a concert.

Director (*amazed*)   Me?

Old Man   The silly girl took the credit. You are naturally a good man. So polite. You seated me on the chair.

Director (*ambiguous*)   Polite . . .

Old Man   You see!

Director   And good, you say?

Old Man   So very good!

Director   I lack malice, it's true. Is that what it means to be good?

Old Man   Of course! (*Looks at him anxiously. The* **Director** *smiles like a child being praised*.) So, the chains . . .

The **Director** *takes a step towards him. He stops, looks at him for a long time, without moving. The* **Old Man** *tugs at the chain, he lets it fall. Little by little his head droops, overwhelmed.*

Scene Five: The Dreamed One's Rebellion

The house. **Ana** *walks in with the* **Old Man**, *barefoot, in her nightdress. From time to time crying can be heard.*

Ana   Come. You're at home.

Old Man   Are you sure about what you've done?

Ana   What did I do? Invite you to my house.

Old Man   Is it yours?

Ana   My brother's. But there's no difference for him between what's mine and what's his.

Old Man   Do you hear?

Ana   What?

Old Man   Crying.

Ana (*listens*)   No. Nothing.

Old Man   You're deaf.

Ana   It must be an echo of all the crying you've heard.

Old Man   Who told you that I heard crying? I'm hearing this crying.

Ana   Which crying? (*They listen. Silence.*)

Old Man   They've stopped. They're gathering their strength.

Ana   Who? There's only Julia in her bedroom. Brushing her hair. She pulls the brush through her blonde hair a hundred times. It makes it shine like gold.

Old Man   Won't he tell me off?

Ana   Who?

Old Man   Your brother.

Ana   He's as good as gold. And his wife is too.

Old Man   Not to me, he'll kick me out as soon as he sees me. And his wife would do the same.

Ana   How untrusting. Goodness me, don't mistrust people so much. Sit down. I'll bring your slippers. And tea. Would you like tea?

Old Man   *mate* I don't want anything. I want to go back to the old people's home.

Ana   But, grandp . . . Mr Pérez, you don't like being there.

Old Man   I don't like being here either. Then I get more disappointed. (*The crying can be heard.*) I can hear it!

Ana   That's not going to happen to you. You'll be welcomed. Nobody will throw you out.

Old Man   Yes they will! I don't believe you. They stole the concert tickets from me, I didn't go to the park. They took me for an idiot! (**Ana** *closes her eyes, brings her hand to her chest.*) You don't convince me by closing your eyes! (*He looks at her, relents.*) Could you take a few years off me?

Ana (*opens her eyes, smiles*)   As many as you want.

Old Man (*laughs*)   Let's see if I appear in a nappy! (*He crumples.*) In a nappy . . .

Ana   Mr Pérez, come with me, come younger, come with your feet snug in slippers.

Old Man   You don't dream of much! Slippers! Why would I want to be shining the floor. If I could! . . . . I could . . . . Nothing.

Julia *enters from inside with dishevelled hair, her face very beaten up, her eyes swollen from crying. She stays next to the door.*

Ana   Anything is possible if you believe it is. Twenty years. Julia will come and brew you a good *mate* tea.

Old Man   Sweet?

Ana   Very sweet. (*She closes her eyes.*) Julia will come with her golden hair. And a black dress, long.

Old Man   And she'll tell me if I can stay?

Ana   Yes.

Old Man (*he notices her next to the door*)   She's arrived! In her black dress. But she's not blonde . . . (**Ana** *opens her eyes. The* **Old Man** *smiles, uncertain. To* **Julia**.) How are you?

Ana (*looks at* **Julia**. *Disconcerted*)   What happened to your face?

Julia   A caress.

Ana   So . . . forceful?

Julia   Idiot. Your brother hit me.

Ana (*disturbed*)   No. Manuel couldn't . . . It wasn't him. He's a kind man, he never had a trace of violence towards me. Towards anyone. (*She suddenly screams.*)

Old Man   My ankle hurts. (*He rubs it.*)

Julia (*crying with rage*)   I hate him!

Old Man (*terrified*)   She's crying!

Ana   I'll get you some ice. I'll talk to him. I'll tell him that he can't . . . under no circumstances can he . . .

Julia   And as soon as you talk to him, he'll ask for my forgiveness. All it takes is one word from you and he's moved. One plea from you and he'll drop to his knees before me, so repentant that he wishes himself dead.

Ana   Yes!

Julia   How pig-headed! He takes as much notice of you as of the leftover food that he either swallows or spits out. Even less.

Ana It's not true! (*She covers her mouth with her hand to stifle a scream.*)

Julia Stupid girl. You might slobber all over him, but you won't be able to have him in your bed. I have him!

Ana He hits you!

Old Man (*nervous*) I'm going. Where do I have to head? Left, right? I don't remember very well . . .

Julia Head anywhere. Who cares about you?

Ana Don't frighten him. I'll take him later.

Old Man I want to go back now! I want to go back home! I want to go back! (*He fastens his clothing.*)

Ana Wait. (*she brings him towards one of the armchairs*) Sit down. Remember, the other day . . . You open your eyes wide, I close mine, and Julia will begin to talk. You have no idea what a witty soul she is! She cracks me up.

Julia I'd crack open your skull. Such bullshit! Take this old man away from here. Who told you to bring him here?

Ana Manuel wants to get to know him.

Julia (*laughs*) He went off in a bad mood. You see? (*She shows her her face.*) He hits hard.

Manuel *comes in from the street.* **Julia** *slips away.*

Ana Manuel! We were waiting for you.

Manuel What for? Don't you work? And this old man?

Ana He's from the old people's home.

Manuel Psssst! Get up.

The **Old Man** *quickly gathers himself together.*

Ana I brought him so that . . . you'd get to know him.

Manuel Pleased to meet you.

Old Man (*calming down*) The pleasure is mine.

Ana (*throws herself around* **Manuel***'s neck*) Darling brother. I knew that you wouldn't mind. Seeing as Christmas is coming and he's on his own . . . (*To the* **Old Man**.) I'll bring you your slippers! (*To* **Manuel**.) He always has cold feet. (*She exits.*)

Manuel What a shame.

Old Man (*happy*) It's age. I hope the slippers are spares. Otherwise it would be . . . I don't know . . . taking advantage . . .

Manuel Yes. They're not spares. They're mine.

Old Man (*pleased*)   This girl . . .!

Manuel (*ambiguous*)   So generous . . .

Old Man   You give me your slippers, you invited me for Christmas . . .!

Manuel (*opens the door*)   I've had enough. Get out. You're not going to piss on my floor.

Old Man (*offended*)   I . . . I can hold it in!

Manuel   Go.

Old Man   To . . . where to? I don't remember where it is, the . . . I'm lost!

Manuel *grabs him by the back of his shirt and throws him out. He closes the door. Then he sits down, takes off his shoes.*

Ana (*comes in with the slippers. Her eyes scan the room for the* **Old Man**)   He left?

Manuel   Just a moment ago.

Ana (*disconcerted*)   Alone?

Manuel   Alone.

Ana   He must have suddenly rejuvenated.

Manuel   Yes. If you could see how agile he was! (*There's a timid knock at the door.*) Thanks for the slippers. (*Points to his feet.* **Ana** *smiles at him going between being frightened and being perplexed. She squats down in front of him and puts the slippers on his feet. She looks at him.* **Manuel** *takes her face between his hands. He brings her face close.*) I told you not to bring anyone. This is my house, not yours.

Old Man (*knocks, pokes his head shyly around the door*)   Forgive me. (*To* **Ana**.) You couldn't . . . ? I don't know where it is, the . . .

Ana   I'll come with you.

Manuel   He can get lost. Make some food. Don't get distracted. Did you see how Julia looked? You'll look worse. (*He pushes her.*) Move it!

Old Man   She forced me to leave the old folk's home! I didn't want to!

Manuel (*he smiles dangerously*)   You forced him to leave . . .

Ana   No! He came so happily! I talked to him about Christmas Eve . . .

Manuel   That we'd have it here. (*He pinches her hard.*) Move it!

Old Man   I didn't want to! And now, what street am I on? I don't remember . . . Where do I go? I don't know, I don't know . . .!

Manuel (*with a dark smile*)   I'll show you. You'll get there straightaway.

Ana   I'll come with you. It's just a second. Or better still . . . (*She closes her eyes, presses them shut with her fingers, brings her hand to her chest.*)

Old Man (*happy*)   I remember! I suddenly recall! Turning left and then . . .! I'm going before I forget! (*He disappears.*)

Manuel (*turns slowly towards* **Ana**, *comes closer, puts his hand on her shoulder*)   Ana. (*She lifts her face, illuminated, towards him. Her smile is uncertain.*) What happened?

Ana   The window.

Manuel (*lost*)   What?

Ana   We made a journey, do you remember? In a boat with three sails. We sailed the open sea. It's moored in the dock, so close to the house that we can touch it. (*She goes towards the window and opens it. There's nothing outside. Perplexed.*) It was here, with three masts and the sails waiting for the wind . . .

Manuel   And where is it? I know.

Ana   You do? In the dry dock after the journey.

Manuel (*ambiguous*)   What a trip!

Ana   Long, but in such a calm and crystal-clear sea.

Manuel (*with effort*)   Knot after knot, the boat parted the water . . .

Ana   Towards the island. It sailed wonderfully. It must suffer being in the dry dock. But it'll come out of there clean, cured of scratches.

Manuel   We carried a lot. You wanted to bring Mum's rocking chair, her bed, the knitted blanket . . . Even the little dog.

Ana (*laughs*)   He got sea sick. There's room, you said.

Manuel   Yes, lots of room in the boat.

Ana   And we unloaded everything onto the island, remember? We felt such joy! You put up a hut with wooden beams, a straw roof . . . Paradise.

Manuel   We didn't spot it.

Ana   What?

Manuel (*mimicking her*)   Remember? We didn't get anywhere.

Ana   Yes, we got to the island! In the boat!

Manuel (*hateful*)   It sank. We'd barely left the port when it sank. It wasn't even a shipwreck. It was a piece of rubbish that the sea sucked in. It was rotten. There was water, rotten woodwork, rotten sails, rotten dreams. You convinced me – I'll be your helmsman and your cabin boy! – and I almost drowned in that wreck.

Ana (*she screws her eyes shut, shakes her head*)   No! It's not true! No, no! It's not true!

Manuel   Yes, yes! It is. I swallowed water, I swallowed muck. I was scared. (*He moves towards* **Ana**, *takes her by surprise and lifts her up in his arms.*) I'll throw you down! Three floors and you'll be pulp! Puree!

Ana (*she struggles*)   No, no! Forgive me!

Manuel (*he holds onto her tightly*)   For what? Wasn't it a lovely trip, wasn't the sailing boat beautiful? Speak!

Ana   No, no it wasn't lovely!

Manuel   A wreck.

Ana (*her tears are falling*)   A wreck.

Manuel   Rotten. (*He smiles.*) I'll throw you down anyway.

Ana   No!

Manuel   No one will suspect me! She went head first. She had nothing inside. One less dot in the world!

Ana   I dragged you, I talked you into it! Forgive me! Manuel, forgive me!

Manuel *lifts her a little higher as if he were about to throw her down. Suddenly he laughs and brutally deposits her on the floor.* **Ana** *screams, no longer out of fear but as if before a horror she cannot bear. She flees inside while the* **Old Man** *bangs at the door, desperate.*

Old Man (*from outside*)   I'm lost! I don't know where it is, I don't know, I don't know! (*Banging.*)

Scene Six: As the Dream Dictates

The old people's home, the two metal beds and a chair. The **Old Man** *sleeps in one of the beds. At the head of the bed is a wreath of mistletoe. The* **Director** *is leaning over the* **Old Man**. *He pulls away, goes toward, the exit, bumps into* **Ana**. *Something has changed in her, as if she had another kind of clarity, more sorrowful and more secret.*

Director   You're late.

Ana   Am I? (*Smiles weakly.*) Two minutes.

Director   I'll forgive you because it's Christmas Eve. And because it's Christmas Eve, I'll let you care for a special resident. So he won't escape! The last time they brought him in here he was a mess. And it was your fault!

Ana   I'm sorry.

Director   It doesn't matter. It would have been better if he'd gone missing. They always pay late! I'm easily taken in. I never learn my lesson. You know what I did?

Ana   No.

Director   I've given him too many sedatives! I doubt he'll escape.

Ana (*looks at him*) He looks dead.

Director Sleeping.

Ana I don't like them to be put to sleep.

Director And who asked for your opinion?

Ana No one.

Director That's what I wanted to hear. I'm going home. They're waiting for me with a little Christmas tree.

Ana I'll celebrate tomorrow. But I'll be sleepy.

Director (*jovial*) You can't do everything! Duty first. (*He belches, raises his hand to his stomach.*) Something made me feel bad. (*Gropes around to find a chair, sits down.*)

Ana Don't panic. (*She stands over him.*) A dizzy spell.

Director Don't panic!

Ana I'll bring alcohol. (*Searches. Wavers between two bottles on the shelf. Chooses one and uncorks it.*)

Director (*sniffs the bottle which* **Ana** *waves under his nose. He sways*) That's not alcohol. Ya dim . . . wit.

Ana (*wets her apron and presses it into his nose. The* **Director** *struggles weakly, then passes out*) You can't do everything. To eat at midday, to eat at night . . . You'll sleep. You'll miss the party, but you'll wake refreshed, a little surprised. (*She drags him under the empty bed. She shakes the* **Old Man**.) Pssst . . . pssst . . .! Wake up.

Old Man Eh?

Ana (*she leans him against the bars of the bed*) Wait for me. I'll be right back. (*Exits.*)

Old Man Eh . . . Merry . . . eurgh . . . (*Mumbles, collapses.*)

Ana (*enters. She pushes a hospital trolley, with two paper cups, a bottle of wine, cake*) Christmas Eve! Silent night, holy night . . . The bells are ringing! Ding-a-ling-a-ling! Ding . . . (*Unintelligible sound from the* **Old Man**.) Come on, wake up! Look what you're missing! Grandp . . . Mr Pérez, do you hear me? (*Unintelligible sound.*) Sit down. (*He sits down, collapses.*) Don't let me down! (*Takes water from the bucket and dabs his face.*) Wake up!

Old Man You're . . . eurgh . . . blurry . . . Where . . . where did you put . . . your face?

Ana Sit up. We're having a party.

Old Man Th . . . th . . . they knocked me out. I'm . . . a good little boy. A baby. Let me sleep.

Ana I'll make coffee. Strong.

Old Man No! No! Not coffee!

Ana Then wake up.

Old Man Coff . . . coff . . . coffee's banned.

Ana Today it's not.

Old Man Dream that I sleep. So I can sleep.

Ana (*saddens*) I don't dream anything.

Old Man How . . . (*Jabbers.*)

Ana There's a big party in my house. But . . . I preferred to come here. I felt like it. Manuel became . . . (*Without conviction.*) so irritated because I preferred . . . (*Abruptly.*) He hit Julia. Did you know that? (*Quickly corrects herself.*) No, no he didn't hit her. He adores her. (*Laughs.*) And he wanted to throw me out the window! (*Straightens out the* **Old Man**. *Uncorks the bottle, pours the wine into the two little cups. She puts a cup in the* **Old Man**'s *hand. He supports it badly, it tips over. She lifts her cup to his.*) Chin chin. (*She drinks.*) Do you want cake?

Old Man Th . . . th . . . they don't let me . . .

Ana But you can eat a little. (*She puts a few crumbs in his mouth. He chokes and spits them out.*) Chew.

Old Man I don't feel like it. Dream . . . that you leave me alone. Go off in your sailing boat.

Ana It sank. It perished somewhere . . .

Old Man (*pulls himself up with some effort. Looks at her*) You saved yourself.

Ana I didn't save myself.

Old Man You're here!

Ana Poor thing, you don't understand when things die.

Old Man Thank . . . thank . . . goodness! I don't under . . .

Ana They do it so silently . . . Did you know? When I woke, I closed my eyes and it was Sunday.

Old Man It wasn't . . . Sund . . .

Ana No, it wasn't. It was only one more day. I had to get up.

Old Man My children . . . they don't come . . . the Sunda . . .

Ana They came today. This afternoon. You were sleeping.

Old Man No . . . I saw them . . .

Ana I was with them. They brought . . . wine, cake. I was with them.

Old Man Who . . . were you with?

Ana With your children.

Old Man They wanted to take me home.

Ana Yes, but the Director said no.

Old Man Why?

Ana A lot of excitement. That: a lot of excitement. It could make you ill. Only then did they accept it. But it was hard for them.

Old Man Sad?

Ana Oh, so sad! If you could have seen them. I saw them. They wanted to accept it, rise above the pain, but they couldn't. Each one was alone, as if they weren't siblings, as if they didn't know one another, their hearts exposed. The distress.

Old Man (*he looks at her amazed. In a whisper*) All this for me?

Ana (*with a different look, almost cruel*) Tomorrow you'll be more lucid.

Old Man Ah, they are so good . . .

Ana The Director will come, he'll tell you the same thing.

Old Man When?

Ana When? Now! He's already here. Come out! (*She drags the **Director** by his feet from under the bed, sits him up sprawled against the wall. The **Director** belches, snores. From time to time he strikes the floor with a limp hand. **Ana**, to the **Director**.*) Tell him how his children suffered. Pale and distressed.

Old Man He's snoring!

Ana Then I'll tell you.

Old Man (*anxious*) With all the details! Don't hold anything back. (*Silence.*) So?

Ana Your children . . .

Old Man (*helping her*) Pale, distressed.

Ana They didn't come.

Old Man Yes, you're wrong! This afternoon. They brought wine, cake . . .

Ana Your children have forgotten you.

Old Man (*pointing*) The cake!

Ana (*with a malicious smile*) I bought it. When they remember you, it gives them goose bumps, their hair stands on end. They're young. They don't want to know about old age, ailments, that life ends as their own life will end. It seems like a burden to them.

Old Man Me? A burden?

Ana An eczema that won't clear up, a bone that aches, a nuisance.

Old Man   What's . . . what's got into you? Why do you want to take everything away from me?

Ana (*desolate*)   Nothing that you have.

Old Man (*helpless*)   I have my children.

Ana   They forgot you.

Old Man   Incredible! They . . . they . . . forgot me . . . I don't believe it. Open the window! I'm suffocating! There's no air to breathe. Go on! Make yourself useful! (**Ana** *opens the window to the light of the night. The* **Old Man** *breathes anxiously*.)

Ana (*she looks at him. Takes pity*)   Breathe slowly.

Old Man   Summer. Fucking weather!

Ana   My dear old man . . .

Old Man   I'm . . . Mr . . . Pérez to you.

Ana   Dear old man . . . I love you.

Old Man (*hopeful*)   You love me? . . . (*He can't accept it*.) I don't love you. You're boring. Odious. You were more entertaining when you were talking about the sailing boat. To think that I believed that there were going to be biscuits!

Ana   It wasn't there. It sank, I said.

Old Man   Then let me sleep. (*He shrugs his shoulders and turns his back on her*.)

Ana   Don't you want to listen? They threw me out of home and I came to celebrate with you.

Old Man   Who asked you to? Celebrate with a dog.

Ana   I get in the way too, like a useless thing. Look. The cake, the wine . . .

Old Man (*facing her*)   It was my children who brought the cake . . . the wine . . . the sugared almonds . . . They thought of everything. Who knows how many things they brought and you made disappear along the way. They brought me a suit. Where is it? They'll come again because they want me at home. Not for tonight, forever.

Ana   I don't know them. I've never seen them sitting by your bedside.

Old Man   . . . Taking my hand . . . (*He reacts*.) And what proof do you have if you haven't seen them? You're envious! (*He turns his back on her*.) To hurt me . . . like this, you're envious . . .

Ana   They never come. But don't suffer. I came to celebrate with you. Don't you care? The two of us together at a great party. I'm your daughter . . . I could be, couldn't I? When you were young you lifted me up in your arms and promised me beautiful dreams . . . So perfect that there was no pain that could puncture them, no power . . .

Old Man (*quietly cries*)   Is it true . . . they forgot me?

Ana (*tries to caress him but the* **Old Man** *stretches out his arm and pushes her away without turning around*)   Don't cry. You have your daughter here, the one you promised beautiful dreams to . . . Remember? With love you were concerned to feed and clothe me, to divert the little stones in life that could hurt me . . . me . . . so clumsy, so silly. But you loved me. You cared for me in health and in sickness . . .

Old Man   They were . . . the light in my . . . pu-pi . . . pu-pi! . . .

Ana   In your pupils. And I forgot pain in your arms. You were kind to me.

Old Man   I cared for them.

Ana   You were kind to me and I never got in your way, isn't that so? And now you are a dear old thing, so old that you cannot dream more than death, and me helpless. I'm your daughter . . . Father, together at the party . . . (*She kneels down on the other side of the* **Old Man**, *her head and shoulders resting on the bed.*)

Old Man (*after a moment, as if* **Ana**'s *sadness has got through to him and he wants to respond in some way, he reaches his arm out behind him. Without turning around he strokes her head*)   Together . . . it's okay, it's okay. Thank you for coming . . . Thank you . . . It's a great party.

They remain still. While the light dims, the open window reveals the masts and sails of the boat in the night air, slowly moving forwards.

Curtain.

Asking Too Much (2004)

The premiere of *Asking Too Much* was on 28 May 2004 in the Orestes Caviglia Theatre of the Cervantes National Theatre in Buenos Aires with the following cast:

Elena   Ingrid Pellicori
Mario   Horacio Peña

Set Design and Costume: Jorge Ferrari

Lighting: Gonzalo Córdoba

Music: Ernesto Jodos

Assistant Direction: Virginia Lombardo

Staging and Direction: Alicia Zanca

Characters

Mario
Elena

Translator's Note

For the most part, the two characters, Mario and Elena, address one another in the formal '*usted*' form which the Spanish language affords. However, at moments in the play, both characters lapse into the informal form of address. This introduces an ambiguity about the nature of the characters' relationship to one another. In English it is not possible to reproduce these subtle, yet crucial, modulations without somewhat heavy-handed solutions. I have chosen to indicate where these changes take place, but leave it open as to how this might be interpreted dramatically.

Laughter can be heard. **Mario** *and* **Elena** *come in from the street, a bit tipsy.*

Elena   It's a good joke. My memory's not the best. I never remember the jokes people tell me.

Mario   I do. Like elephants. Why do they talk about an elephant's memory? Do you know?[1]

Elena   Because if anyone kicks them, they never forget. They remember a hundred years later.

Mario   No, that's holding a grudge. (*Draws close to her face.*) It's the elephant's memory because they remember the place where they're going to die. (*She pulls away. He shows her a photo on the wall.*) Do you like it? You used to like photos of landscapes. I used to look for them for you.[2] Special landscapes, with water. The sea, or a river. Places, currents that carry us away.

Elena (*distancing herself*)   Yes. I like those landscapes. Even now. I told you that back when you put it up . . .

Mario   A year and two months ago.

Elena   You had moved into your apartment. It was the first time I came here. There were a few things to sort out and I came.

Mario   Ah. I was thinking you hadn't seen that photo, that you hadn't been to my place. What are you having to drink?

Elena   Nothing alcoholic. Coffee. I already drank quite a bit at dinner.

Mario (*he puts a glass in her hand*)   So what? A nightcap doesn't count. Drink up. We're not going to get drunk on one glass . . .

Elena (*laughs*)   More! That's debatable. I'm feeling pretty light-headed.

Mario   Light-headed? In what way?

Elena   Like my head's in the clouds. I have to go.

Mario   Yes, at some point you have to go. If it's ten minutes later, half an hour, it makes no difference.

Elena   I'll have a drink and go. They're waiting for me.

Mario   Who's waiting for you?

Elena   I'm married, you know that.

Mario   Ah, how could I forget? My congratulations. (*Silence from* **Elena**.) You don't accept them?

---

1   Mario addresses Elena in the informal form *el voseo*.
2   Here too Mario addresses Elena in the informal form. Elena responds in the formal *usted* form.

Elena Of course I do.

Mario I'm sure you're anxious to get back. I can see it in your face. Do you want to go now? I won't keep you. Not if you don't want to. Not against your will. (*With a certain rudeness he takes the glass from her hand.*)

Elena (*taking it back*) I'll have a drink, I said.

Mario Then, let's drink in peace. Cheers. (*Pause.*) It's hot. Don't you think it's hot in this apartment?

Elena No.

Mario The sun's been pouring in all day. An oven. Is your place cooler?[3]

Elena The same.

Mario Not the same. No two apartments are the same. The people who live in them are not the same. Do you know what Saint Francis used to say?[4]

Elena About apartments?

Mario No. He used to say, forgive me, Lord, for having committed the sin of sadness. Or did someone else say that? I don't know. I've drunk too much. Let's say it was Saint Francis.

Elena (*smiley*) Which one of them? There are loads. Good saints, bad saints. And they all used to call themselves Francis. The one who used to sing to the rosaries? To brother sun, sister moon?

Mario That's the one. Do you see Saint Francis?[5]

Elena Do I see him? Where? (*She cracks up.*) In an apartment? I don't know why I'm laughing. I'm drunk. No, I don't see him.

Mario I do. I see him. Short, skinny, a little dirty, with short nails because he used to bite them.

Elena There weren't any scissors! (*Laughs, she can't stop.*)

Mario (*looks at her, serious. Waits for her to stop laughing. Takes up where he left off*) With short nails because he used to bite them. He had renounced everything this Saint Francis.

Elena That was his duty. If saints are as they should be, they must mortify their flesh. They're all skinny, full of arrows. It's a very sacrificial life. They can't run after luxury, money, women . . .

Mario This guy didn't run. He had renounced everything. His titles, luxury, women. Not out of humility, it was calculated. It was a pure game: to win God, paradise. He

---

3   Here Mario lapses into the informal form of address.
4   Mario addresses Elena in the informal *voseo* form in this line.
5   Mario addresses Elena in the informal *voseo* form in this line.

made a calculated bet on sacrifice, on a serene soul and so pure that he could speak to animals like kindred spirits, as equals. What he wasn't expecting was this: one day, in the sun, the Italian countryside, the hills . . ., everything perfect, the little birds were singing all around him, they would perch on his shoulders, he's eaten hard bread, drunk water: a banquet, he kneeled and, pow! The day got dark, the little birds turned into vultures, paradise turned into a nightmare because he couldn't imagine it.

Elena (*taking her distance*)   And why did that happen to him? I don't understand.

Mario   *You* don't understand?

Elena   I do business deals. With everything else . . . maybe I lack a little shrewdness, I don't know. You're skilful at some things and useless at others. (*Points.*) What does that window look out on?

Mario   On an airshaft.

Elena   And why did they make it so small? If you changed it into a bigger window, the apartment would be cooler. Air conditioning would also be a solution.

Mario   I can't now. Work, you know?

Elena   You lost your job?

Mario   No, no. But the situation's uncertain. So uncertain that . . .

Elena   You shouldn't have spent so much tonight.

Mario   On a meal? I wanted to make a good start. Our first, long meal since . . .

Elena (*interrupting him*)   I think I can smell gas.

Mario   Can you?

Elena   I can smell it. Can't you?

Mario   I can only detect . . . a delicious, chaste perfume. (*Draws close to her.*) A scent of lavender, mixed with . . .

Elena   Better to make sure. There could have been a leak.

Mario   A leak? No . . . Everything's new here. Even your perfume.

Elena   Distractions are dangerous. Listen to me. Go.

Mario   Hmmm! Actually, I bet you're scared of other risks. (*Winks at her.*) Let's see. (*Goes out.* **Elena** *puts down her glass, stands.* **Mario** *comes back in.*) Everything in order. One of the knobs wasn't turned off properly in the kitchen. It only let out a small whiff. Good sense of smell.

Elena   A small whiff in the end can form a cloud. Don't be reckless.

Mario (*laughs, mocking*)   You're looking out for me! You wouldn't miss much, believe me.

Elena (*picks up her things*)   It's time for me to go.

Mario (*takes them from her*) A bit longer.

Elena They're waiting for me, I told you.

Mario Oh, whoever's waiting for you must know that you had a date with me. (*With intention.*) You wouldn't have hid that from him, would you?

Elena Not in any way.

Mario So he won't be very worried? Or will he?

Elena It's late.

Mario I'm not asking you to spend the whole night, for it to be hours before you appear, until dawn, for example, but . . . for a moment . . . It's okay, there are clingy types who always pressure you. They'll use any excuse to make a fuss. Is he one of those?

Elena (*categorical*) No. Not at all.

Mario Isn't there jealousy between you? A lack of trust?

Elena No.

Mario He doesn't follow you around like a sad bastard? There are men who . . .

Elena Suffocating.

Mario Very difficult to put up with.

Elena Very difficult. With them, the air gets thinner.

Mario Speaking of suffocation . . . some people commit suicide with gas. They don't mind the tang. They seal the windows. Stuff newspapers in the cracks around the doors. Blankets . . . Then, when the guy has achieved what he wanted to, if it occurs to anyone to investigate the smell in the hallway . . ., forces the door . . . and lights a match, pum! He dies with them. Even though it was because of someone else's death, he's obliterated. I think it's inconsiderate.

Elena (*coldly*) Committing suicide is always inconsiderate.

Mario Yes, to let other people do your dirty laundry, for other people to bury it.

Elena It was an exquisite meal. I enjoyed it a lot. I come from a village where we're used to eating badly.

Mario Out of poverty?

Elena Not always. Out of a lack of refinement. It sounds awful, but that's the truth. Cooking is a laborious art. Not everyone knows how to do it.

Mario (*laughs*) How you used to cook![6] (*Rapidly pours himself a glass of water and Elena observes him.*)

---

[6] Mario addresses Elena in the informal *voseo* form in this line.

Elena (*gently remarks*)   You're very thirsty!

Mario   It's hot in this apartment.

Elena   Having a big window would solve the problem. Or air-conditioning.

Mario (*serves himself another glass of water, drinks it*)   Aren't you going to ask me?

Elena   What should I ask you? Why you're drinking so much water?

Mario   Precisely!

Elena (*shrugs her shoulders*)   You're thirsty! Because it's hot. Or the food was salty . . .

Mario (*laughs*)   To put out so much fire! You lose![7]

Elena (*yawns*)   I said that if you don't want air-conditioning, a big window would solve the problem . . .

Mario (*impatient*)   Yes, yes. I heard you. I'll consider it. At some point I'll take the measurements, the builders will come, break everything, put in the big window . . . (*Abruptly.*) My wife left me. Maybe it's because I didn't make up my mind in time. About the window. (*Uncomfortable, her expression is engaged.*) I knew she was going to leave me, I tried to convince her otherwise.

Elena   And you didn't succeed.

Mario (*points*)   You see! She made up her mind to separate and there was no way of moving her. And not because she was a stone. She was . . . sweet. I talked to her about how I felt, about being abandoned, and her face flushed, her eyes began to fill with tears and I regretted having told her. But deep down she was unmoved.

Elena (*dryly*)   Sorry, why are you telling me this? I'm happy, I don't want to know. You're even trying to make me feel sorry for you.

Mario   Your face is flushed.

Elena   No. I've done my crying.

Mario   You feel like laughing, you feel like crying. I never would have believed it.

Elena   But I prefer to save my tears. They never gave me relief. They make me weak, and even humiliate me, most of all when they're useless, when I can't help.

Mario   That must happen to you a lot.

Elena   What?

Mario   That: not being able to help.

---

7   Mario addresses Elena in the informal *voseo* form in this line.

Elena Where did you get that idea? I'm referring to the fact that some people will take the nearest shoulder to cry on. I appreciate it if they don't. You'd also be grateful.

Mario (*joking*) I only complained about the heat!

Elena Then don't feel this applies to you.

Mario How can I not? It was very direct. I used your shoulder? (*Shakes his head.*) I'm immune. To crying. People can tell me about the greatest disasters and it doesn't move a hair on my body. Leaves me cold. Someone else's sorrows don't affect me.

Elena (*acidly*) Only your own.

Mario Not even my own. I'm a man. (*He opens the drawer of a dresser, then another.*) Where was it? I put it somewhere here. (*Taking up the thread again.*) My wife left me.

Elena (*irritated*) So you said.

Mario She left, crying. She filled her suitcase with clothes, picked it up and walked through that door. Her own tears didn't move her. I loved her. And I told her so. Useless. As if she were listening to rain.

Elena (*hard*) Perhaps it wasn't like that. Otherwise why did she leave crying?

Mario (*doesn't listen to her*) What a lack of imagination. The terrible thing about someone who stops loving you is that they totally lose their imagination in relation to the other person who *does* go on loving. They can't even imagine the desperation. (*Looks at her.*) Your imagination doesn't keep you awake at night, does it?

Elena Not in order to worry me. It only keeps me awake about some things.

Mario Yes, only about some things. (*Smiles.*) About business. (*Looks through the drawers.*)

Elena What are you looking for?

Mario This. (*Takes a gun out of the drawer. Looks at it and puts it down.*) I couldn't beg her. Out of pride. I made jokes, from time to time I invited her out for dinner, as I've invited you. Deep down, Saint Francis was naïve, sadness is always all around us. Tempting us.

Elena Where is that animal barking? What a racket. Can you hear it?

Mario It's the neighbour's. It's gone to sleep now. Before she left me, she confessed that she'd fallen in love. I found it difficult. I'd been in cloud cuckoo land. If you could have seen her face!

Elena Flushed, I suppose.

Mario Guilty.

Elena She was honest.

Mario   What for? What good was her honesty to me? It only gave her relief. It sunk me.

Elena   Oh, you're never satisfied![8] If she hadn't been honest, you would have accused her of lying. What did you propose? Deception? One lie after another?

Mario   She didn't ask me about my preferences. Perhaps that's what I wanted. Many people live happily . . . like this. Knowing and not wanting to know.

Elena   Until the roof caves in on top of them.

Mario   She didn't take long. In bringing the roof down on top of me. She had fallen in love. Not with me. Was it possible? Not with me. Not with me anymore.

Elena (*harshly*)   Not with you anymore. And?

Mario   Do you think that I made a scene? You're wrong. I held it together. Unmoved, as I said. I didn't get angry, I didn't make reproaches . . . She objected to me carrying her suitcase, if she hadn't . . . imagine. I would have carried it to the taxi. I acted like a gentleman. With such serenity! Such grace! Do I not seem to you like a gentleman, a courteous guy?

Elena (*violent*)   No! No you don't. A gentleman doesn't talk about . . . anything!

Mario   I didn't tell her about . . . anything. I didn't tell her that when she packed her bag and walked out, when she closed the door behind her, my world collapsed. I threw myself head first against the walls. How childish, eh? I cut myself down to the bone. I caught myself on the edge of the window. Can you see the scar?

Elena   You can hardly notice it anymore.

Mario   After I banged myself, though not because my head was split open, what did I do? I howled like a lunatic, like the wolf man. Desperate. This howl was something I'd never uttered to her. It could have moved her. What do you think?

Elena   I don't know. Perhaps she was moved, a part of her was desperate, and she hid it.

Mario (*laughs*)   A part of her was desperate? Desperate in subdivisions, in little pieces? You know nothing of desperation, my friend.

Elena   If she could have made something better, I don't know, comfort in some way that was within her reach, don't you think she would have done it? She left with her suitcase, you said, and I could say to you that she didn't come back to look at that man she'd abandoned because . . .

Mario   Because she had all the cruelty of someone who's happy.

Elena   And what solution do you propose? What? How could she make things better? I can't think of anything. Pretend to feel what she didn't feel?

---

8   This is the first time Elena lapses from the *usted* form and addresses Mario in the informal *voseo* form, after which she immediately reverts to using *usted*.

Mario You can always make a kind gesture. I wanted to touch her. So strange, isn't it? I wanted to touch her. But I didn't tell her that. Out of pride. (*Looks absentmindedly at the gun on the dresser, spins it round his fingertip.*) And she didn't have the imagination to be able to know it without me telling her.

Elena I've been watching you for a while now. Why don't you stop playing with that gun? You're having fun but it's annoying me.

Mario Are you scared?

Elena It annoys me. That gun doesn't scare anyone. It's a relic; if it isn't rusted it won't be long until it is. It hasn't worked for years.

Mario Not so. I sent it to be fixed when this story started . . . (*Smiles.*) about burglars. You have to protect yourself, don't you? To shoot first.

Elena The cure's worse than the disease. Don't you read newspapers? This thing about firing first, you don't always get it right, they fire back. And with greater precision. (*Abruptly picks it up. Puts it back in the drawer, closes it with a dry slam. They look at each other. With a mute violence, staring at her, he opens the drawer and she closes it again. He tries two or three times more and she refuses to let him. Mario ends up moving her aside with his own body, a little brutally, and then, giving up with a contemptuous shrug,* **Elena** *relents and returns to her place.*)

Mario (*spins the gun on his fingertip*) I don't hurt anyone. But if it annoys you . . . (*Puts his hand up.*) She was very . . . inflexible. When she decided to leave me there was no going back. Done deal.

Elena And why did you keep on at her? It's not smart to go on about it. It's also irritating. You have to leave people in peace.

Mario Don't be odious.

Elena Why? All I'm saying is that we're not the masters of anyone.

Mario Masters? Who thinks that? I never felt like the master of anything, or anyone. Least of all of her, who was so . . . inflexible. If I needed her for something, it was with so many precautions, so many fears . . . Sometimes I thought that she was moved, that she was on the point of agreeing to . . .

Elena Never come back.

Mario To make love to me. Not love. To make tenderness, compassion, to repeat love like brother and sister. Because she had loved me so much.

Elena She was wary. She would have felt bad. You both would have felt bad afterwards.

Mario Who knows? Who can be sure of it with any certainty?

Elena She didn't love you.

Mario She said she did . . . fraternally. And why couldn't we have made love . . . fraternally? Or with some other feeling, not passion but . . . a remnant of affection.

Elena It's not enough. You need . . .

Mario What? There isn't only one kind of love, is there? There are so many, good or not, generous, cruel . . . And ultimately, they all have their place. The thirsty can be thankful for murky water. There was a time when we were reading a book together. Not together. I was reading it at night, she in the day.

Elena I don't read much. I think I've missed out. Was it interesting? But don't tell me! Books are like nightmares, better not to talk about them. Only the bare bones of it remain, and the poor sod who listens to it doesn't understand the pleasure, the admiration . . .

Mario Or the anguish, in the nightmare.

Elena You try to look like you're interested and you die of boredom.

Mario You're not going to get bored. I'll tell you. In two seconds. A big-boned woman falls in love with a small hunchback and the hunchback himself falls passionately in love with a bodybuilder who's a pervert. How they suffer, they abuse each other, even hate each other. And despite everything, this book was only talking about love. Actually . . .

Elena You protect yourself from this kind of love.

Mario Go for the safe option.

Elena Yes, get away from problems if you can. And better still any feeling that's driven by pity.

Mario And who wants pity? Is that all there is in the larder? Only pity? (*Spins the revolver on his fingertip. A silence.*) Are you scared[9]?

Elena Of what?

Mario I could fire it.

Elena At who? (*He looks at her mocking. Allusive.*) At me? Two people celebrating a deal go to dinner on friendly terms, drink a little more . . . there's no motive. No, no I'm not a bit scared.

Mario You could be.[10] I could shoot myself. 'Dying is an art. / Like everything else, / I do it exceptionally well.'

Elena (*laughs*) Do you want to scare me?

Mario (*after a moment, he laughs too*) Yes, I think so. You got me!

Elena You're not that kind of man. You don't get depressed easily. And that gun is pure scrap metal.

---

9 Mario addresses Elena in the informal *voseo* form in this line.
10 Mario addresses Elena in the informal *voseo* form in this line.

Mario Hmmm . . .! You seem like the other woman. Immovable. After the separation, the divorce was later, we remained friends. She thought it was possible. That, to remain friends. To meet up from time to time and to tell each other the little things that make up a life.

Elena Why not?

Mario Because I loved her. (*Looks at her.*) I couldn't touch her. (*Strokes his face.*) Not even this. Impenetrable.

Elena You give too much importance to love. I prefer friendship, like you and I have between us. It's a friendship I would call . . . affectionate . . . – but not intimate – that's why it's good. Tonight the drink changed the goalposts, I'm sorry.

Mario When she left me, I didn't only cry out. I got thin, drank too much. Not like tonight, much more. Without enjoying it, out of neglect, perhaps spite. I also thought about lying down on the train tracks like someone who takes a siesta, to stay there, very quietly . . .

Elena (*making fun of him*) To terrorise yourself, to scream with panic, and jump far away at the first sound of the train! Yes, sometimes these ideas go through your mind. But acting on them is another matter.

Mario I had made up my mind. I lost resolve for another reason: I thought it was very harsh.

Elena (*joking*) Yes, it is harsh.

Mario It wouldn't have been for me. The train crushes you, chops your body in half like a wild animal, and then . . . into pieces. If a child was walking by and saw them. It would have ruined his childhood. And then what an unpleasant job for those people who were going to have to pick up the torso, the head, the little arms . . . some fingers! Put them in a bag. That stopped me.

Elena You've got a balcony! I hadn't seen it.

Mario I *do* have a balcony.

Elena That's exactly why you need the big window. The air would flow from one end to the other.

Mario (*takes her by the hand*) I'll show you. Come!

Elena No, no. Not to the balcony.

Mario (*laughs*) I'm not going to throw you over it. We could look at the moon together, at the stars . . . A little bit of romance never did anyone any harm, did it? I'd put my arm around your shoulders, (*He does so.*) draw you closer to me . . . (*Brusquely tries to kiss her.*)

Elena (*violently pulls away*) I didn't come for this.

Mario Then what did you come for? You might imagine that I would try to. You're not stupid. Or so innocent.

Elena I came because I knew you would like to share a last drink at home. The dinner was pleasant, to talk like friends. What's wrong with you? Don't misinterpret.

Mario Forgive me. You saw that I wanted to keep my distance. Until now . . .! (*Lifts his hands up with open palms.*)

Elena Carry on keeping your distance.

Mario You're bad tempered. Any other woman would feel flattered.

Elena That's what men think.

Mario Don't get irritated. 'And suddenly there came a sound from heaven as of a rushing mighty wind.' That is desire.

Elena When it's shared. Otherwise you can't hear the noise or the wind.

Mario So drastic. So sure of yourself. So much certainty must give you such peace.

Elena You're wrong. Sometimes it doesn't make sense to ruin two lives.

Mario When you can ruin just one.

Elena Why did St Francis ask for forgiveness for the sin of being sad?

Mario You want to change the subject.

Elena Yes.

Mario That's why! Because it was a sin when he had everything. But he didn't have everything. Who knows whether he missed St Clare, who knows if he discovered that he couldn't stand little birds and couldn't turn back because everyone was talking about him treating all animals as equal. Everyone admired him: Oh, Saint Francis, oh, oh! (*Pale, closes his eyes*.) And the poor man didn't know what to do with his sorrow.

Elena (*gets up*) He felt too sorry for himself, I think, your Saint Francis.

Mario You don't have sympathy for him.

Elena (*delays for a moment in answering him*)   Yes . . . But perhaps the birds wanted him to leave them alone, not to annoy them any more with his little breadcrumbs and his chat and his whinging.

Mario He didn't whinge about anything.

Elena No? It's better that way. It's late. I'm going. (*Picks up her things*.)

Mario (*takes them from her hands*)   Not yet. Wait. I have an idea, and don't dismiss it.

Elena What idea? You don't have many, only a fixed one.

Mario That's nasty! Why are you so nasty? Listen . . . (*Beats his hands against a piece of furniture then, steadying himself, soon begins a catchy rhythm. He looks at her, charming and smiling. Suddenly,* **Elena** *smiles back, joins in with him beating the same rhythm with her hands. There is a brief, complete moment of release. And then* *he begins to hum and they dance separately, with the same mood of release, until* **Mario** *suddenly forcefully dances with her, buries his mouth in her neck.*)

Elena (*she resists, pulling away*)   Stop it now.

Mario   Why? Aren't we having fun? Music? A little tango? We don't need to talk. I won't torment you anymore.

Elena   We've talked a lot.

Mario   I've talked a lot, you said very little. Come on, fair play. It's your turn now. And don't hold anything back.

Elena   You really want to listen to me?

Mario (*a silence*)   No . . . I don't think so.

Elena   So . . .

Mario (*as if he won a bet*)   I talked! I told you about the other woman, the one who left with her suitcase without looking back. I talked!

Elena   Excessively.

Mario   No, no. Not excessively. How long's it been? A year, two months, that I haven't talked.

Elena (*laughs*)   How did you do it?

Mario   I don't know. It happens. But now the dam has broken. I have more to tell you.

Elena   No, no. Stop. Have mercy. There's more still? It really is something, this story of yours!

Mario   Interesting.

Elena   You get to the point, one thinks: thank goodness it's come to an end, and no, it goes on, it goes on! You ended up making me into your confidant.

Mario   Yes I did, when someone pays you attention . . .

Elena   I don't give you my attention.

Mario   Don't lie.

Elena   Or I give it to you out of politeness.

Mario   You're lying. You like listening to me. You like me telling you that every minute I think about that woman, who doesn't love me anymore. More than that. *I go to sleep* thinking about that woman, who doesn't love me anymore. Did I tell you that? I didn't tell you. But pain doesn't last, does it?

Elena   Not even the deepest of wounds.

Mario   Everything comes to an end. It's true. Even though you try to resist them, feelings take their own course, kill us with love, with anguish, and one day, puff! They disappear. They never existed.

Elena   Yes, they existed! They disappear for some reason. Because passion deceives us, we get bored. That's what must have happened to her, to that woman who left with her suitcase without looking back.

Mario   It'll happen to me. Some morning I'll wake up and her memory will hold no weight any more. In the end it'll be the languor of hunger at the mouth of the stomach.

Elena   We survive, that day always comes.

Mario   And in the meantime?

Elena   Take your mind off it. (*He bursts into brutal laughter, almost grotesque.*) Did I say something funny? At least tell me what you find so funny. So that I can share the joke.

Mario   Nothing. There's no joke, not even sleep is a place where she could leave me in peace. Even *there* she doesn't leave me. She comes and goes. Sometimes it's like before, other times like now. And as she comes and goes, coming into my bedroom or waving goodbye from the door, I wait for the moment when falling out of love doesn't mean anything. A small bare wall.

Elena   So, before the bare wall, you'll realise that she really isn't worth so much pain. That she too can be replaced.

Mario   Don't be so sure. There are days I wake up and the wall's there. She's leaning against the wall. Who is she? Her face is any face, her mouth any mouth. And yet I recognise her gestures and those gestures don't provoke nostalgia in me anymore. Then, how strange, before that empty figure against the wall, do you know what I feel?

Elena   Peace.

Mario   Noooo . . .!

Elena   You jump for joy. So much hitting your head against the wall . . . You think: how foolish, how over the top I was!

Mario   I think: how foolish! But without any happiness. How? She's already a stranger, doesn't matter to me anymore? She's not even a wound, a pang? How could I forget like this? So . . . banal. I can't bear it.

Elena   (*ironically*)   You'd rather remember her. You want to hold on to the suffering. You're very contradictory.

Mario   Yes! Yes, I'm such an idiot! (*Furious.*) And you are for not getting it. At least she's in my suffering! And I want her to be!

Elena   Oh, my God, why don't you shut up? You make me uncomfortable, wear me out. You've lost all your dignity. You display your pain like a gift. You offer it to me. I don't want it. It's a gift with thorns. Your problems don't belong to me. I've problems of my own. Perhaps they'll leave me some day, and then . . . I'll see. But I won't make this exhibition, do this . . . guilt tripping.

Mario Shut up!

Elena Wasn't it my turn? You only want to hear words that suit you, that's what you want. To be returned to the mother's womb, to be cradled, to be comforted. By whom? You're looking in the wrong place. Not by me. I can't do anything. More than have dinner sometimes with you and to talk about one thing or another, nothing that concerns ourselves too much.

Mario And how does that help me?

Elena You asked me to come.

Mario And you agreed.

Elena I made a mistake. I didn't need to see you. I'm not dying to know every second how you are, how you're suffering, how you lick your wounds. Least of all now, when . . . (*She falls silent.*) I can spend time in your presence perfectly well. And in the presence of many other people at that.

Mario (*after a silence*) You're happy.

Elena I am. And to hide your own happiness is difficult. Happiness isn't so easy to come by, is it, so that we hide it, so that it's a stain, so that ashamed we deny it? It wants to show itself, happiness. And the one who's unhappy has to have the strength to be able to deal with it.

Mario Deal with it? How easy. Why don't you ask that of the people who've never experienced it?

Elena I'm only talking about you.

Mario About me . . . specifically, about me?

Elena About this poor creature who is suffering. And if you want to make a comparison, then compare yourself with those who suffer hunger or death, not 'because she left me'. That's sorrow, yours isn't.

Mario Mine isn't?

Elena No! I think it's pathetic.

Mario (*ironic*) It's not worth the bother. My sorrow. *In comparison.*

Elena In comparison, yes. She's happy without guilt. *In comparison.* She got lucky.

Mario She did quite a lot in order to get lucky.

Elena But not as much as having luck itself. Yes, she helped. She wasn't indifferent. She took care of that situation which brought you a different person.

Mario And displaced the other one.

Elena She was already becoming a different person before then. And she got lucky by enjoying life. And in the name of what cause would she have let that pass her by? Like I said, happiness isn't so easy to come by.

Mario And I couldn't let mine pass me by, the difficult time.

Elena She can't be celebrating it. And neither can I, believe me.

Mario That's lucky.

Elena But it irritates me. Your pain irritates me.

Mario Good protection, getting irritated.

Elena What do you expect? It's self-defence. Your pain descends over me like a net. You want me to share it, make it better, I don't know what you want.

Mario Not your pity.

Elena Really? When bread's scarce, anything will do. Even this exhibition of suffering. Put an end to it, for God's sake! She left you with her bags, so hate her, bite your tongue before asking for the impossible. (**Mario** *looks at her, turns his back to her. When he does, she doesn't stop looking at him, sighs, relaxes the tension in her. A change occurs, a heavy expression surfaces on her face. After a long time, she goes towards the music system.*) Mario! (*He turns, looks at her sadly, probing, also distant.*) We could . . . listen to music. Calm the wild beasts. (*She smiles.*) The rows. (*She turns on the machine.*)

Mario (*he turns it off*) Some other day.

Elena Why not today? To end the night in a more . . .

Mario Favourable way? I'm tired. Not of you! Simply, the tiredness has suddenly hit me, I'm sleepy. I'm sure to go out like a light. I've been inconsiderate. Forgive me. Also for having kept you. (*He hands her her scarf, carefully winds it around her neck.*)

Elena It doesn't matter. It was a good meeting, the dinner. If we fought afterwards it was . . . We have lively personalities.

Mario Exactly. (*He goes towards the door.*) Goodbye.

Elena (*laughs, uncomfortable*) Don't throw me out![11]

Mario I'm not throwing you out. Please! But I have to get up early tomorrow. I already told her, the other woman, everything I had to say. Immovable.

Elena Perhaps . . .

Mario (*he covers her mouth with his hand*) Sshhh . . .

Elena Your hands are cold.[12]

---

11 From this point, Elena addresses Mario in the informal form while Mario responds to her in the formal form.

12 Elena addresses Mario in the informal form.

Mario Yes. After so much heat . . . Come to think of it, I don't need the big window. Go on. It's very dark, so silent . . . Picture the street. Even this room seems empty, as if we weren't here anymore.

Elena (*joking*) Oh, if we're not here anymore that's because you really want me to go.[13]

Mario If you take it like that . . . No. I really do have to get up early.

Elena I'm going. (*With a glance towards the gun.*) That gun is not a very nice ornament. Put it away, please. Does it work, like you said? Or was that a joke?

Mario It's not even loaded. It's an old gun. How could it work! It's scrap metal.

Elena Goodbye. Thanks for dinner. You shouldn't have spent so much. Look after yourself. (*She kisses him. She doesn't pull away immediately.*) Give yourself time.[14]

Mario I will. Goodbye. (*Before leaving, she takes his hand in a vague attempt at a caress, lets it fall. Goes out.* **Mario** *remains still for a moment. Then he goes to the dresser, spins the gun on the tip of his finger.*) It's not revenge. It's not revenge. You'll understand, won't you? It isn't because of you.[15] It's because Eden belongs to nowhere. (*He picks up the gun.*)

Curtain.

---

13 Elena addresses Mario in the informal form.
14 In these final words to Mario, Elena addresses him in the informal form.
15 Mario addresses Elena in her absence in the informal form.

Persistence (2007)

The premiere of *Persistence* was in July 2007 in the Casacuberta Theatre of the Teatro San Martín in Buenos Aires with the following cast:

Zaida	Carolina Fal
Boris	Gabo Correa
Enzo	Horacio Acosta
Silent Man	Sandro Nunziata

Set Design and Costume: Graciela Galán

Lighting Design: Jorge Pastorino

Music: Edgardo Cardozo

Assistant Direction: Tanya Barbieri, Ana María Converti

Staging and Direction: Cristina Banegas

Characters

Zaida
Boris
Enzo
Silent Man

As in the majority of dramatic texts, including Persistence, *the stage directions or instructions accompanying the characters and the action in their original conception may or may not be transformed into the staging. But in the case of the* **Silent Man**, *apart from drawing his character, the directions are themselves the text for the role, determining him through gesture and image and therefore have that level of importance.*

The idea for this play arose from the Beslan massacre, in Russia, appearing in the newspapers. On 3 September 2004, a group of thirty-two Chechnyan rebels took hundreds hostage in a school in Beslan, where parents and students joined to celebrate the first day of classes. The Russian government did not agree to negotiate with the captors and in the immediate repression the school was attacked with flame throwers and tanks. The operation, in which only one Chechnyan rebel was captured alive, had a high and unforeseen cost: 331 hostages died, the majority of which were children. As we know, no work is entirely imagined.

Scene One

Interior of a primitive-looking hut, a chest, two long benches. Scarce provisions, some belongings are kept inside the chest and some in the leather pouches hanging on the walls. On one of the benches, a jug of water, a basin and bowls. Suspended from a tripod, an iron saucepan over the fire on the earth floor. **Zaida**, *dressed in dark colours, is crouched down in a corner, her face hidden, hands over her head. Seated on one of the benches,* **Boris** *looks at her as he caresses a small wooden box. In the darkest area,* **Silent Man** *remains still and always apart. He is of tall stature, wears a full cloak down to his feet. When he moves, he does so with curiously slow movements, cautious and at times uncertain. The few occasions on which he dares show his face, it is a white face, inexpressive. Gusts and other noises made by the wind are heard.*

Boris (*gets up, comes near to* **Zaida** *and crouches down in front of her with the little box between his hands*)   Zaida . . . I found his little box . . . Look. It didn't break. Only a few scratches so faint that . . . you can't even tell they're there . . . It was under the rubble. (*She looks at him fleetingly, hides her face.*) Don't you want it? He used to play a lot with this . . . (*He takes out a few stones from the box, shows them to her.*) He had filled it with stones, little stones. They're all round like they've been touched by the sea. (*He smiles weakly.*) If we had sea here . . . Zaida, would you like that? So much water, blue, green, with little stones . . . round . . .

Heartbroken, he returns them to the box and closes it. He puts out his hand to **Zaida**, *begins a caress which does not conclude, returns to his place, sits down. Hunched over, he deposits the box under the bench and continues observing* **Zaida** *looking sad and concerned. A moment later* **Enzo** *comes in. He has strong features and a bitter expression.*

Enzo (*shakes his cloak*)   All the way from the town hall I've done nothing more than swallow dust. (*He spits.*) Bloody wind!

Boris (*listens to the outside*)   It's over now. Suddenly.

Enzo (*with latent animosity*)   Just now. I'm unlucky. (*With intent.*) You were fine in here, weren't you? Sheltered. (*He shakes out his cloak, holds it hanging from his outstretched arm.*) Zaida! Zaida! (*Seeing as she doesn't react.*) Hey, Zaida! Are you asleep? (*She collects herself and takes the cloak. She hangs it on a nail and, indifferent, returns to her corner. Without force,* **Enzo** *prevents her from doing so.*) I want to eat something hot. I left on an empty stomach and it was a long meeting. (**Zaida** *fills a metal bowl from the cooking pot over the fire, puts it down on the bench.* **Enzo** *sits down and eats.*) Give me bread. (*She takes bread out of one of the pouches, cuts off a piece and puts it down on the bench.*) Have I got the plague? On the bench? You can't touch me? (**Zaida** *picks up the bread and puts it in his hand. He holds on to her. Calmly, almost persuasive.*) I slept alone. You got up out of bed, the whole night you stayed there. Tonight you won't get up. Enough. Enough, okay?

Zaida   Yes.

Enzo (*looks at the bread in his hand*)   I'm frugal, but not that frugal. Just this? What do you think? That my stomach is a child's fist? (*She cries out and backs away as if he slapped her.*) What's wrong? What offended you? Or did you wake up on the wrong side of bed, like you always do.

Zaida *opens her mouth, tries to speak.*

Boris   That word.

Enzo   Which one?

Boris   Fist.

Enzo   No. Child. *That* is the word. I said fist. Fist of a *child*.

Boris   If it disturbs her don't say it.

Enzo   Oh yes. We won't say it and we'll also hide the children in the village so she doesn't suffer.

Boris   Just so she suffers less.

Enzo   A year's gone by. It's very little, but so many things have happened to make us forget our loss. And if not forget, to attend to what is first and foremost.

Zaida (*lifting her head. With a flat tone of voice*)   What did you say? A year?

Enzo   A year!

Zaida   That we haven't seen him for? No . . . A day. It's just . . . happened. (*Comes near to* **Enzo**.) Was it this morning? Enzo . . . was it this morning?

Enzo   Stop talking nonsense! Mend our cloaks, they're falling to pieces.

Zaida   It was this morning, I know it. That's why I didn't sleep . . . waiting for it to happen.

Enzo (*in agonising exasperation*)   Shut up. Dogs and women are quiet. I prefer you over there. (*He points. Seeing as she doesn't move, fixing her with a tormented expression he bellows.*) Child, child!

Zaida   No, no! (*Covering her ears she runs to her corner.*)

Enzo   I utter it like any other word. Or am I going to grieve for a word when there are so many other things I don't allow myself to grieve for? He was also my blood. And that blood doesn't exist anymore. It's hate. That's what my son is now. (*He eats.*) They've thrown salt on our crops. (*He goes near the cooking pot, registers how little it contains.*) We're hungry. And sad as if we'd never been light-hearted, had celebrations, parties. But I remember them, the parties. (*To the* **Silent Man**.) What do you say, sir? Do we deserve this? This bitterness? Forgive me. That deranged woman drives me round the bend. I shouldn't ask you. (*Points to* **Boris**. *Contemptuously*.) The person who's never going to ask questions is this guy.

Boris   I ask questions.

Enzo   I don't hear them.

Boris   What did you decide?

Enzo   Before answering your question I have another one: Why didn't you come? All the men were there, except for one.

Boris   I stayed with her.

Enzo   Ah! To comfort her? Watch over her? Babysitting? Is that your role?

Boris   I didn't want to leave her alone.

Enzo   I look after her, even in my absence. She has me. She doesn't need anyone else.

Boris   She's my sister, we grew up together. How can I not worry?

Enzo   Maybe she asked you to? Went moaning to you behind my back? I've let her cry for long enough.

Boris   Who's keeping track of that time? But she didn't say a word, or ask for anything. That's why I was worried.

Enzo   Now the war is our only concern, our only goal. You forgot that for a moment – because of your sister – but you keep it in mind, don't you?

Boris   Yes.

Enzo   You barely hesitated, (*With a twisted smile.*) despite appearances.

Boris   You got that right with barely hesitated. And it's *didn't* hesitate. You can do without the barely.

Enzo   I might be mistaken. Who knows what matters more to you, consoling your sister or finding out about our next move in this war.

Boris   It does matter to me. What will it be?

Enzo You should have been there to find out.

Boris But I wasn't.

Enzo Perhaps it was better that way. Because there was no voice of dissent.

Boris What did you decide?

Enzo What could we decide? A banquet for our enemies? A round of tea?

Boris I'm asking you. Answer me.

Enzo We'll leave before night falls. You'll guide us to the mountain, seeing as you've looked after sheep and guided them along all the paths. You learned that. But what a shame. It came at such a cost. You caught something from the sheep!

Boris It gives you pleasure to insult me, doesn't it?

Enzo None.

Boris Stop mocking me then! (*They look at each other hard.* **Boris** *gives in.*) We cross the mountain?

Enzo Towards the lion's cave. Do you dare?

Boris Stop mocking me, I said! Don't insult me, Enzo! I dare to do everything!

Enzo Calm down . . .! You'll waste your energy. For what? To get angry and shout that you dare to do everything between four walls? Save your energies for our enemies. They won't be wasted against them: they grow. If there's courage. We want to arrive – and surprise them – tomorrow morning, early.

Boris Surprise them? How?

Enzo (*ironically approving*) Well, well! Now this is how you ask questions! With that enthusiasm! Where are they not expecting us, where do they believe themselves to be safe?

Boris (*disbelieving*) Through . . . the northern path? Is that what you're wondering?

Enzo *We will go* via the northern path. They don't patrol it. Good choice of ours, perfect for our mission.

Boris It's not good. They are sheer drops, steep gradients and . . .

Enzo And stop.

Boris It's an impenetrable path.

Enzo Just difficult. We won't trip up. We have strong legs. And if someone falls down a precipice, others will jump over it. Didn't you dare to do it once – or so you said – for pleasure, as a game, to prove to us that you were brave?

Zaida (*absorbed*) He came with his clothes torn, ripped . . . I almost didn't recognise him . . . And he had lost an arm . . . Boris, his arm!

Boris No, Zaida. No . . .

Enzo (*he heard but doesn't blame* **Boris**) You'll guide us along the northern path. All the men made that decision and, because you weren't there, you didn't object. Now it's too late.

Boris On this border there's deserted countryside and then a village.

Enzo Pretty, they say. With cobbled streets.

Boris Will we attack the village?

Enzo Not exactly. Guess.

Boris I don't know.

Enzo A sacred place.

Boris The temple? Is it the temple?

Enzo If we attacked the temple, God would forgive us. But it's not the temple.

Boris What then?

Enzo A school.

Boris (*confused*) A . . . I don't understand.

Enzo Bit by bit they take away our most fertile land, they'll never stop setting their sights on what doesn't belong to them. What don't you understand?

Boris Why attack a . . .?

Enzo Exactly! To surprise them. We'll be waiting from dawn, hidden like snakes, little vipers with gunpowder venom in their fangs. They'll all fall in the trap, children and adults. Mothers and children. They'll be struck dumb, dogs with their tails between their legs. (*Laughs.*) Am I the only one who has any fun in this hut? No one's going to join me?

Boris The school? I won't attack children. I don't fight against children.

Enzo No? No child was injured? Not one died of hunger, of a fever? Children haven't died?

Boris Not like this.

Enzo I don't see the difference. Death is death, however it comes.

Boris What will we be left with?

Enzo That their mothers will suffer as our mothers did. Look at her. Pain has turned her stupid.

Boris And how does revenge make things better?

Enzo Ah, no, it's not just revenge! Though it might be a good driving force, revenge. If all turns out well, we'll make demands and they'll have no other choice but to back down.

Boris Are you sure?

Enzo They'll realise that we exist.

Boris They already know.

Enzo They'll know it in another way. That they can't stamp out blood and fire without the blood and fire spreading. The fact is bothersome, irritating, that they wish us dead and can't satisfy this desire, because for each one that falls, another rises. This gets them all twisted up inside. We'll close the doors with us inside. We'll hold their children hostage, we'll make them suffer fear, hunger, thirst, forbid them to move, their hands behind their heads like ordinary criminals. The two-year-olds, the five-, the seven-year-olds? We'll use them as shields if they attack us.

Boris And in order to kill us they'll shoot them against their enemies, because their hate is not inferior to ours.

Enzo Their hate doesn't matter, only our own counts. Let them hate us!

Boris They'll say that the flesh which protects us as a shield is made of iron, an iron shield, and they'll shoot the iron.

Enzo All the better! Murderers of their own children! All the better! (*Laughs. Darkens.*) Whose side are you on? Or you're happy to live with the humiliation, to take solace in the misery? An eye for an eye. Eh, Zaida? Yes, pain has turned her stupid. We're allowing you to listen, aren't you glad? Give up stupidity, seeing as you've gone into quite enough of it, open your ears! (*He violently pulls her hands apart. She doesn't lift them again.*)

Boris Leave her in peace.

Enzo Yes, perhaps I should. Because her brain is like this. (*Puts two fingers together.*)

Zaida Says who? It's only my heart that's scorched, not my brain. (*Strikes her forehead.*) I think, I think!

Enzo Think with me, not on your own. (*Points to the* **Silent Man**.) Last night, while I was sleeping, he came up to me and whispered his design: a perfect plan. Like this, like this! I thought I heard him. He rested his hand on my shoulder, and when I woke up, I knew exactly what I should do, as if it were written in stone. Tell this weak man what your order is, sir. Our children die when they shower us in bullets and our enemies, the hypocrites, don't count them in the casualties so the hypocrites of the world don't shudder with pity. We conduct ourselves honestly, our faces open, with the pride of cruel people. We can be cruel because we never receive kindness. We're well qualified! We'll take advantage of the night and tomorrow, early, in the school, on that first day of hymns and ceremony, it'll be us who are the teachers. And what teachers we'll be! Sir, thank you for dictating to us what is just. (*The* **Silent Man** *has moved amongst the shadows.*) Where are you?

Boris He's there, are you frightened of losing him? What would you do, eh?

Enzo The same. But he never lets go of my hand. If my eyes, stinging with dust, don't see him, he sees me. Sir, thank you for your words in the night. (*Looks. To* **Zaida**.) Why is there no meat in this dish?

Zaida Women don't kill the animals. And the meeting with your men lasted longer than the morning.

Enzo Milk? (*She shakes her head.*) Water, then! So that he can transform the water into nectar. (*She gets up, serves water in a bowl and returns to her place.* **Enzo** *takes the bowl and offers it to the* **Silent Man**.) Drink, sir. (*As he remains still, after a moment* **Enzo** *lowers the bowl and deposits it on the floor at his feet. He observes the bowl, fascinated.*) The water's thickening, it's turned an amber colour, like honey . . . (*He smiles. He picks up the bowl and reverently places it on the bench.*) The water and the nectar are yours. You transformed our hearts like this. Our life is air, our parents wood, our women clutter, there is no other dream but this one: to get rid of our enemies. And later, when the universe is clean, we'll have another life and when we die you'll bring us to this place which you prepared for us, those of us who are faithful to you.

A silence of vague expectation.

Boris He's silent.

Enzo If you have doubts, don't come with us. We have other guides. Because you might know the mountain like the back of your hand, but you're no good to us. Doubters are of little use to us. You can say no. But the risk of deserting us is greater than facing the fight.

Boris I'll guide you. I'm with my people, I suffer with my people. But we've never gone so far.

Enzo Hate opens avenues.

Boris Aren't you allowed to have doubts?

Enzo Is it that you turned into a woman, less than a woman? Look at her. Her eyes are shining a little, she feels revived. She lost a son, our son, and she gained more. She feels chosen. (*Squats down in front of her.*) Isn't revenge sweet?

Zaida Yes.

Enzo (*he brings his fist to her mouth*) Bite. My hand is full of hate. And hate is the only thing which wipes out pain. (*He pushes her head down.*) Bite! Swallow it down. (*She sinks her teeth into it.*) Not with so much fear! With rage, with fury. Without mercy. (*She obeys. Without releasing his fist, tearing it with her sunken teeth, she moves her head from side to side. Then she opens her mouth, wipes it.* **Enzo** *runs his hand over the bite.*) You bit hard. (*Smiles.*) The teeth of a hyena.

Zaida (*lifts her hand to her chest*) I suffer . . . I suffer less . . . A scab, a wound. It hurts, it's bearable the way it hurts.

Enzo Bearable. Hate is more comforting than a hand on your cheek. More than this. (*He caresses her cheek. With rare tenderness he engages* **Zaida**, *and for a moment* *rests her against his chest. He stands up.*) Are you coming with us? (*She nods. To* **Boris**.) Put on your rags. You deserve them.

Boris   I only hesitated.

Enzo (*turns towards the* **Silent Man**)   Sir, we're going. We will return fewer than we left. For us it's a detail, a number. (*He puts his hand out to* **Zaida**; *she stands. She remains still, her arms at her sides.*) If you find death, you won't go alone. You'll take children with you. And hopefully lots of them! They'll warm your bones, your blood will be warmed, with those dead, and they won't weigh on your back because in this world no one is innocent. (*To* **Boris**.) You realise that, right? Let's go. (*He puts on his cape, looks at* **Zaida**, *who stands absorbed.*) Zaida!

With sudden decisiveness, she envelops her head in a dark hood and leaves with **Enzo**.

Boris (*he drops before the* **Silent Man**)   Sir, what should I do? Guide me, sir.

Anxiously, he looks at him. Slowly, the **Silent Man** *opens his arms in a vague gesture of uncertainty.* **Boris** *stands, picks up his cape and goes towards the door. Before reaching it, he turns back towards the* **Silent Man** *with the same anguished questioning. He goes out. When he's left alone, behaving with extremely halting movements, the* **Silent Man** *picks up the bowl and drinks, then he goes up to the chest, opens it, searches and takes out a piece of cloth from inside it. He sits down on the bench, feels around his cape and from the inside of the collar takes out a needle. The cloth upon his knees, he hunches over and sews with concentration.*

Scene Two

Enzo, *looking tired, is sitting on one of the benches.* **Zaida**, *dishevelled, her hair loose, the same tired look, tends to a wound on his arm. She throws fleeting looks towards the door. The* **Silent Man** *remains still, amongst the shadows.*

Enzo   Wait.

Zaida   I haven't finished.

Enzo   Tie your hair back. (*She looks at him, gathers her hair on the back of her neck. He looks at his arm.*) It's stopped bleeding.

Zaida   You lost a lot of blood.

Enzo   Not as much as I wanted to. And your leg?

Zaida   A strike, a bruise spreading. But whoever caught me by surprise with that strike can't do it again to anyone.

Enzo (*brushing her cheek with a finger*)   Is it hurting?

Zaida   Only when I walk. (*Looks towards the door.*)

Enzo What are you fretting about?

Zaida Boris.

Enzo That man is safe, for sure.

Zaida He didn't come back. I fear . . .

Enzo Don't fear anything. Do you think he's wounded, that he's dead? He's not one of those who'll take a risk.

Zaida (*she bandages the wound. Appealing*)   Enzo . . .!

Enzo Enzo, Enzo! Look at what you're doing, or is your wound the door? He'll come back, don't worry. And if he doesn't come back, you can think that sometimes those who have no virtue are rewarded. Sir, it's not a reproach. We were lucky. It was a great disaster for our enemies. I would have liked to fall like so many of our people fell, but your wisdom is obviously keeping me for other tasks. And I will fulfil them. (*With one of* **Zaida**'s *movements as she bandages the wound, tenses with pain.*) Be careful! What are you thinking, woman? That I don't feel pain? (**Boris** *comes in, his cloak in tatters, dirty with soil. He registers the presence of the two with a weary smile. Exhausted, he collapses on the floor.*)

Zaida Boris. (*Relieved.*) Boris!

Enzo (*impatient, pushes her away*)   Get out. Enough's enough! Didn't I tell you? He came back. Safe.

Zaida So did we.

Boris I had this picture of the hut deserted. Zaida, Zaida . . . that you wouldn't be here!

Enzo She's here. She came back only a little dishevelled, a little dirty. As unscathed as you. I didn't have luck on my side. But not because I got hurt but because I wasn't hurt enough. (*He shows his arm.*) You see? A bullet which wavered when it got close. It came towards my heart and hardly brushed my arm. He didn't want me to fall.

Zaida (*to* **Boris**)   You came back so late . . . Everyone's back home, tending to their wounds, praising those who didn't return. For a moment I thought . . .

Enzo That we would be praising you. But it's not our turn yet, is it Boris? Your gun? It didn't get jammed, did it? Ours were so well oiled they'd go off by themselves. And they hit the target! (*Laughs.*) Did you give it back?

Boris Did I . . . . did I give it back . . . ?

Enzo (*his expression hardens, he moves towards him*)   That's what I said. To our pitiful arms store where they're serviced. Your gun!

Boris My . . . my gun?

Enzo Do you not understand my question? What's strange about it? Is it stupid, silly, something a fool would ask? Where's your gun? Outside, against the door?

Where? (**Boris** *looks at himself; just then he seems to realise he's lost it. A gesture reveals this.* **Enzo**, *furious*.) Even every one of the dead returns theirs! You lost yours! You abandoned it! (*He slaps him.*)

Boris No, no!

Enzo As if we had too many of them! As if paying for each one doesn't take the food out of our mouths. They cost us hunger! The first one of ours that falls will be shot with your bullets. An enemy will make good use of it. Idiot!

Boris No. It was on the way back! I fell down a ravine. It slipped out of my hands.

Enzo And how were you going to stop and get it back? (*Using his unwounded arm he stands him up violently, pats him.*) Not a scratch, right?

Boris (*he touches his side*) A graze.

Enzo A graze isn't a wound. How did you escape?

Boris I don't know. We weren't fighting anymore. I saw an open wall. I ran. They all ran.

Enzo We didn't. Fire and smoke protected us, a smoke as dense as a sandstorm at night. But we didn't run.

Boris An explosion took out half a wall. Then I fled.

Enzo Or was it before then?

Boris Before?

Enzo Before we were stepping on the bodies of children, the blood of children.

Boris And women.

Enzo Women too. What difference does it make? None. There are no innocent people, I told you. And what happened? . . . If you were there. Wasn't it good? (*Unable to speak,* **Boris** *shakes his head.*) Yes, very good! Zaida, how was it?

Zaida (*with an inane smile and a flat voice*) Very good.

Enzo To kill the seed in the furrow, the first shoots of the weed. If they had grown, they would have been our enemies. We got rid of so many! So many! And you're right. They were of no use to us as shields. In order to kill us, they took it out on their own children. But for this, only we are to blame, that apart from brutes they're also hypocrites. (*He squeezes his arms against his body. Groans irritably.*) Ow, it hurts! Sir, why didn't I fall? Only this wound as a triumph. Our comrades are having their bodies bathed in honeys and oils, surrounded in eternity by beautiful women. (*Points.*) Look what I have to put up with! Oh, forgive me, forgive me, sir. If this is your design, I accept it. And I simply take new orders, that you tell me in a dream what you expect of me. (*Exits.*)

Zaida Let me wash that graze.

Boris It doesn't hurt. I did it when I fell down. A scrape against a rock. Give me a bit of water, I'm thirsty. (**Zaida** *serves him. He drinks*.) I saw you.

Zaida (*ambiguous*) I saw you too.

Boris You fired at the children in the school.

Zaida (*in a flat voice*) That's why I went.

Boris Didn't they look like your son?

Zaida Oh, yes. They're the same . . . In some sense.

The **Silent Man** *looks sideways, troubled. In a moment he will lift the hem of his cloak and will sew a tear on the edge with the concentration of a child who doesn't want to listen.*

Boris And how could you?

Zaida I could because . . . I bit Enzo's hand, (*She smiles, on edge*.) which is not a compassionate hand! And Enzo was right. Hate gives relief. Relief!

Boris You were . . . the most maternal of all women, the kindest . . .

Zaida (*coldly*) Sometimes I think you're stupid. We all changed, even the lambs are hard and the goats scream themselves hoarse with their voice of grit. (*She changes her tone, lowers her voice*.) We never found my son's arm. In that attack in the village, do you remember? All they left us with was rubble. Under the rubble, my son was missing an arm. (*She points to her shoulder*.) From here to here . . . nothing. That missing arm won't let me sleep. (**Boris** *tries to hug her*.) Don't touch me! Don't even think about it! Many people died yesterday, (*Lowers her hand*.) small like this. Some didn't have legs, or heads, holes here, and others had bled so much that their flesh had turned into blood, in revolting clots on the tiles they once played on. Bruises, wounds, but they all had arms! Maybe if I'd found one without . . . I would have remembered my son and then . . . *maybe* I would have been sorry . . . (*She laughs*.) But I didn't find one! It was easy to be fierce with those children, well fed at the expense of ours, so blonde, *all of them* with their arms!

Boris Why did I guide you? Why didn't I make you all fall down the mountain? Why don't you shut up?

Zaida (*malevolent*) Oh, yes. Better than I shut up. It's more convenient for you.

Boris Nothing's convenient for me anymore. (*He strikes himself*.) I showed you all the way!

Zaida You'll have to be accountable.

Boris Yes.

Zaida I didn't see you firing. Your gun must smell of roses. If you had died yesterday, paradise would not have been yours.

Boris (*turns his head towards the* **Silent Man**) Nor is that heavenly brothel yours, is it? I can't believe that you imagined it. (*To* **Zaida**.) Death would not have been punishment. And if I die, I want dust for my corpse, earth. A handful of ashes is enough for me. As grey as they can be, and as dirty! No paradise.

Zaida   Don't blaspheme. The only thing you need to lose yourself completely. But don't worry too much. There are few of your comrades still here to blame you.

Boris   You would blame me.

Zaida   I'm your sister. I have to think it. I don't like you now. I saw you, your hands were trembling.

Boris   Thank goodness my hands were trembling! They're trembling right now!

Zaida   Mine didn't. I said to myself: he's a coward. If Enzo had discovered you . . . . trying to make yourself invisible. Whereas I . . . did you see me?

Boris (*with a kind of horror*)   I saw you. And I didn't know who you were anymore.

Zaida   Me. I was me. The woman who's been in that corner for months. And I felt good, liberated. The first child that fell was scared, he didn't see the weapon, he ran towards me with relief, happy, a woman who would take him into her arms. Such tenderness!

Boris   How could you, Zaida? If all the children in the village were your children . . . if you were talking about the one who had grown taller in the last few months, about the one who was ill, the one who was better. . . . You never tired of talking about the beauty you found in their faces, no child was ugly, no child was stupid . . . How could you?

Zaida   I don't fool myself anymore. That's how. I'm not fooled anymore by the children's candour, their delightful smiles, their milk teeth, their cute babbling. I don't even love our own, but I pretend to. I accept them, I put up with them. For the others I only harbour disgust. They're our enemies, as small as they are, with their milk teeth, their fear of the dark. Frauds. They're not scared, they've got fangs, their eyes murky with evil thoughts, traditions that are not our own. I'm gloating: we do well to kill them!

Boris   Who poisoned you in this way? Not even hatred goes that far. You cannot know what a child will be but for the fact he's defenceless I won't touch him. He might commit a crime but his cruelty, his malice is put upon him. Even though he takes a gun and fires, even though he stabs his brothers in a dream. Who poisoned you so that you deny innocence?

Zaida   What strange kind of innocence! (*She laughs.*) Like Enzo, I don't accept it. But it's not because of him that I don't accept it. Everything I told you is true. Who else but a mother could know it? Your *innocent* creatures are not so innocent. That they're defenceless? They're pretending. That they need protection? They're lying. I looked at their children and I withered in disgust. Cut them down, cut their lives off quickly so that they don't spread their poison. My cutie pie, my little angel of the earth, my baby, what soft downy hair!, as fluffy as a new born chick, what benevolent little eyes. Lies! They'll be our enemies with as much certainty that the day will come and night will fall. They already are. They deserve to die: to cry with hunger, to not find their mother's breast when they're born, to be strangled by the umbilical cord. They should feel the bite of pain like sheep with broken feet and whine and whine and bleat. They should explode!

Boris Swallow those words! I don't want to listen to you! You have dry eyes, dry stones! (*He lets out an animal sob. He shakes her with rage.*) Cry for your dead son, cry for those children you murdered!

Zaida (*pushes him away*) Cry? For those children? My job is to hate them. I have no pity, (*Pointing to her eyes.*) stones! And I think . . . I don't know . . . that I hate them to prevent the hypocrisy of loving them. Because . . . what kind of love do we have for children? If we love them, if we really love them, the earth would topple from its axis, with each death we'd come out howling dishevelled and ferocious, tearing at our clothes in desperation. But where is it? The desperation. It doesn't exist. Not even I have it! If I had had it I wouldn't have allowed Enzo to come to my body taking refuge from his own. Even now I open myself to his desire and I let him dump his seed in my body and I even hope, I do! I hope that I won't reject it to hold off his rage. Each month, Enzo is disgusted by my blood, he doesn't touch me, furrows his brow, silent with reproach. And I promise him. The next time, yes . . . Yes, yes! That's what I promise. Meek, submissive. Whereas, desperate, how would I be? I'd strike a fist to his heart, I'd cut off his testicles, never again another child! Not one more child on the surface of this earth! After the last old man, from the last sterile old woman, extinction. But I'm not desperate, I live another turn of the wheel, my belly is my greatest ally, it only bears pain, a little pain, a bottomless sorrow . . .

It doesn't know desperation and yes, hypocrisy. The kind which says that they're the most precious creatures on earth, the light of our eyes. No, not even the earth knows what to do with them, they're burdens, the earth doesn't understand what they're for if we erase them with such ease. So, why are you playing the good guy, Boris? Hypocrite. Why do you pretend like the others? Why this pretence that it matters to us when they're born, when they're in the belly? Ah, most of all they matter to us in there. After that they can look after themselves! (*With a twisted smile.*) Or can't they look after themselves? Yes, they can! They're happy, they play. Did you see how they play? A few little stones in a box and . . . Boris, Boris. I'll have more children for Enzo, but none of them will be equal to the one I lost. Do you remember my child? Even his father's frown softened. Do you remember?

Boris Every day I remember. I loved him.

Zaida Ah, but not as much as me! Every day I look for his arm in the rubble. His face has faded away, but not his arm, its shape, the skin like silk . . . It was . . . the right one? Yes, the right, the one which reached out to me. And it doesn't reach out anymore. (*She laughs.*) Nor does the left, let's be honest! Perhaps you didn't want this, sir? That the women hate like men? With even more abandon. (*To* **Boris**.) In the next attack, do you know what I'll do? I'll bring the sharpest dagger, or better still, I'll sharpen it myself, and I'll cut off arms, only arms, I'll put them together in a bag and I'll bring them here, and I'll scatter them over my son's tomb for him to choose one, for him to play with them in his coffin, for him to scratch them, bite them, and talk to me. Because he doesn't talk to me anymore. Angry because I let him die.

Boris   It wasn't you.

Zaida   Yes, it was me. Luckily hate came to save me. It didn't console me as Enzo believed it did. No, no. Hate doesn't know about contemplation. It's an orphan no mother no father, it knows no offspring, it doesn't see or hear or console. It doesn't grow grass, the slightest patch of turf, it is a wind which drags the soil along and leaves a desert. But what a desert! Sand, sand between your teeth, in your eyes, and a desire to kill!

Scene Three

Leaning on the bench, the **Silent Man** *cleans a small surface with a rag with very slow movements, looking sideways as if he feared being taken by surprise.*

Zaida *enters holding some logs for the fire. She is heavily pregnant.*

Zaida   What are you doing, sir? (*He freezes immediately.*) Wasn't it clean? Sorry. I'll do it. (*Leaves the logs, cleans the surface of the bench. He remains like someone deprived of a task he enjoys. Passively, he folds his hands together, still.*) Sorry, sorry. (*Then, with difficulty she leans against the tripod, cuts the wood into small pieces.*)

Enzo *enters pushing a wheelbarrow, followed by* **Boris**.

Enzo   Don't light the fire.

Zaida   Why?

Enzo   We're going to the mountain.

Zaida   All of us?

Enzo   Yes, the whole town. Not many because they decimated us. (*Points.*) Load our things on here.

Boris   I'll do it. (*Opens the chest, takes out some blankets which he settles in the wheelbarrow.*) They beat us.

Enzo (*rattled*)   What did you say? No, while one of us remains living, and even when we're dead, the war will never be over. (*To* **Zaida**.) Don't worry about the child. We'll look after him. He won't suffer any distress. We'll protect you from the cold, we'll give you our scraps so that he's born strong. (**Boris** *puts some bags in the wheelbarrow. He goes to take down another one. To* **Boris**.) Not that one. A few things.

Boris   It'll be needed.

Enzo   The only thing we need is our courage. Take hold of your own. What's in there?

Boris   Tools.

Enzo   Tools. To rub rocks together, tweak some roots, stir up moss? Fine work for a fool. Stay here, Zaida. We still need to sacrifice some animals. The ones we won't take with us. We'll leave nothing behind. We'll burn the huts so the only thing they'll have to make use of is ashes. (*Exits.*)

Boris   Do you want to keep it? (*Shows her the small wooden box.*)

Zaida   No.

Boris (*he opens it*)   There are little stones inside.

Zaida   It doesn't matter what's inside. Just a few things, Enzo said.

Boris   He played a lot with . . .

Zaida   A few things! (*She snatches it from him, throws it far away. The box falls near the* **Silent Man**.)

Boris (*goes to pick it up*)   It's not big.

Zaida (*she stops him*)   It's not yours. Leave it where it is!

He looks at her. A silence.

Boris   I'm not coming with you.

Zaida   What?

Boris   I'm not coming. Others can lead the way through the mountain. There are more than enough shepherds who know it as I do, they'll find shelter, some caves.

Zaida   You'll be alone.

Boris   Yes. But I won't touch blood.

Zaida   Does Enzo know?

Boris   No. He wouldn't let me. I'll leave with you and I'll take another path at night, when everyone's sleeping. You won't say anything, will you?

Zaida   I covered for you before. I didn't say that you were trembling. And when others blamed you, I defended you.

Boris   I'm grateful, sister.

While they're talking, slowly and with stealth the **Silent Man** *picks up the little box. He sits down in the shadows, concentrated like a child, and he shakes the box; every now and then the sound of the stones is heard.*

Zaida   But now you're asking too much. To keep quiet about a deserter. I don't know if it's what I want. And anyway, how will you manage? When you were looking after the sheep you had your bread, some olives . . . who will provide for you? You're clumsy.

Boris (*smiles*)   Not that clumsy.

Zaida (*takes a bag*)   I'll give you a little bread, some water. At least for the first few days, until you find your feet . . . (*She remains absorbed. She abandons the activity.*) No, this is good for nothing. Do we have time?

Boris What for? They're all outside, sacrificing the old animals, the thin animals, the ones that are of no use . . . And I'm in here. I wouldn't want . . .

Zaida (*she sits on the bench*) For Enzo to get annoyed with you? He's already annoyed. Sit down with me.

Boris (*looks at her*) What do you want? (*Reaches his hand out to her face.*)

Zaida (*pushing his hand away*) I think that . . .

Boris (*sits down*) To talk? Did you think you wanted to talk?

Zaida Yes. (*A long silence.*) It's not easy.

Boris We lost the habit. (*Silence. He tries.*) Why did you call me clumsy?

Zaida Because you always were. (*She goes quiet.*)

Boris I've defended you since you were a little girl.

Zaida (*distant*) Who?

Boris The clumsy guy.

Zaida Oh, yes. You were.

Boris Where did you get that idea? I never lost sight of a sheep! I brought them back to the fold fat, sleepy, swollen with food.

Zaida They used to send you for water and you spilt it all over the path.

Boris How old was I? Seven? But later I grew up and then, who was the one who challenged the rules? Our father: don't do this, don't do that, not a little girl, not this.

Zaida (*she faintly smiles*) Yes. And you were the skinniest of my brothers, those brothers who died. (*Looks at him.*) And you're alive.

Boris (*he absorbs the impact of her words, sad*) I shouldn't be.

Zaida I don't know. I know very little now.

Silence.

Boris They used to forbid you to go out, remember, Zaida? And I secretly I would go to look for you . . . I would give up my friends who played with slings, with stones . . .

Zaida Oh, yes!

Boris I would take you to places that only I knew in the mountains.

Zaida (*without enthusiasm*) I remember. Those places . . . are they still there? . . .

Boris You would run, you would climb the mountain like a goat.

Zaida It pains me that you're abandoning us like a traitor. Why do you always dither? Why were you never brave?

Boris   I wasn't brave? If they had found me out . . .! (*Laughs, crushed.*) They never found me out!

Zaida   Come with us. Don't abandon us. There aren't many of us.

Boris   I can't. They don't want me anyway. And when I lead the way, they'll put someone at my side who won't take their eyes off me.

Zaida   They only suspect. But it would be enough that in the first attack – because they didn't beat us – you'll shout like mad and you'll kill with hate to win their confidence. Now I can't cover for you like I did in school, killing for me, as well as for you. With this belly . . . I have to take care of it.

Boris   Sweet mother.

Zaida (*coldly*)   No. Don't kid yourself! Don't get carried away. Do you think I changed with this? I'm only thinking that it's going to be born, it will be born and I'll rejoice when it grows . . .

Boris   So?

Zaida   I'll watch over him like the light of my life. I'll see him sprout muscles, the tendons in his neck like ropes, the silly look of his first few years transform into rage . . . The cold rage of someone who hits the target. I'll wait, I'll wait for him to grow. It won't cost me anything to look after him, to take food from my mouth. Nothing will be too much for me!

Boris   I get it. Everything for rage.

Zaida   Yes! As soon as his beard appears on his face, even before, he'll eliminate an enemy. As soon as he has the strength in his arms to hold a gun.

Boris   Maybe he won't do it.

Zaida   He'll want to! We'll still have hate. There's nothing more difficult than stopping it, nothing easier than causing death. So much fragility! The other is only an object which falls down. I wish it on our enemies. I wish it on the half-hearted who don't come with us.

Boris (*after a silence. Lucid*)   You wish death on me?

Zaida (*with a strange accent*)   Brother, brother . . . I don't wish for anything, the situation wishes it for me.

Boris   What?

Zaida (*avoids answering*)   Let me look at you. I wouldn't want your face to fade away from me.

Boris   You have it right here.

Zaida (*runs her hand over his face*)   But you'll go. You'll disown us, now, when we're weak, when we are so few . . .

Boris   We better go.

Zaida Enzo will call us. He won't me! (*She touches her belly. Like* **Boris**, *she turns towards the wheelbarrow.*) Where are you going? They're still not ready. (*She seeks him out and takes him by the hand to the bench.*) Come, here with me. Let's go on talking. Don't you want to?

Boris I don't think so.

Zaida I do. A moment longer. We don't know what can happen . . . on the mountain. Summers under the fig tree . . . You told me stories under the fig tree. There was one . . ., the one about the woman who told endless stories to delay her death. (*Laughs.*) So they gave her more time!

Boris And sometimes they spared her.

Zaida Very few times. And there was another one, another story about a giant!

Boris (*shrugs his shoulders, sad*) I don't remember. Suddenly everything's wiped out.

Zaida One winter we went out in the snow. It was night and everyone was sleeping. Just us, trembling with cold, do you remember?

Boris No.

Zaida Oh, that sky! I'd never seen it before like that nor have ever since, shining with so many stars . . . And I remember the giant! After many sorrows, he brought joy.

Boris I don't remember. Why do you remember now?

Zaida A rest. (*Brief silence.*) I'm thirsty. Can you give me some water? (*He stands, goes across the hut towards the bench where the jug of water is.* **Zaida** *follows him. When* **Boris** *realises, he turns around and smiles, crushed, comprehending, as if he knows what she has decided to do.* **Zaida** *returns the smile, they look at each other for an instant. In his surreptitious way, the* **Silent Man** *looks on. He hunches over the little box in his lap and from this point on he doesn't look up.* **Zaida**, *through her teeth.*) I'm thirsty. (*When* **Boris** *turns his back again as he faces the bench and picks up the jug, she pulls out a dagger from her clothes, raises it up and brings it down stabbing him over and over again shouting desperately and ferociously.*) I'm thirsty! I'm dying of thirst! (**Boris** *staggers, makes a final and agonising effort to hold the jug and set it on the bench. Then he turns around, looks at* **Zaida** *and puts out his hand which doesn't reach her. He collapses.* **Zaida** *remains still for a moment, then she lets the dagger fall, taking jagged breaths. Looks at* **Boris** *at her feet. Softly.*) Coward.

Enzo (*enters carrying two old guns*) Zaida! Let's go. We'll go ahead. Others will be at the rear guard to set fire . . . (*Looks, continues on autopilot.*) the huts . . . (*Puts the guns on the wheelbarrow. Then he comes near* **Zaida**, *puts his arm around her shoulders.*) Why?

Zaida I didn't want to do it . . . but I did it. He was thinking of defecting.

Enzo I thought as much. I've questioned his loyalty for some time. In the school someone saw him trembling and when he came back he wasn't injured.

Zaida   Just a graze. A scrape against a rock, he said. He didn't allow it to be dressed. It must have been a scratch made by nails. Maybe he scratched himself. He was capable of that. Now he is wounded! Now he does have the mark of war! I want to see! Show me, Boris! (*Bending over him, she begins a movement.*)

Enzo (*stops her*)   Don't

Zaida (*bursts out laughing, with a kind of death rattle to her laughter*)   Yes, I won't! What do I need to check for? It's obvious! There's a lot of blood. Like there was in the school, remember, Enzo? The same colour, it smells the same, the same blood!

Enzo   Stop, Zaida!

Zaida   Stop, stop. He didn't want paradise. For his corpse he wanted dust, earth. He's managed it with a fist full of ashes! He'll be happy! He'll be happy! He'll be ash when they burn the huts.

Enzo   He wouldn't have won paradise anyway.

Zaida (*abruptly stops laughing*)   Why? Didn't he have a right to it? No . . . He wasn't always like this. He led us through the mountains. He led us!

Enzo   What other choice did he have? To fake willingness.

Zaida   And this didn't cost him? He didn't just fake it. He tested the sturdiness of the rocks to prevent us from falling. He even . . . even changed the landscape to suit our desire, we found no precipices, impossible inclines, not one trip-up, or an accident. Not even you did who hated him . . .

Enzo (*interrupts her*)   I didn't hate him. I despised him.

Zaida   Not even you, who hated him, could fault him. He protected us with the care of a father.

Enzo   Because he felt our eyes on the back of his neck. If afterwards you hadn't defended him . . . you fought his corner so much . . . I didn't believe you.

Zaida   You didn't believe me? You're wrong. I did well! To defend him. I saw him kill foaming at the mouth in pleasure. I saw him risk his own life, his gun smoking.

Enzo   The gun he lost.

Zaida   So what? Do you think you're perfect? With these eyes I saw when he smashed the head of an enemy with his boot.

Enzo   It wasn't a child's head.

Zaida   A child's head as well! Lots of them! He didn't spare the women either. In that moment I recognised him, my brother, a wild beast like me. My brother, my brother . . . (*She leans towards* **Boris***, looks at him for a long time, even with curiosity.*)

Enzo   He always wavered.

Zaida (*with difficulty she crouches next to* **Boris**, *kisses him. Unable to stand again*)   Help me. (*He helps her.*) But he didn't have enough hate. (*With a soft voice, kind.*) It ravaged me but him . . . so weak . . . it didn't even touch him . . . How was he able to stand up to it? What did the fool think?

Enzo   What men don't think.

Zaida   After the school he fell to pieces like a house razed to the ground.

Enzo   Let's go. (*He softens his tone, touches her belly.*) We'll have another child. Don't be scared, eh? Give your word. Don't be scared anymore.

Zaida   No. Now I know why we're bringing them into the world. (*She smiles vaguely.*)

Enzo   They're waiting for us. Let's go.

Zaida   Oh yes! The war goes on. (**Enzo** *pushes the wheelbarrow towards the door.* **Zaida** *points to the* **Silent Man**.) And him?

Enzo   He'll come with us. As always.

They exit.

The **Silent Man** *moves with his habitual slowness. He picks up the jug of water, drinks. The water drains from his mouth. He drinks without stopping, with the sound of drowning.*

Curtain.

Dear Ibsen, I Am Nora (2013)

The premiere of *Dear Ibsen, I Am Nora* was performed in the Cunill Cabanellas Theatre of the Teatro General San Martín in Buenos Aires in September 2013, with the following cast:

Nora	Belén Blanco
Henrik	Alberto Suárez
Ana María	Pochi Ducasse
Cristina	Victoria Roland
Krogstad	Agustín Rittano
Rank	Leonardo Saggese
Torvald	Ezequiel Díaz

Staging and Lighting: Gonzalo Córdova

Art Design and Costume: Renata Schussheim

Music: Pablo Cécere

Assistant Direction: Horacio Larraza

Direction: Silvio Lang

Characters

Nora
Henrik
Torvald
Cristina
Krogstad
Rank
Ana María

To Alicia Zanca (1955–2012)
In her memory and in the memory of so many plays and days spent working in the theatre that we shared.

Scene One

Nora   He lent me his voice. Before I noticed, he warned me about what was happening. He was an intelligent man, wide awake, while I was a woman unable to sleep upon cotton wool that concealed needles. And those needles pierced me more and more as time went on. A kind of bland pain, a restlessness. And yet my loves were firm, my husband, my three children. Perhaps in dreams or in nightmares I asked for his help, and he came.

Henrik *enters. He crosses the room as he takes off his top hat, he sits down and puts his hat next to him, on the floor. They look at each other for a moment.*

Henrik *(flatly)*   It's a difficult situation, isn't it?

Nora   I don't know what's wrong with me. What I lived before with courage, as a challenge, today annoys me. And it annoys me all the more to feel irritated by a contemptible cause.

Henrik   Which one?

Nora   You're asking me? Money, first of all.

Henrik   The lack of it.

Nora   The lack of it, naturally. To ask for it, beg for it, to depend. Even for the minimum. These Christmases I want to buy presents. For everyone, Torvald, the children, the servants. Too much expense, says Torvald. The children, yes. The servants . . . they can go without. He treats me like a little girl. Too extravagant. (*She faces him.*) Is this why I asked for your help?

Henrik   Torvald is very strict. He's careful with money. A loan, a debt, would be a stain on his honour.

Nora *(teasing)*   How very proper! You . . . could intercede, couldn't you? Torvald would listen to you.

Henrik   You confer more powers on me than I possess.

Nora   You are a man, of . . . similar persuasion to Torvald, one could say.

Henrik *(laughs)*   Nora . . .! I also live in my century, I cannot unknow it's rules.

Nora   You infringe upon them all the same.

Henrik   Oh, in little things! The scandal will be further ahead.

Nora *(unsettled)*   What do you mean?

Henrik   That I will make unexpected choices . . . For my century.

Nora   And me? How will your decisions affect me?

Henrik   They will change you. Don't be impatient. You *must* wait for the events to change you.

Nora (*after a silence*)   They have already changed me.

The doorbell rings. **Ana María**, **Nora**'s *elderly wet nurse crosses the room to open the door.*

Henrik   No, no. Now you will be docile, you will laugh a lot.

Nora   No.

Henrik   You will laugh so that they'll believe you're a sweet, enchanting creature . . . a little girlish.

Nora   That's not how I am!

Henrik (*he puts a finger to his lips*)   Sshh!

Nora   You're the one who makes me laugh. Too much. Oh how happy I am all the time! Like a moron.

Henrik   Sshh!

Ana María *comes back.*

Nora   Who is it?

Ana María   A surprise awaits you, madam. A friend of yours, Mrs Linde.

Nora   Mrs Linde? Show her in!

Henrik   It's been a long time that we haven't seen her . . . three years?

Nora   No, much longer, ten, fifteen years! (**Mrs Linde** *enters.*) Cristina! (*She embraces her.*) It's been so long!

Cristina   I married without love, with a vested interest. He had a fortune and with that fortune I could care for my mother and my brothers. But later, when he died, he left only debts, a fortune built on pillars of mud. I was left ruined. My mother died, my brothers grew up, they didn't need me anymore. I am . . . incredibly alone.

Nora (*searching and fleeting look at* **Henrik**)   So much unhappiness!

Cristina   I can see looking at your house that you're in a good position.

Nora   And I will be in a better one. My husband, Torvald, was promoted to being the director of the bank. (*To* **Henrik**.) Thank you. Sometimes I think that you're hard but with the promotion of Torvald you've been generous.

Henrik (*smiles*)   You saw that?

Nora   In the future, goodbye to money problems! (*To* **Cristina**.) Now I can help you.

Cristina   Really?

Nora   Yes. With what you need, Cristina.

Cristina   I'm looking for work.

Nora I will speak to Torvald.

Cristina Thank you. I think that fortunately you have never known suffering or difficulties. And for not having known them, your gesture is worth all the more to me.

Nora (*laughs*) That I haven't known them! Listen to what she says!

Henrik She doesn't know.

Nora Three years ago, Torvald got ill. The only thing which would save him would be a trip to another country with a mild climate, without this cold, this snow, this darkness of winter. (*She protests facing* **Henrik**.) Honestly! The climate can cure you!

Cristina Did you travel?

Nora Yes, at noon from France. We were there a year.

Henrik In Italy.

Cristina How were you able to?

Nora (*slightly disconcerted*) How were we able to what?

Cristina To travel. Torvald wouldn't work naturally, so much expense . . .

Henrik A loan. It's not possible that you could have forgotten.

Nora I didn't forget it. That loan sucked my blood.

Cristina How did you secure it, Nora? From a bank it's difficult.

Henrik More than difficult. No bank lends to a woman.

Nora Through other means. (*Teasing*.) I had . . . a friend.

Cristina What do you mean?

Nora (*smiles*) You think badly of me.

Cristina Were you the friend?

Henrik It wasn't me.

Nora No. He only gave me the idea.

Cristina Torvald recovered.

Henrik (*taking revenge*) The climate *cures*. It's not the same to live in the sun as to live in the gloom. Nora . . .

Nora He recovered, yes. And you've no idea how well! Of course I lied to him. The loan: a gift from my father, who was already very unwell. I even said that it was *me* who wanted to travel. Oh, how I insisted! I became unbearable, petulant. I dreamed of France . . .

Henrik Of Italy.

Nora What's more, I was pregnant and you don't ignore the whims of a pregnant woman. Not even on death's door would Torvald have been able to bear owing me favours.

Cristina You were his wife.

Nora Oh, yes. His extravagant crazy wife.

Cristina How did you pay back the loan? Because . . .

Nora Oh, I had my ways! Losing out on hours of sleep, copywriting at night, doing dress making . . . (*To* **Henrik**.) Tell me, do you really think that with these jobs it's possible to pay back a large sum?

Henrik Yes, saving each penny.

Nora I spent each penny: clothes, food, unforeseen costs . . . I saved the crumbs left over from *each* penny. Only you can think that . . .

Meanwhile the doorbell has rung, **Ana María** *has crossed towards the door; she comes back.*

Ana María I beg your pardon, madam. A gentleman wishes to see your husband. And seeing as your husband is with Dr Rank . . .

Henrik (*to* **Cristina**) Rank is a friend of the family, a doctor.

Krogstad (*appears*) It's me, Mrs Helmer.

Nora (*she startles, turns towards* **Henrik**) Why did you send him to me?

Henrik Remember? He's linked to you by the past.

Ana María Forgive me, madam. I didn't realise . . .

Nora It's fine, it's fine. (**Ana María** *leaves.* **Nora** *to* **Krogstad**.) What do you want? To speak with my husband? What do you intend to say to him?

Krogstad I have a job at the bank. That's what I want to talk to him about. Not about any other matter.

Henrik The gentleman lawyer is with a visitor. He can't attend to you.

Nora (*pays no attention. Unsettled, to* **Krogstad**) So, if you wish to speak with him, take the trouble of going into his study. (*Pointing*.) It's there. (*With a bow,* **Krogstad** *exits*.)

Henrik Nora, why did I say it wasn't a good time . . .?

Nora To see my husband? How many times will I be able to stop him? On the other hand, it seems that he is only concerned about his little job at the bank.

Cristina I know that man. Krogstad. I knew him when we were young and . . . He's very changed. For the worse.

Nora (*laughs bitterly*) And that's saying something! A bad marriage. Widowed with a lot of children. He doesn't have a good reputation. Actually, I know very little about him and wish I didn't know anything.

Rank (*appears, speaking towards the inside of the study*) No, no I don't want to bother you. I will talk for a moment or two with Nora. (*He notices the presence of* **Cristina**.) Oh, forgive me. I think I'm going to cause just as much bother here.

Nora Not at all. Doctor Rank, Mrs Linde. Mr Henrik.

Rank Madam . . . (*He ignores **Henrik**, only giving him an unfriendly look.*)

A moment of uncomfortableness.

Nora (*bursts out laughing*) I think Torvald will be able to make some heads roll and replace them with others in the bank. I already know the first to fall! Krogstad's!

Henrik It won't be so easy.

Nora Don't throw a spanner in the works for me! He's an odious man, odious. Cristina will take up his post.

Cristina (*laughs*) Nora, aren't you rushing things?

Nora (*also laughing*) No! (*Takes out a packet of sugared almonds from her pocket.*) Would you like one, doctor?

Rank Sugared almonds. I would have thought that Torvald forbade them.

Nora He fears for my teeth. (*Irritated, to **Henrik**.*) It's a bit much, isn't it?

Henrik It is a bit much, but that's Torvald for you. A man of his time.

Rank You shouldn't . . .

Nora Have bought them? I didn't buy them. Cristina gave them to me.

Cristina Me?

Nora Come on, don't be scared. You couldn't know that Torvald had forbidden me to eat them. For my own good he prohibits everything I like. (*She laughs.*) Sugared almonds! Bad words!

Rank (*smiles*) Which ones?

Nora (*she opens her mouth wide about to say one. Her mouth claps shut on seeing **Torvald** come out of his study. She hides the sugared almonds*) Torvald! Did you throw that man out?

Torvald He left of his own accord. He used the door from my study.

Nora Torvald, I want to introduce you to a childhood friend, Mrs Linde.

Torvald A pleasure, Mrs Linde.

Nora She has made a long journey in order to speak with me.

Henrik With Torvald.

Nora With you, rather. Cristina understands a lot about office work. She's looking for a job. Could you do something for her, Torvald? When she learned from the newspapers that you had been appointed director of the bank . . .

Torvald (*to **Cristina***) Do you have experience?

Cristina A lot. And I always dreamed of working with a great man, a capable man.

Torvald (*flattered*) Would that be me?

Cristina Exactly.

Torvald Then, it's likely that I can provide you with a post. You came at a good time.

Nora You see!

Cristina I don't know how to thank you . . .

Torvald Oh, let's not speak of that! (*He takes his coat.*) Now, if you'll excuse me . . . I have to go out.

Rank (*mirroring him*) I'm also leaving.

Nora Don't take too long, Torvald.

Torvald Only an hour.

Nora (*seeing that* **Cristina** *takes her coat*) Are you going too, Cristina?

Cristina I need to find lodgings.

Nora What a pity that in this house I can't . . .

Cristina Don't mention it. Thank you and goodbye.

Nora See you later because you're coming for dinner tonight, aren't you? And you too, Doctor? How do you feel today?

Rank Fine. (*Looking at* **Henrik** *with aversion.*) In spite of some people.

They leave.

Nora I have a deadline of the New Year to repay my debt. I will pay the last instalment. Then free. Like a fluttering skylark, Torvald would say. End of worries, of sneaking around trying to get money together. Money slips through your fingers, he tells me. I will end the lies. (*Directly to* **Henrik**.) Although having no choice but to lie, because others don't give space to the truth, is not exactly lying, don't you think? Are you staying? I'm going to entertain the children for a while . . .

Henrik Wait. I said no . . . not everything would be so easy.

Nora But nor would it be so difficult, right? The worst is already over. Although . . . there are shadows . . . disquiet because Torvald and I . . . Torvald with me . . . It's fine. What we haven't talked about has never existed. And I won't talk and Torvald won't find out . . . (*Sighs.*) I don't know . . . (**Krogstad** *appears.*)

Henrik I think you've got a visitor.

Krogstad Excuse me, Mrs Helmer.

Nora What can I do for you now? How did you come in?

Krogstad They forgot to close the door.

Nora My husband isn't at home.

Henrik He knows that already. He saw him walk past with someone.

Krogstad Opportunity makes the thief. That is why I came. Because your husband was not at home.

Nora You committed an offence. But you're used to doing that. What do you want?

Krogstad I will tell you. Before that allow me a question: the lady who was with him was Linde's widow?

Nora Yes, she arrived today.

Krogstad I had dealings with her in another era. May I ask something else? Mrs Linde hopes to get a post at the bank?

Nora Yes, she will get it thanks to me. I vouched for her. I exercise some influence over my husband, so measure your words and take care with what you say, my good sir.

Krogstad I say this. (*Ironically*.) With care. Seeing as you have such influence, would you have the kindness to use that influence in my favour?

Nora What?

Krogstad Your husband is thinking of reorganising his staff. It will leave me unemployed. Use your influence to reverse his decision.

Nora I have no influence, Mr Krogstad.

Krogstad You have just said the opposite.

Nora (*to* **Henrik**) He's right.

Henrik It's in your character to contradict yourself. You lie a lot.

Nora I don't want to anymore. Why do I have to go through this? Haven't I suffered enough?

Henrik No suffering in the past absolves us from more suffering. No one can say 'It's not my turn to suffer'.

Nora Nice way to keep me happy, Mr Henrik! (*To* **Krogstad**.) You're blackmailing me with my debt? I'm soon to pay the last instalment. I'll be free from you.

Krogstad Do you have the money?

Nora Not yet.

Krogstad And how will you find it in a week?

Nora It's not your concern. You won't be able to threaten me anymore. You'll lose your job? Well, others have lost theirs. (*To* **Henrik**.) And how will it be settled?

Henrik The issue is that he *doesn't want* to lose his job.

Krogstad I'll fight to keep it as a matter of life or death. Take heed, Mrs Helmer.

I will back down from nothing. That job was the first step in clearing my name, which I myself muddied a few years ago. Don't sink me.

Henrik A fraud. Some scams . . . He got away with it.

Nora Then what's he complaining about? You get what you deserve. I can't help him.

Krogstad I have ways of making you.

Nora Don't tell me! You're about to tell my husband that I owe you money? It doesn't scare me. He doesn't know, but he'll appreciate what I did. He'll pay the rest of my debt.

Krogstad He'll pay it just like that? Calmly? Your husband is a fool.

Nora Don't insult him!

Krogstad (*goes on*) You should fear public opinion. You will not be able to cover up the matter and your life in this house will change a lot. The grumbling, the scorn. And he will prevent contact with your children. You will be a bad influence.

Nora On my children? You're mad. You don't know the kindness of Torvald.

Krogstad I know it well. And I might be mad but you are forgetful.

Nora Really? Why?

Krogstad You were so desperate when you asked me for money to attend to your husband's illness that you didn't pay attention when you signed.

Nora Of course I paid attention!

Henrik You didn't pay attention, Nora.

Nora (*to* **Henrik**) But, *why* didn't I pay attention? If everyone knew this man was not to be trusted.

Krogstad Do you remember who countersigned the loan?

Nora My father.

Krogstad Your father was very ill.

Nora Dying.

Krogstad Do you remember the date of his death?

Nora These dates are not forgotten.

Krogstad Of course. (*He takes out a piece of paper from his pocket.*) And that's why I can't explain . . .

Nora What?

Krogstad Why your father would sign this guarantee three days after his death.

Nora (*to* **Henrik**) Was that how it was?

Henrik Lamentably.

Nora (*looking at him incredulously*)   Why didn't you warn me?

Henrik   Should I have done? At that point, you were supposed to know what you were doing. And I didn't move your hand.

Nora   But you took me to such extremes! (*With a gesture of impotence she turns towards* **Krogstad**.) Very well. I falsified my father's signature, so what? He was very ill, I would have had to explain the situation to him and embittered his last days.

Krogstad   You would have forgone the trip.

Nora   And let Torvald die? Because without the change in climate (*Pointing to* **Henrik**.), according to him and the doctors, Torvald would have died.

Krogstad   That doesn't absolve you of responsibility.

Nora   Towards whom? My responsibility was towards Torvald, towards my father.

Krogstad   The law does not concern itself with motives. Just so you understand, I will tell you that the crime I committed was no worse than yours.

Nora   Completely different! And if the law doesn't account for this, then the law is bad.

Krogstad   Bad or not . . . if I show this document to the courts it will be judged according to the law.

Nora   I doubt it. I had a right to save my father from suffering, a right to save the life of my husband. I don't know much about the law, but somewhere it will be said that those motives are worth more than others. You, being a lawyer, don't you know that? You seem poorly skilled as a lawyer, Mr Krogstad.

Krogstad   Perhaps. But matters like the ones we're dealing with, you will admit that I understand them, eh? Perfectly. If you don't want to intercede on my behalf, don't. But keep in mind that if I have to pay again for my mistake, you will keep me company. Good day, Mrs Helmer. (*Bows, leaves.*)

Nora (*looks at* **Henrik**)   Should I be frightened?

Henrik   I would say so.

Nora   No. Acts committed out of love are not judged.

Henrik   Ah . . . if you believe that . . . Society doesn't believe it.

Nora   You put stumbling blocks in my way.

Henrik   And you trip over them. Besides, don't get upset. You never know if what we consider misfortune has some other purpose beyond the misfortune itself.

Nora (*ironically*)   Of future benefit, you say?

Torvald *enters from the street with a folder of documents.*

Torvald   Did someone come?

Nora No. No one.

Torvald That's strange. I saw Krogstad leaving.

Nora Krogstad?

Torvald The man himself.

Nora Oh, yes! I'd forgotten. He was here for a moment.

Torvald What did he want?

Nora Er . . . (*To* **Henrik**.) What did he want?

Henrik I can't think of an excuse to . . .

Torvald Let me guess: he came to beg you to intercede on his behalf, that you speak in his favour.

Nora Yes.

Torvald That you pretend it was your idea.

Nora Yes.

Torvald Nora, Nora! How could you act like this? Meeting such a person and making a promise! And to make matters worse, lie to me!

Nora Lie to you?

Torvald You told me that no one had come. 'Who was here? *No one*!' (*He threatens her with his finger.*) My little singing bird won't do that again, will she? My pure and clean beaked songbird. My little bug.

Nora (*to* **Henrik**) Why does he talk to me in such a ridiculous way? I can't stand it!

Henrik He loves you.

Nora I love him too. But I don't call him my little bug or my little singing bird. Torvald!

Torvald (*going through his papers*) Yes.

Nora Krogstad . . .

Torvald Ah no! Enough of Krogstad! Not a word more about him! (*He gathers his papers and goes into his study.*)

Nora I have to silence myself, don't I? You never amend Torvald's plan.

Henrik With some characters it's not possible. They need to suffer more blows.

Nora And where will they come from? From whom? From me, correct? (**Henrik** *is silent.*) Why don't you answer me?

Henrik I don't know yet.

Nora Then, what do I do? Krogstad, one way or another, will tell him everything. Did you hear his threats?

Henrik   They were to be expected.

Nora   For you. Torvald could have listened to me. What would I have asked him for after all?

Henrik   Something he couldn't give you. He's inflexible.

Nora   And Krogstad? Krogstad could have said to me: I cancel the IOU, or after the last payment you won't see me anymore. Don't be afraid of me because I admire you. I admire your integrity. He and Cristina could have worked together and fallen in love. They know each other from another era. Instead, before Christmas, Torvald gets annoyed and doesn't listen to me, Krogstad threatens me. What a great present! A catastrophe.

Henrik   Perhaps Krogstad changes his mind, doesn't deliver on his threats. Still not everything has been said. At least not for me.

Nora   And meanwhile, I will be on tenterhooks. I asked for your help!

Henrik (*picks up his hat*)   And I am helping you. I will see what I can do. I must go, can you manage on your own? Don't make the decisions for yourself.

Nora   What? I should manage on my own and not make decisions? You make me live in limbo and that limbo is hell!

Henrik   Trust me. Torvald is so annoyed with Krogstad that he won't accept any more visits from him.

Nora   But Krogstad can send him a letter! Torvald won't stop reading a letter! Don't you understand? If Torvald finds out what I've done, that not only did I lie, but that a document exists with my father's signature falsified, how do you think he'll react? He'll consider me a bad woman, he'll take away my children. My little singing bird, my skylark, my little bug, how could you deceive me like this? he'll say.

Henrik   Don't anticipate misfortune.

Nora   So I don't anticipate it, help me. You can't leave me in this uncertainty, it's cruel!

Henrik   I'll look for another solution. I'll think about this.

Nora   And in the meantime? And in the meantime? (**Henrik**, *with his hat in his hand turns towards the exit. The light gets weaker*.) Come back!

Henrik   I told you to trust me. You are not alone. (*Exits*.)

Nora   I am. It is as sure as it is true that I exist. Alone.

Ana María *enters.*

Ana María   Madam, shall I turn on the lights? What are you doing here in the darkness?

Nora   Don't turn them on.

Ana María (*she comes close, looks at her intently*)   Are you upset?

Nora   No.

Ana María   So? Oh, I know well what sorrows are! They come even though you might be happy, and you don't know why. Is that it?

Nora   Ana María . . . Do I seems like a bad person to you?

Ana María (*laughs*)   Oh, madam, what ideas you have! I raised you, I know you. Do you remember when your father forbade me to fuss over you? He was afraid that you would become spoiled. But when I put you to bed at night, I fussed over you, kissed you and sang you songs to make up for everything I hadn't been able to do during the day. Do you remember? (*Laughs cheerfully.*) That really is being a bad person! I certainly was bad, madam! Come on, come with the children, they're waiting for you. (*Exits.*)

Nora   I'm coming right away. (*But she doesn't move.*)

Scene Two

Nora *and* **Ana María.** **Nora** *holds up her dress for the Stenborgs' party and examines it. She drops it brusquely over a chair.*

Nora   Has a letter arrived?

Ana María   No, madam.

Nora   And by hand?

Ana María   Some documents for the gentleman. (*She looks for them on a small table and hands them to her.*)

Nora (*she rifles through them feverishly, gives them back*)   Leave them on the desk in his study.

Ana María   Yes, madam. (*Exits.*)

Nora   Nothing. Still nothing. No, Krogstad will not carry out his threats. It's Christmas. Tomorrow there'll be a party upstairs at the Stenborgs' house. And what does he expect? That I dress as a Napoleonic fisherwoman and dance the tarantella. Ridiculous. Me, with the ice that I carry inside, move like a southern Italian! From the south or from the north it's the same. A fisherwoman! When the only fish I know are the ones I've eaten. (*Laughs bitterly.*) Cristina will come to help me with the costume. And I will watch her sew while I die of restlessness.

Cristina *enters accompanied by* **Henrik.**

Cristina   We met on the road.

Henrik   Has something happened?

Nora   Don't you know? Not yet.

Cristina I really enjoyed the supper last night. Even though Dr Rank seemed so downcast . . . What's wrong with him?

Nora (*violent, to* **Henrik**) No! I won't tell her that!

Henrik Tell her.

Nora That pleasure corrupts? That if we do not lead a decent life, our children will suffer the consequences? Please, Mr Henrik. Look for other storylines.

Henrik (*firmly*) Through his father's vices, Dr Rank inherited a terrible affliction in his marrow.

Cristina Will he be cured?

Henrik Nora believes he will be (*He surreptitiously shakes his head at her.*)

Nora Haven't you seen anyone circling the house?

Henrik Little birds.

Nora Luckily you take it that way. I can't. I'll check to see if there's a letter in the mailbox.

Henrik Don't go. There's no letter for Torvald. (**Nora** *goes out briefly.*)

Cristina Why is she so nervous? Not because of the ball, I hope.

Henrik No, although that adds to it.

Cristina To what?

Nora (*returns*) There's no letter for Torvald.

Henrik It's almost as if you wish for it.

Nora I wish for something better than this uncertainty.

Cristina (*she moves away towards the chair where* **Nora** *left the dress. She picks it up*) Nora, does it fit you well?

Nora Long. And I think the sleeves . . .

Cristina They're unsewn, yes. I'll sort it out for you. (*She sits down next to the little table with the dressmaking tools. As she sews.*) Nora, does Dr Rank come often?

Nora Daily.

Cristina And how does he commit that lack of discretion?

Nora How?

Cristina Don't pretend, Nora. Wasn't he the one who lent you the money?

Nora Him? Have you lost your mind?

Cristina It isn't him?

Nora Of course not! Although no doubt if I asked him, I'm sure that he would . . .

Cristina Without Torvald knowing?

Nora Torvald doesn't have to know anything. At the beginning of the year I have to settle my account, the last I will pay. If I can't raise the money, I'll go to Dr Rank. I want to get out of this problem, although it gives some pleasure to prolong it.

Henrik I'll only prolong it just long enough. (*Offended.*) And I'm not taking any pleasure!

Nora Cristina, I want to ask you . . .

Cristina What?

Nora When everything has been paid, even the last penny, the guarantee will be returned, won't it?

Cristina Naturally.

Nora The foul piece of paper torn into a thousand pieces!

Cristina (*stops sewing*) Nora, what are you hiding from me? You haven't been the same since yesterday. What's this about? The truth!

Henrik Shhhhh! Speak quietly. Torvald's at home.

Nora Oh, yes, he's at home. Cristina, don't sew. He gets irritated if he sees me sewing. (*To* **Henrik**.) Why's he so touchy? Or does he believe that his trousers sew themselves? Wash themselves?

Henrik Nora. It disgusts him. Actually, it doesn't seem elegant to me either when a woman sews, if she knits a lot . . .

Cristina (*smiles*) Thanks for the part I play.

Nora Oh, you're ridiculous too!

Henrik Besides, why provoke a quarrel for unimportant things?

Nora They are important.

Henrik (*pleasantly*) Cristina, go to the children's room.

Nora Do as you're told, Cristina. No doubt I should speak to Torvald alone.

Cristina I will sew there. (*She laughs.*) If they'll let me . . . (*Exits.*)

Nora He dislikes watching sewing! You could have come up with another excuse.

Henrik Has Cristina gone? Then the excuse is a good one.

Nora You always have the last word. (**Torvald** *enters.*) Are you going to work?

Torvald Yes, in my study.

Nora Torvald . . .

Torvald Yes?

Nora Can I ask you something?

Torvald   Anything you want, my little bug.

Nora   Is it so terrible what Krogstad has done?

Torvald   I will speak of that gentleman for the last time. Yes, it was terrible. He embezzled funds.

Nora   Was he not driven by misery?

Torvald   Perhaps. I am not so cruel as to condemn a man for a single crime, provided that he acknowledges his fault, that he redeems himself and suffers his punishment.

Nora   His punishment?

Torvald   But Krogstad did not choose that attitude. He is morally lost. That's why I don't want to keep him at the bank. His presence offends me. What's more, I've known Krogstad since my youth. We trusted each other, but that trust has come to an end. He has so little tact that he allows himself to address me informally in front of everyone. It's disagreeable.

Nora   Torvald, can't you think about what you're saying. How can such a petty reason bother you?

Torvald   Petty? Are you calling me petty?

Nora   No. On the contrary. You are generous and that's why . . .

Torvald   It's the same. My motives are petty, therefore I am too. Thank you. It's time for this to end, stop talking about Krogstad! Ana María!

Nora   What are you going to do? For God's sake, don't get annoyed!

Torvald   Luckily I have the decision in my pocket. (**Ana María** *enters.* **Torvald** *takes out an envelope, hands it to her.*) Take this. The address is on the envelope. Take it by hand.

Nora   What's that letter?

Ana María *exits.*

Torvald   Krogstad's dismissal.

Nora   No! Ana María! (*She tries to run after her.*)

Torvald (*stops her*)   Please, Nora! Why such anguish?

Nora   Krogstad can do bad things to us! He could plan to take revenge!

Torvald (*laughs*)   In what way? Against me?

Nora   He'll slander us. The newspapers will lap up his infamies.

Torvald   Nora, you don't think I'm going to fear what a resentful poxy lawyer might say, do you? Whatever happens, the responsibility is mine.

Nora   Yours? What do you mean?

Torvald   That I take care of all the responsibilities.

Nora (*with a thin thread of a voice*)   Even my own?

Torvald (*laughs*)   What are your responsibilities, Nora? To look after your children, the house, make yourself look lovely for me?

Nora   And if there were others?

Torvald (*he doesn't take this seriously*)   Hum . . .! The same. I take care of them.

Nora   Never, you'll never do that!

Henrik   Being challenging doesn't work with Torvald. Modesty, Nora, seduction, perhaps . . .

Nora   Forgive me, I'm worried for us, for you. I love you so much!

Torvald   I know, my little bug.

Nora   Will you take back the letter? Will you reverse your decision? Krogstad's dismissal will only hurt us. He will take revenge.

Torvald   Let him. And enough, Nora! I take care of all the responsibilities, I told you.

Nora   You will never do that!

Torvald   Then, as husband and wife, we share them. Are you happy?

He goes into his study.

Nora   Which part will he share? (*To* **Henrik**.) If you don't help me, I'll go to Doctor Rank.

Henrik   To Dr Rank? Soon he'll be dying.

Nora   No! Promise me that he won't! Please.

Henrik   I don't know . . . His father was a licentious . . .

Nora   Dr Rank will live for many years and he'll help me make sure Torvald doesn't find out . . . (*Some knocks on the front door are heard.*) It's him. (*She opens it.*) I recognised him by his way of knocking on the door. Come in. Torvald is busy.

Rank   And you?

Nora   For you I have all the time in the world.

Rank   Then I will make the most of the time I have left.

Nora   A lifetime.

Rank   A short one. I hoped but . . . I didn't believe that it would be so soon. (*Allusive.*) Some are in a hurry to get me out of the way.

Nora (*to* **Henrik**)   You promised me . . .!

Henrik I said 'I don't know'. He's ill and not because of me. His end is drawing near. You'd be better off worrying about Krogstad. When he receives his letter of dismissal, he'll carry out his threats.

Nora The end of Dr Rank . . . is drawing near?

Henrik Yes. It's inevitable and I am sorry about it because . . . He is a good man.

Rank I don't want Torvald to visit me. He has such horror for disagreeable things . . . and death is one of them. I want to die alone. As soon as the end draws near, I'll send him a card with a cross. That way he'll know they've begun, the hours of . . . (*A gesture.*)

Nora It's sad. Infinitely sad! (*She covers her ears with her hands.*) I don't want to know it. Let's be cheerful! Let's be cheerful, Dr Rank! (*To* **Henrik**.) What nonsense do you make me say? (*To* **Rank**.) My friend . . . my punctual visitor, my companion . . . You're not going to die. Be sure. I don't want you to.

Rank Ah, if only that were enough! No, my dear, I will die and you will see that it is not so painful to endure it. After all I am only a friend. You'll miss me for the first few days and then . . .

Henrik Nora, show him the silk stockings that you'll wear at the ball. They're in the box. (*He points.*)

Nora You want me to show him the stockings? Dr. Rank is telling me what he's telling me and you want me to show him my stockings?

Henrik Why not? The more frivolous you are now, the more remarkable your change will be.

Nora If I go on like this, if today I am insensitive to the death of a friend, I won't be a heroine later, Mr Henrik.

Henrik Do you think I reserve that fate for you? In any event, don't let Dr Rank's condition make him forget your troubles.

Rank Troubles, Nora? Why not confide in me? If you tell me, perhaps I can do something. You will be grateful to me and with that I will be satisfied. Gratitude is quite similar to love, don't you think?

Nora Why do you speak of love?

Rank Surely you're not oblivious to it? Ever since I met you, I . . .

Henrik A woman can be totally oblivious to another person's feelings which don't concern her, above all when she doesn't feel the same way.

Nora (*to* **Rank**) I've always known. I didn't tell you about my suffering so as not to worry you. What's more, the gratitude I could have towards you if you were to help me is small compared to the great fondness I feel towards you.

Rank You don't say so as not to cause me distress. Or to keep me at a distance?

Nora No, because of how fond I am of you.

Rank (*murmurs sadly*) Fondness, fondness . . .

Nora Which is the most similar to love. (**Rank**, *moved, kisses her hands.*)

Henrik Actually, Nora, it doesn't seem proper to you that Dr Rank . . .

Ana María (*enters*) Madam . . . (*She comes close to* **Nora**, *murmurs something in her ear and hands her a visiting card.*)

Nora *looks at her and takes it; her expression darkens.*

Rank Something bothersome?

Nora No, nothing like that . . . It's my new dress.

Rank Wasn't Mrs Linde fixing it?

Nora This one is new. I ordered it. A surprise for Torvald. Go to his study and don't let him come out. Doctor! (*Just as he's about to enter the study,* **Rank** *turns.*) The two of us are going to fight so that you don't die. (**Rank** *smiles sadly. He goes into the study.* **Nora** *to Ana María.*) Where is he?

Ana María In the kitchen. He came in through the servants' entrance.

Nora Didn't you tell him I had a visitor?

Henrik He didn't care.

Ana María He says he won't leave until having spoken with you.

Nora Then show him in. (**Ana María** *exits.* **Nora**, *to* **Henrik**, *bitterly.*) There's nothing to be done, is there? (**Krogstad** *enters.*) Speak quietly because my husband is at home.

Krogstad I have received the dismissal, madam.

Nora I wasn't able to avoid it.

Krogstad Perhaps that's true.

Nora And . . . your threats . . . ?

Krogstad I wanted to see you. All day I've thought about you. It pained me. I won't make any accusation, Mrs Helmer.

Nora Oh! I knew it!

Krogstad We can deal with this matter on friendly terms. We'll keep everything between the three of us.

Nora Three? Who is the other person? My husband must not find out.

Krogstad How will you stop him from finding out? You can't even pay the rest of your debt.

Nora Not immediately. I can't.

Krogstad Even if you paid, it wouldn't do you any good. Even if I don't make an accusation, I plan to keep the document.

Nora (*to* **Henrik**)   Can he do that?

Henrik   Not legally, but . . . (*He shrugs his shoulders.*) with this man . . .

Nora   I'll offer him a greater sum.

Krogstad   Even offering me a greater sum, I won't return the receipt.

Nora (*to* **Henrik**)   Do you think that's fair?

Krogstad   I want to keep it. The receipt and the guarantee. No stranger will find out. (**Nora** *strikes her forehead with her fists.*) So if you thought about making an extreme decision concerning your life . . .

Nora   No.

Henrik   Yes, you thought about it, Nora. It would be a painful solution for you, but it would demonstrate to what extremes the acrimony of some people can take you to, their rigidity, their lack of understanding of others . . .

Nora   No! I do not want death, neither for me, nor for Dr Rank.

Krogstad   Or if you thought about abandoning everything and fleeing . . .

Henrik   That would be possible . . .

Nora   I don't have those ideas.

Henrik   You could have had them. In the situation in which you find yourself, one thing or another leads us to a logical ending.

Nora   Death, flight? And my children? What do you think I'm made of?

Krogstad   And yet, I had those thoughts. I was at the point of making them into reality. But I lacked courage.

Nora   I do have courage. To face up to things, Mr Krogstad.

Krogstad   Don't do it. When your husband finds out and the first storm passes, he will accept the situation. Especially since I am not going to make it public. Here, in my pocket, I have the letter informing him.

Nora   My husband doesn't have to read that letter. Tear it up! I'll find the money to pay you back.

Henrik   He told you he didn't want money.

Nora   What does he want then?

Krogstad   Money doesn't interest me anymore. No. I want to progress and your husband can help me. I have struggled through dreadful adversity. Not anymore. I've been honest the last few years. What good is honesty to me if I lose my job, if they throw me out like a rat. Now it's not enough for me that your husband takes me on again as a favour. I want to progress. I want to have a better position in the bank than the one I had and your husband will create that position for me.

Nora   He'll never do that! You don't know him.

Krogstad   He'll do it. I know him. He will not dare to blink and within a year I will be his right hand. It will be me, Krogstad, and not Torvald Helmer, running the bank.

Henrik   Given how Torvald is, I doubt it. He can't contradict his character.

Nora   But this man, who's a rat, contradicts him. Where did that ambition come from?

Krogstad   From a lot of suffering, Mrs Helmer. (*To* **Henrik**.) Then, if her husband does not give in, she will suffer the consequences.

Nora   You won't dare to!

Krogstad   Yes, I'll dare to do everything.

Nora   Do you want me to commit suicide, to run away? Is that what you're proposing to me?

Henrik   No, I don't want . . .

Krogstad   Killing yourself won't help you either. Your memory would be in my hands, your name dragged through the mud. No idiocy, Mrs Helmer. Your husband will receive my letter. We will see what happens. I'll leave it in the mailbox.

Nora   Think of my children!

Krogstad (*he turns fleetingly*)   Your husband never thought of mine. (*Exits.*)

Nora   He'll leave the letter?

Henrik   I think so. I'm sorry.

Nora   Already . . .? We're done for! If I had the key to open the mailbox and . . . Oh, my God, I don't have the strength . . .!

Henrik   Yes, you do.

Cristina (*enters holding* **Nora***'s dress*)   I fixed everything I could. It looks good. Nora, do you want to try it on?

Nora (*shaken*)   No. No!

Cristina   What's wrong?

Nora   Krogstad is going to give me away. He left a letter in the mailbox.

Cristina   Nora . . .! Was it Krogstad who lent you the money?

Nora   Now he demands . . . Torvald will know everything.

Cristina   It's better that way.

Nora   I forged a signature, Cristina! My father's.

Cristina   I'm going to talk to Krogstad right now. Where does he live?

Nora   I don't know. Yes I do. (*She takes out* **Krogstad***'s card from her pocket.*) Very near. Don't go to see him. He won't give up.

Cristina   Nora, there was a time when he would have made any sacrifice for me.

Nora (*to* **Henrik**)   Did you find a way out?

Henrik   I'm trying to.

Nora   But the letter . . .! It's in the mailbox, and how . . .?

Cristina   Does your husband keep the key?

Nora   Always.

Cristina   It's fine. Krogstad can reclaim it with an excuse before he reads it.

Nora   But it's exactly the time when he collect his letters. (*She looks at* **Henrik**.) All wrong! All wrong!

Cristina   You can distract him with an excuse. Show him your dress, sit down at the piano, anything. I will come back as soon as possible. (*She exits at the same time as* **Torvald** *and* **Rank** *appear from the study*.)

Torvald   Has Cristina gone?

Nora   She's going out for a moment.

Torvald   What a face, Nora! Are you worn out?

Nora   Oh, talk about weariness!

Torvald   So much so? Why? I'm going to collect my correspondence.

Rank   Come, Nora. Sit down.

Nora (*doesn't pay attention to him*)   No, Torvald, don't go! I'm so troubled . . .

Torvald   By what? (*Silence from* **Nora**.)

Henrik   The ball.

Nora   The ball, the tarantella.

Torvald   By that? Ah, what a crazy girl!

Nora   No letters this evening, no business, eh? How's that?

Torvald   Are you really so scared, my little Nora? Of a ball?

Nora   It's just that I won't be able to dance tomorrow if I don't practise today.

Rank   Well then, let's practise. (*He sits down at the piano and plays.* **Nora** *doesn't move.*)

Torvald   Come, my skylark, my startled little skylark. Didn't you want to rehearse?

Nora   Yes, but . . . (*She smiles weakly.*) my legs are limp, as if I'd been struck down.

Torvald (*joking*)   Did you strike her down, Rank? (**Rank** *stops playing, gets up and looks at* **Nora**.) Or you, Mr Henrik?

Henrik Rehearsal or no rehearsal, Nora will dance the tarantella. I'm looking forward to it.

Cristina (*enters*) Am I intruding? I went out to buy . . . some threads. (*Looks at* **Nora**. *Surreptitiously shakes her head.*)

Torvald Come in. Perhaps you'll calm Nora down. (*He smiles.*) She's paralysed with anxiety.

Nora I am mad with fear.

Torvald It's not so bad.

Nora Yes it is! Will you guide me, Torvald? Promise? Will you guide me to the end?

Torvald Of course. Your dance will turn out fine and I will be proud, so very proud of my darling little Nora.

Nora Neither today nor tomorrow should you think of anything other than me. You're not going to open any letters . . . not one.

Torvald Why such insistence? There's something else, isn't there? The fear of that Krogstad again?

Nora A little . . .

Torvald I know your face. No doubt there's a letter from Krogstad in the mailbox.

Nora I don't know . . . It's possible . . . But now your time is mine . . . isn't it Torvald?

Torvald Ah, my capricious little crazy girl.

Nora (*reticent*) Yes, your little crazy girl.

Rank Our Nora is strange today.

Nora Go now. Cristina will help me to get dressed. To rehearse the dance, the tarantella.

Rank (*as they go out*) All this . . . Nora's behaviour . . . does it foreshadow something in particular?

Torvald No. Dealing with the children again, no! (*Laughs.*)

Nora (*to* **Cristina**) What happened?

Cristina He wasn't there. He went to the countryside. He's coming back tomorrow night. But I've left him a note.

Nora You shouldn't do it. What am I preventing after all?

Henrik What you prevented until today. That Torvald is disappointed, that your marriage may be thrown up in the air when Krogstad has his revenge. But trust me. I do not abandon you.

Nora I no longer have strength, Mr Henrik. I can't bear much more. And yet . . . deep down there might be a pleasure in waiting for a scandal. The end . . . like a hope. The end. Whatever it may be.

Cristina No, Nora, no! I will help you! (*She embraces her.*) Nora, Nora, don't cry!

Ana María *leans in. She looks at them distressed*

Scene Three

Cristina *and* **Henrik**. **Cristina**, *sitting, leafing through a book distractedly, looks towards the door, checks her watch.*

Cristina He's not here . . . And yet, it's past the time.

Henrik He'll come.

Cristina (*impatient, she goes towards the door, opens it. She sees someone in the half light*) Ah, at last. Come in. I am alone.

Krogstad (*enters*) And who opened the door . . .? To you.

Cristina To me? The maid. She's sleeping now.

Krogstad I received your note.

Cristina I needed to talk to you.

Krogstad And you chose this place? Precisely this house?

Cristina The Helmers are at the ball. I couldn't receive you at my home.

Henrik It seems like an excuse but it isn't. A lady receiving a gentleman alone . . . at night . . .

Krogstad What, the Helmers are at the ball? What good humour! If there's a problem, let's dance! (*Laughs.*)

Cristina We have to talk.

Krogstad (*he darkens*) What do we still have to say to one another?

Henrik There are many things that you still have to say to one another.

Krogstad I wouldn't have believed so.

Cristina But then you never understood me.

Krogstad What was there to understand? It happens every day. Between us the matter was simple. Don't you remember? You abandoned me for a more advantageous proposition.

Cristina You suppose the break-up wasn't hard for me? I was destitute with my mother and my brothers, and you were poorer than I was.

Krogstad And that gave you the right to reject me for another.

Cristina I don't know. I've asked myself many times. I paid a very high price.

Krogstad (*lowering his voice*) And me? When I lost you, I felt the ground part beneath me. Look at me. A castaway clinging to a plank of wood, that's what I am.

Henrik Cheer up, Cristina. Confess that this Krogstad still attracts you, that you never managed to get him out of your head.

Cristina (*shakes her head nervously. After a silence*) Perhaps salvation is near and you don't see it.

Krogstad Whose? Yours or mine? I had a job in the bank and you took it away from me. That was my salvation.

Cristina Until today I didn't know that it was you I was going to replace.

Krogstad I believe you, since you say so, but now that you know, will you resign?

Cristina It won't do any good.

Krogstad Ah!

Henrik Cristina, give him reasons. Despite his flaws, if the roles were reversed he would resign, surely.

Cristina I have learned to act wisely. (*To* **Krogstad**.) Life taught me, hard necessity. If my resignation would be helpful to you, I would speak to Torvald today.

Krogstad Well, what life has taught me is to mistrust words.

Cristina Would you believe the facts? My shipwreck is bigger than yours.

Krogstad You wanted it.

Cristina I wasn't able to choose.

Krogstad Where do you want to end up?

Cristina With something very simple. For those two shipwrecked souls to reach out to one another.

Krogstad What?

Cristina Clinging to the same life raft. Otherwise we will drown, Krogstad.

Krogstad Cristina! How can I trust you again?

Cristina For what reason do you think I brought myself to this city?

Krogstad You were thinking of me?

Cristina All my life I have worked. For others. Now I have no one. Just a gaping hole. Krogstad, tell me, for what and for whom am I going to work?

Krogstad I struggle to believe it. You want to sacrifice yourself. Like all high-minded women, it seems to you like a good destiny.

Cristina Have you ever seen me be high-minded?

Krogstad You would do it? You would do it knowing my past?

Cristina Yes.

Krogstad My reputation, you know about it? You could have saved me.

Cristina Is it not possible to repair everything? That is what you live for. To repair.

Krogstad Cristina! Would you have the courage?

Cristina I need to serve as mother to your children and your children need a mother. I love you, Krogstad. With you nothing frightens me.

Krogstad (*with hope*) Is it possible . . . ?

Cristina It is certain.

Henrik The Helmers are about to come back. They'll return after the tarantella. I can hear it.

Cristina How can you hear it from one floor to another? With these walls! (*Looks at her watch.*) It's twelve! (*To* **Krogstad**.) Go now.

Krogstad One more minute. You know the step I have taken against the Helmers.

Cristina Against Nora. I forgive you. I know what desperation can do, sometimes it's not a cry, it's hatred. And very bitter.

Krogstad Oh if only I could undo what I have done!

Cristina The letter is still in the mailbox. You can retrieve it.

Krogstad Ah, that's why you accepted me. To retrieve the letter. For your friend you are prepared to make any sacrifice.

Cristina Yes. Except sharing your life, Krogstad, is not a sacrifice. (*Smiles*.) Are you being mocking, my friend? (*They look at each other for a long time.*)

Krogstad I will await Torvald's return. I will ask him for the letter, I'll tell him it's just about my dismissal . . . that he doesn't need to read it.

Cristina No, Krogstad. Don't ask for the letter yourself.

Krogstad What? I don't understand.

Henrik Don't punish Nora yourself, Cristina.

Cristina What do you know about my friendship with her? Doesn't Nora suffer enough with so much deceit and subterfuge? It's better that she ends the lie once and for all.

Krogstad I'll wait for you downstairs. I've never been so happy, Cristina! (*Exits*.)

Cristina Me too. Dear, dear Krogstad! (The voices of **Nora** and **Torvald** can been heard. They open the door. **Cristina**, to **Henrik**.) Already! Won't they bump into Krogstad?

Torvald Come on, Nora darling! The ball's finished!

Nora No, it's still going, it's still going! Let's go up again.

Torvald (*discovers* **Cristina**) Mrs Linde! You're here?

Cristina Forgive the intrusion. I wanted to see Nora.

Nora With my dress on? (*Opens her arms, laughs.*) How does it suit me? (*Abruptly removes the ornament from her hair, flings off her jacket.*) I hate it!

Torvald Nora. This is excessive. (*He holds her lovingly, hugging her from behind. To* **Cristina**.) Everyone applauded her dancing. She would have been able to be better but I don't know why . . . We had agreed to leave after the ball but she objected, my crazy little girl.

Nora (*dryly*) Let go of me, Torvald.

Torvald Yes, sorry. (*He releases her. Moves away.*) A little light. (*He switches on the light bulbs.*)

Nora (*quietly, to* **Cristina**) Any news?

Cristina Nora . . . You have to confess everything to your husband.

Nora Ah, Krogstad! That wretched creature!

Cristina You have nothing to fear from his part. He repented. But even so you have to talk to Torvald. It's the best thing for the both of you.

Nora I will not speak to him. I have doubts, Cristina!

Cristina (*grips her shoulder*) In that case the letter will speak for itself. I am going now.

Torvald (*comes closer, hands her some knitting*) Is this yours?

Cristina Yes. I forgot it.

Torvald Do you knit?

Cristina Yes, Mr Helmer.

Torvald You should embroider.

Cristina Why?

Torvald It's prettier. You hold the embroidery with your left hand, like this, and you carry the needle with your right hand . . . Do you see the curve that is formed, long and light . . .? Isn't it prettier?

Nora (*to* **Henrik**) What's he talking about?

Henrik What a bad mood! Torvald drank a lot, he's tipsy. Can't he be a little frivolous?

Nora No. He doesn't know how to be frivolous. When he's frivolous, he's an idiot.

Henrik Nora! Why so much effort in preserving your marriage, protecting Torvald, so much love if you think like this?

Nora Can't I? Is it not *permitted*?

Cristina Goodnight, Nora. (*She embraces her.*) Think about what I told you.

Torvald (*accompanying her to the door*) Good night. Forgive me not accompanying you. But you live so close! (**Cristina** *exits.*) Thank God she's gone! What a drag! How nice that at last we're alone!

Nora (*to* **Henrik**) Yes, too many people come and go in this house.

Torvald I was looking at you tonight at the ball, I found you so attractive! I imagined that we had just got married and couldn't wait until it was time to . . . (*He embraces her.*)

Nora I'm tired, Torvald.

Torvald Me too. Let's go to bed together, eh? (*He kisses her neck.*)

Nora (*pulling away*) Get him off me! I don't want him to touch me.

Henrik (*clearing his throat*) He's your husband.

Torvald Nora!

Nora (*to* **Henrik**) Oh, no! You too?

Henrik You asked me for help. Why are you taking it out on me?

Nora I'm sick of it! (*Someone's knocking at the door. Hysterical, to* **Henrik**.) Stop this constant coming and going! How many times has Cristina entered and exited, Krogstad entered and exited, how many times has Dr Rank appeared?

Rank (*from outside*) It's me! Can I come in for a moment?

Torvald What will this man want now? What a pain! (*Opens the door.*) Do come in, how nice of you that you can't pass our door without visiting us.

Rank I thought I heard your voice and that I'd come in for a moment. I wanted to ask you . . . I live alone and I never tire of sharing a piece of this home, so peaceful, so happy.

Torvald I saw you happy at the ball as well.

Rank Didn't I have the right to have a little fun?

Nora (*to* **Henrik**) What do you get out of him dying?

Henrik And what do you want me to do? Do you want him to end up as an impossible lover?

Nora Yes! I want to count on his love into my old age!

Rank (*referring to* **Henrik**) He's always had something against me.

Henrik Me! Who helped you to be so noble!

Rank Being noble is of little use to me. (*To* **Nora**.) I have certainty.

Nora About what?

Rank An absolute certainty. That I will be invisible.

Nora The end . . . ? (*To* **Henrik**.) Be coherent. If he is really ill, how could he have danced like he danced?

Henrik With his last strength.

Nora I don't think you know anything about illness.

Torvald What illness are you talking about, Nora? It's not the appropriate . . . (*He makes a gesture.*)

Rank I've completely forgotten what I came for. Ah, yes. Helmer, give me one of your cigars. (**Torvald** *gives him the box.* **Rank** *chooses one, cuts the tip.*) Thank you.

Nora (*strikes a match, brings the flame near*) Allow me to light it for you.

Rank Thank you! And now I'm going.

Nora (*to* **Henrik**) I want to say goodbye with an embrace. A very strong embrace.

Torvald Nora, my darling! Our friend Rank can be trusted, but . . .

Nora (*to* **Henrik**) You have the perfect reply for him!

Rank Fate intervenes in the lives of everyone, except mine. Condemned. Goodbye, Helmer. Goodbye, Nora.

Nora Sleep well, Doctor Rank.

Rank I thank you for the good wish.

Nora Wish me the same.

Rank You? Very well . . . seeing as you ask me . . . Sleep well. And thank you for the light. (*He nods goodbye and exits.*)

Torvald *takes the keys out of his pocket.*

Nora What are you going to do?

Torvald (*selects one of the keys*) Empty the mailbox. (*Exits.*)

Henrik He'll realise that you tried to force the lock.

Nora With a hairpin. I couldn't.

Torvald (*brings a pile of letters in his hands*) Someone tried to break into the mailbox. Who was it?

Nora The children . . . The servants . . .

Torvald I'll soon find the culprit. Do you see how many letters there were? One day without collecting them and they pile up . . . What is this?

Nora (*to* **Henrik**, *with a thin thread of a voice*) The letter? (**Henrik** *shakes his head.*)

Torvald A visiting card from Rank . . . with a cross over his name. He must have left it when he went. How curious! Some joke in poor taste! As if announcing his death to us.

Nora That's what it's about.

Torvald Did he say something to you?

Nora That this is how he would say goodbye to us.

Torvald He's going to die? I knew he was very ill, but . . .

Nora And he wants to do it alone.

Torvald Poor Rank! He'll hide himself away like a wounded animal.

Nora I wouldn't like to die like that. (*To* **Henrik**.) Why don't you surround him with the people who love him?

Henrik He doesn't have any friends, except you and Torvald, he doesn't have family . . .

Torvald But perhaps it's preferable. Poor friend! Maybe it's better for us too.

Nora How so?

Torvald Because no one's going to knock on our door when I feel like embracing you. (*He embraces her*.) Nora, my little woman, my songbird. I wish some danger threatened you so I could protect you, to give my blood, to risk everything, everything!

Nora (*pulls away*) Read the letters, weren't you anxious? In the face of Rank's death, a letter is so inconsequential, and especially the fear of a letter . . .

Torvald I won't read one letter. Not tonight. I entrust it to you. (*He embraces her*.)

Nora (*pushing him away*) Don't you think about your friend?

Torvald Of course I do! But all the same . . .

Nora (*to* **Henrik**) How can he say *all the same* . . . ?

Henrik It's beyond him. He is affected.

Torvald A lot. This missive from Rank with its black cross has robbed me of joy, the wish to . . . You understand, Nora? Forgive me. It's better I read the letters. Perhaps this way I'll forget . . . (*Exits*.)

Nora And now? I wait . . . ?

Henrik You'll find out . . . You're going to get a surprise.

Nora What kind of surprise?

Henrik I still haven't decided.

Nora You're lying.

Henrik   No.

Nora   Then decide that Rank is cured, that Torvald reads the letter and it doesn't matter to him.

Henrik   Don't be hasty.

A shout from **Torvald** *is heard.*

Torvald (*appears at the door, shaking the letter*)   Nora! Nora! What is this?

Nora (*foolishly*)   A letter, Torvald.

Torvald   I know! Is it true? This letter from Krogstad tells the truth? How dreadful. It's not possible, it can't be! My songbird sings only lies! You showed me an innocent face and hid the other one, hypocrite!

Nora   I was capable of that because I loved you more than anything in the world.

Torvald   Let's stop the nonsense please!

Nora (*moves towards him*)   Torvald! I love you.

Henrik   Very good. And Torvald loves you. And with love, everything is resolved. (*Screws up his face, sceptical.*)

Nora   I'll take responsibility, Torvald. You don't have to answer for me.

Torvald   I wouldn't dream of it! But it will still affect me all the same. You are my wife. Whether I like it or not, your actions compromise me. Stupid woman! Do you understand what you've done? The outrage you caused?

Nora (*with an opaque voice*)   Yes, now I begin to understand. (*To* **Henrik**.) Is this what you wanted? That I begin to understand? And who told you that I wasn't harbouring a storm? I forced myself to be what others wanted and understood too well that this Nora could not satisfy anyone.

Torvald (*he paces around in agitation*)   Hypocrite! Charlatan! Even worse: a criminal who forges a signature in total oblivion. Shut up! Not a word. (*He stops before* **Nora**, *who is staring at him.*) I should have seen it. And for eight years I didn't see anything. Now I see what you are: a woman without principles. What a way to annihilate my happiness, my future! You put yourself at the mercy of an unscrupulous man who can do whatever he pleases with me: blackmail me and ask me for whatever he wants without my daring to breathe!

Nora   What if I died, Torvald? You would be calm.

Torvald   Not a bit! What would I gain if you died? Nothing. Krogstad wouldn't hide the facts and people might even think that I was the one who incited you to do it. Stop looking at me! How dare you?

Nora   What shall I look at then?

Torvald   Your guilt! I will appease Krogstad however I can to drown this scandal.

Nora   And us?

Torvald There's no *us* anymore! But we will give the appearance of the same harmony. Henceforth, there is no need to think about happiness. Only to save remains, ruins, appearances . . . (*There is a knock on the front door. He shudders. He mutters an expletive and goes to open it. He returns with a letter.*) A letter from Krogstad. For you. But I won't let you read it.

Nora It doesn't matter.

Torvald I hardly dare. Perhaps he plans to extort me in another way. The degradation knows no limits in this man. (*Opens the letter, reads it, examines two documents attached. He exclaims.*) Nora . . .! Nora! Can you believe it? He has repented! (*Laughs.*) Thank God I'm saved! Yes, I am saved!

Nora And me?

Torvald You too. Look. He's returning the receipt.

Nora Wonderful.

Torvald And the guarantee. He says that he's regretful, that he's sorry for what he's done. That a happy event washed away his resentment . . . Bah, it doesn't matter what he writes. We are saved, Nora! No one can harm us anymore! (*Glances at the papers.*) No, I don't want to see anything, I'll assume I had a nightmare and it's over. (*He tears them up.*) Nora, poor thing! What testing days you must have gone through!

Nora Yes, they've been hard.

Torvald Because you despaired. And you didn't come to me. But now we'll forget, eh? Everything is over. Let's change faces. You don't seem to understand . . . Embrace me. Oh you think I don't forgive you. Yes, I forgive you! I know that everything you did was out of love for me.

Nora It's true.

Torvald Please forget the reproaches I levelled at you to begin with. I was scared. It's just that I thought everything was going to collapse on me. I've forgiven you, Nora. I swear I have forgiven you!

Nora Thank you, Torvald. Thank you for your forgiveness! (*She goes inside.*)

Torvald Where are you going?

Henrik Where is she going at this time of night? To get changed, to sleep, perhaps . . . she'll come out . . .

Torvald Tomorrow she'll see the situation differently.

Henrik Do you think?

Torvald Yes, a loving overture, a good sleep . . . and when she wakes up the ties will be strengthened, the landscape different. That Krogstad repented came just in time. I don't want to think about what my life would have been like. Now the curtain will drop on this story, won't it? I will protect Nora, I won't lose my footing and she won't be able to make a mistake like the one she made.

Henrik Something's missing. If not, what sense would it make?

Nora *enters. She's wearing a coat.*

Torvald You got dressed again? With a coat?

Nora Yes.

Torvald What for?

Nora I'm not going to sleep tonight. We have to talk.

Torvald (*to* **Henrik**) Everything's already been said.

Henrik There needs to be a little bit more like this. Very little. Nora, a happy ending would be good.

Nora Is that what you say? For the legacy of unhappiness to be seen all around? Sit down, Torvald.

Torvald Ah, my capricious little girl! (*He sits down.*)

Nora I'm not your little girl nor am I capricious. In eight years of marriage we've never spoken seriously.

Torvald (*joking*) Well, let's speak seriously!

Nora It was all games and laughter. (*To* **Henrik**.) I owe that to you. (*To* **Torvald**.) You and Dad have been very unfair to me.

Torvald (*getting up*) Unfair? Us? Who have loved you more?

Nora I don't want that love. You've never really loved me.

Torvald You can doubt everything, except for this.

Nora Sit down!

Henrik Sit down, Torvald. Listen to her.

Annoyed, **Torvald** *sits down.*

Nora I remember Daddy lovingly sharing his ideas with me. They seemed horrible, but I kept quiet because he wouldn't have liked other different ideas.

Torvald It's good that you recognise it. He didn't have many principles, your father.

Nora Shh! He called me his little doll and played with me like I played with my dolls. Then I came to your house, from Daddy's hands I passed to yours.

Torvald You were very lucky! Another husband would not have been so generous. What I found out today . . .!

Nora I have been a big doll in this house as I was a little doll in Daddy's house. Our union has been that.

Torvald You exaggerate.

Henrik She doesn't exaggerate, Torvald. I've seen it.

Torvald And if you saw it, why didn't you intercede to get those ideas out of her head?

Henrik I had other plans.

Nora I'm going to leave you, Torvald.

Torvald (*getting up*) You've lost your mind! You'll abandon your house, your husband, your children, in a fit of rage? I spoke harsh words, but justified. I spoilt you.

Nora Tonight I'll go to Cristina's house.

Torvald (*to* **Henrik**) Since when does she make decisions of this level? Since when has she had so much pride? Did you instil it in her?

Henrik Maybe . . .

Torvald It's better he leaves my house.

Nora No. He wanted us to talk.

Torvald And we talked! Will you abandon me when I have had so much patience with you? After what you did?

Nora Together. How many times would you remind me?

Torvald I forgive you, Nora!

Nora For what sin? I am free, Torvald, from forgiveness, from sin, from love too.

Torvald And your children? Have you forgotten them? (*Snaps his fingers.*) Just like this?

Nora How? Those who ignore what I lose will say I'm a bad mother. I am willing: not to see them sleep every night, to miss out on their laughter, their embraces, the things they say . . . because what would they receive from me? My own humiliation. I would poison them with a sweetness as bitter as I would feel if I did not dare to leave. Better that Ana María be their mother, take care of them as she did with me. Some day they will understand.

Torvald It's free to bet on the future, isn't it? But it is not safe, Nora. They will never understand why you have abandoned them. (*To* **Henrik**.) She didn't warn you?

Henrik No . . . In that regard I have my doubts . . . Actually, I myself find it difficult to accept Nora's decision as reasonable.

Nora You imagined many motives. Do you regret them?

Henrik (*piqued*) Not at all! But that doesn't stop it being an extreme decision.

Torvald Which means only one thing. (*To* **Nora**.) You don't love me anymore. Is that it?

Nora Yes. Tonight I hoped for a miracle. That you would accept me. You don't love me either, Torvald. If you loved me, my guilt would have been yours too, your fierce indignation would have been because I refused to share it with you.

Torvald (*to* **Henrik**)   The two of us surrendered to contempt and shame. Good ending! (*To* **Nora**.) Is that your last word?

Nora   I don't believe in miracles anymore. Tomorrow Cristina will come and collect my things.

Torvald   I can't know where you'll go? Write to you? (**Nora** *shakes her head*.) Help you? You will need it, Nora. You don't know the world. Now you see that I am generous with you.

Nora   Goodbye, Torvald. Take care of the children.

Torvald   No, no! You also sink me in this way! I cannot risk this separation. (*Takes her hands*.) Nora, Nora! I do want to believe in a miracle. I'm going to change! We will both change! (**Nora** *pulls away*. **Torvald**, *to* **Henrik**.) Stop her! Nora! I can't see you go! I cannot! Oh, what an injustice! What despair! (*He exits clenching his fists. He bumps into* **Ana María** *in the doorway; he pushes her away violently*.) Get out of my way!

Ana María (*with a coat on over her nightclothes*)   Forgive me, madam. I woke up. I heard . . . the argument. (*She bursts into tears*.) Oh child, child, where are you going?

Nora   To Cristina's house. I was sorry not to say goodbye. Hold me. Tight. (*They embrace*. **Nora** *whispers in her ear*.) I'll send you news. (**Ana María**, *crying, runs inside*. **Nora** *takes a few steps towards the door, stops, listens. To* **Henrik**.) Don't my children call me?

Henrik   No. It's blackmail I won't use.

Nora   Goodbye.

Henrik   Wait! You would go out that door first. (*Points*.) Then Torvald, after a moment of intense pain, reflecting and glimpsing a future . . .

Nora   Of impossible miracles. He left because he was humiliated by feeling upset. It seems to me that at the last moment you did not dare at all, you had to give up hope. The miracle. You've disappointed me a little, Mr Henrik.

Henrik (*smiles*)   I felt it, I felt your dissent. Nevertheless, you asked for my help.

Nora   And I am grateful for it. But I wouldn't have let Dr Rank die. I would not have been foolish enough to falsify a document that was being placed in the hands of Krogstad. *I* would have told Torvald that he was about to die and that we had to have a change in climate – since you came up with that – if he wanted to save himself. And in the face of his death, Torvald, perhaps . . . he would have accepted that I would have moved heaven and earth to save him . . . That I humiliated myself, begged, went to no matter who, to that despicable Krogstad, and would falsify not one, but a hundred signatures to get the money! . . . Nor, in the name of love, would I have put up with Torvald so much. The embroidery and not the knitting, you don't know, you can't . . . my wide-eyed little bird, my songbird . . . Ah! His petty rigidity that was not integrity, no, my good sir, it was not integrity.

Henrik When I made you suffer, it was to make you realise. You could finally decide what you wanted, couldn't you? If I contrived painful circumstances, those circumstances led to you being a different woman.

Nora I always was. Not so different either. Simply a woman like many who drowned obeying her father, her husband, some rules dictated by others. Remember? The restlessness.

Henrik Without me, you wouldn't have spoken, Nora. Without me, you would not have known how to face adversity.

Nora Do you really believe that? Before, long before you tried to speak for me, Mr Henrik, I was already writing myself. You just copied me in your own way. (*She is about to leave. She comes back.*) Thank you, thank you anyway. (*Embraces him lightly.*) Goodbye.

Henrik Goodbye. (*After a moment he smiles.*) Good luck.

Curtain.

The Gift (2015)

The premiere of *The Gift* was performed in July 2015 in the María Guerrero Theatre of the Cervantes National Theatre in Buenos Aires with the following cast:

Márgara   Cristina Banegas
Sonia   Belén Blanco
Efraín   Marcelo Subiotto
Renata   Claudia Cantero

Staging and Lighting: Gonzalo Córdova

Costume: Renata Schussheim

Music: Pablo Cécere

Choreography: Diana Szelnblum

Assistant Direction: Marcelo Méndez

Direction: Silvio Lang

Characters

Márgara
Sonia
Efraín
Renata

Márgara I declare the world is ending and no one believes me. That a comet will come and crash into the earth. The earth will spin in pieces and in pieces the infinite will welcome it with more mercy than when it was whole. I say that one day we will stop eating and drinking, that the skin will fall from our bodies, so you can see the tissue of our muscles, and then the muscles will fall in threads and we will show our bones in the dark. I say. Or we will be shadows of non-existent bodies branded against a wall. A ball of fire will bless us and the smoke, in the shape of a singed mushroom, will rise until it is lost in the altitudes, spilling particles of ash and poison. (*Pause.*) It happened.

Or we'll drink gas. And that gas will have a simple name, beautiful even. Our lungs will seal with no time to scream, just our breath cut short in a simple and almost beautiful asphyxiation. It happened. Uninhabited planes will drop bombs on houses and no one will be saved. (*Laughs.*) Not even the worms! It happened!

Trees will disappear, pastures and blades of grass, and we will live in sterility until we die of helplessness. I say this and nobody believes me. But I insist. Whoever granted me clairvoyance does not allow me to ignore it. (*She makes a kind of moan and is overwhelmed, rocking herself with her arms crossed over her chest. Suddenly she straightens up, smiles with vague sarcasm, a certain mockery.*) Am I different? Will I remain healthy while others explode? Those will not be my prophecies. No. I see thousands of little horses their heads adorned with coloured plumes going round a circus ring. And in the stands of the world the children look at them dazzled and the parents applaud, happier than their children because they have finally heard me, and from troubled waters they fished out good sense. Everyone – not one evil person left out – now knows that goodness reaps reward. Oh, what a light heart! What beautiful humanity I foresee, and I do not contradict myself. I follow my desires and whoever made me clairvoyant can do nothing against me. I also decide! My heart light, such beautiful humanity.

Sonia *and* **Efraín**. *In the fireplace a weak fire. You can hear the sound of the wind between gusts of rain of different intensity. In front of the window,* **Sonia** *looks out.* **Efraín**, *sitting at the table, pounds it repeatedly with his fist, his face resentful.*

Sonia (*turns around*)   Efraín . . .! That noise . . .!

Efraín   This? (*Pounding.*) The rain bothers me more.

Sonia   It's died down. I think that . . .

Efraín (*rattled*)   She sent us the water. Your mother sent us the water.

Sonia   What do you mean?

Efraín   Since she arrived – what a coincidence – it rained, five days of work . . . (*An irritated gesture.*) On top of that, we'll die of hunger. What did you bring her for, I ask myself.

Sonia   There was no one to look after her. My brothers had done their bit. Now it's my turn.

Efraín Why not face the truth? Your brothers would have thrown her out on the street (*Emphatic.*). I don't judge them, I would do the same, but your pleas, your tears . . .!

Sonia She's no trouble. You hardly notice she's here, Efraín.

Efraín She brings bad luck.

Sonia Efraín . . .! She's an innocent old lady. Don't you see how innocent she is?

Efraín Innocent? Living? She has a lifetime behind her!

Sonia Like you. Like me.

Efraín Ours is much shorter! With less years. Less sins! What does she do? She comes, eats our food and goes to her kennel like a dog. But, what's she doing?

Sonia Dozing.

Márgara (*enters, walking with difficulty, although she can be upright and be energetic*) Yes, yes. I sleep all day. (*Laughs.*) But now I've woken up!

Sonia (*pulls out a chair for her*) Mum. Come.

Márgara (*stumbles, clings to the table*) No. I'm fine on my feet. (*She looks at* **Efraín** *curiously.*) He's angry. (*Smiley.*) With me I think. Things are going badly for you. With this rain. I brought it. (*Shrugs.*) It could be . . . Sometimes . . . I want a little kindness. If you ask me nicely . . . the rain stops.

Efraín She's raving mad! But she's right about the misfortunes. What did I tell you? She brought us bad luck.

Márgara Because of the rain? It will last a week, two, but if I want it . . . (*Shudders.*) It's so cold! This fire gives no heat, pure ash. I'm also cold in my room. Stingy people! (*Laboriously goes to the fireplace, puts on a log.*)

Sonia (*moves her aside*) Leave it. (*Adds others, revives the fire.*)

Efraín You waste firewood that this fool pays for. All needs are provided for by the fool. Enough is enough! Sonia!

Sonia (*looks at him with hardness for a moment. To* **Márgara**) I'm going to find you a shawl. (*Goes to leave.*)

Efraín (*grabbing her*) That look . . .

Sonia It's the same look I have every day, Efraín.

Efraín (*dangerous*) Yes, it's the one you have every day . . .

Sonia *pulls off his hand and exits.*

Márgara (*Abandoning her place by the fire. Searching in her look.*) What happened? Why did she go?

Efraín She got angry. She can't stand you.

Márgara   Her? My darling daughter! (*Refusing to accept it, reassured.*) Psst, psst . . .! It's you who can't stand me. Do you ask me nicely?

Efraín   What?

Márgara   About the rain. It bores me too. Ask me. Nicely.

Efraín   What for? To bind your wishes to mine? Over my dead body! (*Exits.*)

Márgara   I should go. Why does he hate me so much? It gnaws at his guts, hatred. One day he'll come to my room and club my head open.

Sonia (*Enters. She's carrying the shawl, she drapes it over* **Márgara***'s shoulders.*)   Efraín?

Márgara   He went out to get wet. He can't stand me.

Sonia   Don't say that.

Márgara   I say it, I accept it. I irritate him. He believes I bring bad luck. I'm not a young girl who's easy on the eye. Do you like to look at me?

Sonia   Of course.

Márgara   Hmmm . . .! He hates me. And you're in the middle between him and me. This morning I heard you arguing, I always hear you even though I'm deaf – thirsty, he wouldn't give me a glass of water – and I decided not to sleep anymore. I decided . . .!

Sonia   Yes, Mum. Whatever you want it's fine.

Márgara   I come from a glorious past, did you know that? I still have guts. (*She strikes her body.*) This won't beat me. I've decided.

Sonia   Good . . . That's fine, Mum.

Márgara   You don't believe me. Nobody, not even you, sets any store by people like me, old, with hardly any meat on their bones. And how are they going to have faith if we tremble, if we show our saliva, with our rheumy eyes, our paper thin skin? Tell me, say it to me, when I chew, is the food visible, do bits fall out of my mouth?

Sonia (*she lightly shrugs her shoulders, smiles*)   Sometimes. A little.

Márgara (*final*)   It won't happen again.

Sonia   Aren't you cold anymore? Get closer to the fire.

Márgara   Ah, the fire, the fire! I will drink the fire, I will grind the fire with my teeth. (*She leans perilously towards the flames.*)

Sonia   Mum! be careful . . .

Márgara   Sonia, believe in me!

Sonia   I do believe, Mum.

Márgara   If I put my hand in, I don't burn. (*She touches it.*)

Sonia You don't burn? (*She gently pulls out her hand.*) And okay, you don't burn.

Márgara I just need someone to believe to feel safe.

Sonia You are safe.

Márgara (*spiteful*) But cold!

Sonia (*draws a chair closer at a sensible distance*)   Sit down. And stay sitting there for a moment. By the warmth. Sitting nicely, eh? Keep your hands still!

Márgara (*she pushes the chair closer, sits down placidly. She looks at Sonia, changes her position*)   What shall we talk about? Your husband isn't here, let's make the most of it! (*Gets up, takes a few steps and stops. Flamboyant.*) I declare that the world is ending and . . .

Sonia (*quickly interrupts her, brings her to the chair*)   Yes, Mum, yes. Let's chat.

Márgara (*doesn't hear*)   What?

Sonia Let's chat.

Márgara (*disconcerted*)   About what?

Sonia The women used to come see you, do you remember?

Márgara I remember. They queued up on the street. And I used to charge them! (*Laughs.*) They wanted to know if they'd get a boyfriend, if they'd be lucky . . . There's no such thing as being blessed with luck. I never told them the truth, just a fragment. But now . . . now I'm old, . . . if I don't say . . .

Sonia It's always better to tell the truth, isn't it?

Márgara (*continues*)   A lie has short legs. So the saying goes. Sonia, fly a little!

Sonia I don't follow you, Mum.

Márgara Now I will decide! I can . . .! Change everything. The future is coming to me and it's not inert. Nothing is immutable. Nobody. This is why I grew old, to know that I can change everything.

Sonia Yes, Mum. You can.

Márgara To turn the unjust inside out like a glove, the black into white, the darkness into light. If you want it, if the crowds want . . .!

Sonia Yes, Mum. I want it, I want . . .

Márgara You speak like a toad, a parrot. I'm not stupid.

Sonia I know.

Márgara Well then? Why don't you trust me? Neither me nor what I say?

Sonia I do, Mum.

Márgara But not totally. Or were the roles reversed and I'm a little girl who has to behave?

Sonia (*laughs*) Who's making you behave? Impossible, I wouldn't even begin to try.

Márgara (*comes near*) Look me in the eye. (*Scrutinising her.*) Do you trust me?

Sonia (*Remains still. With an uncertain smile.*) Okay, Mum, yes. . . .

Márgara (*dismissing her*) Silly! You're a brick wall. Words bounce off you.

Sonia (*irritated and patient*) In *what* do I need to trust? *What* must I hear?

Márgara My prophecies! I don't predict catastrophes. Not anymore. I expelled them from the world. I see thousands of little horses adorned with coloured plumes going round a circus ring . . .

Sonia That's really lovely, Mum.

Márgara (*excited*) There are little black horses with white spots and little white horses completely white, all with plumes and the colours move when they tilt their heads from one side to the other.

Sonia Is that what little horses do?

Márgara I'll show you!

Sonia No, no. I see them. They're very funny, their dainty little legs . . .

Márgara Sorry?

Sonia Dainty!

Márgara They trot! And everyone looks at them and their faces become lighter, happy, and evil vanishes.

Sonia How lovely!

Márgara Then, the misfortunes become small and there are no bitter words in my mouth, the usual ones – misfortunes – an illness, death . . ., only for old people after they've lived a lifetime, a lifetime! . . . This is what I prophesise, this is what I decide! But they must hear me.

Sonia (*distractedly*) Of course, Mum.

Márgara Elephant ears! Otherwise they will continue with their sadnesses, their lustreless comings and goings without realising that it could be different. That's why I asked Efraín that if the rain bothers him, to kindly ask me . . . (*Gets lost.*) because kindness . . .

Sonia Makes things easy. Are you still cold, Mum?

Márgara (*unsettled*) I have to go to the beach.

Sonia Another day.

Márgara At the beach, the sea helps me, my words come out better, louder, more firm. (*She goes towards the door.*)

Sonia (*stopping her*) It's raining. Let's have something to eat, shall we?

Márgara (*helpless*) To eat . . .?

Sonia Yes. I'll make you something tasty.

Márgara You didn't listen to me.

Sonia Yes, Mum. I listened to you.

Márgara I want to save them! So that they understand that goodness reaps reward, it takes away hatred, wars, death . . .

Sonia (*moved*) Yes, it'll take away everything, Mum . . . All the suffering.

Márgara We will go together to the beach.

Sonia Tomorrow, okay?

Márgara Tomorrow. (*She thinks about it.*) Tomorrow is a long way away. Even if Efraín does not ask me – kindly – I make prophecies now – I can't wait – I'll decide *right now* . . .! In this very instant!

Sonia (*tired*) What will you decide, Mum?

Márgara A clear sky! A little cloud here, there . . . And . . . seeing as we're here, the sun! Not just any sun, a burning sun that wipes out the humidity in a flash, dries the earth. (*She signals to* **Sonia** *to wait.*) Don't rush me. (*All the noises of the storm cease. After a moment,* **Efraín** *enters.*)

Efraín (*his face is impassive*) The rain stopped. About time, wasn't it?

Márgara (*lights up*) And the sun hasn't appeared . . . yet? (*Happy, signals again to wait.*) Don't be impatient. A moment! In a moment . . .! Now . . .!

A pale sun shines through the window.

Márgara *and* **Sonia**. **Márgara** *seems younger, she's knitting.*

Márgara (*cheerfully*) I see the stitches! Yes. I see the stitches, purl, knit, butterfly stitch, seed stitch. What I don't know (me, the one who can predict things!) is what will come of this. A scarf, a sweater?

Sonia This morning I went into your bedroom and you weren't there.

Márgara What?

Sonia You weren't there.

Márgara Oh, I had to do an invocation.

Sonia You went to the beach. Alone. You shouldn't do that.

Márgara To invoke in a very loud voice so that humanity can hear me!

Sonia Why not do it in your bedroom, in peace.

Márgara I like the beach more.

Sonia You could have fallen on the way.

Márgara Yes, I could have. But I didn't fall. I stopped before the waves, which were serene, like tame water, and I felt content, full of strength, I invoked the past and the future.

Sonia (*smiles*) The past you know. You went very crazy.

Márgara I read the cards, and how right I was! (*Laughs.*) But to the women who came to see me I didn't tell the whole truth. Only the good.

Sonia I know. They went away happy.

Márgara (*laughs*) Even though they might have been struck by lightning afterwards! (*She abandons the knitting.*) I took pity on them. They didn't hold a grudge against me. After a month they returned. If they weren't lucky, it made them believe they could be. Gross error.

Sonia Aren't you tired, Mum?

Márgara No. It was a nice job, always heralding good news! They paid me with pleasure, some more, some less . . . What do you think if now . . .?

Sonia No, Mum, no.

Márgara I would earn money. They would be one to one sessions! Tell my fortune, fortune teller, attend to me, madam? (*She laughs.*) Your husband, who owns three boats but still complains, would look at me with different eyes.

Sonia Give him time.

Márgara To that man?

Sonia For him to get used to things.

Márgara To me? That man will only get used to what he wants. He got used to money.

Sonia He'll be here any minute. Why don't you go to your room? Not because you annoy him. To take a nap.

Márgara (*following her own train of thought*) I will rid your husband of his vices and tricks! I'll transform him into a lamb! What did you say?

Sonia That you go to your room, to take a nap.

Márgara You're sending me to my room? Now? When I'm so entertained? I come out of one nap and go into another. It's not fair, you go to sleep! (*The door opens.* **Efraín** *appears accompanied by* **Renata**.)

Efraín I bring you company. She wants to see your mother.

Márgara (*happy*) To see me! What a state, you see, Sonia? I can't take a nap!

Sonia (*to* **Efraín**) What for?

Efraín (*acidly*) To have a bit of fun, isn't that so madam?

Sonia   Come in. It's Renata, isn't it? We met once.

Renata   In the market.

Sonia (*points to* **Márgara**)   Do you want to talk to her?

Renata   I'm worried.

Sonia   But what . . .? She doesn't converse much, except with me. She's a bit deaf.

Renata   They say she sees beyond the present. That's what the children say. They spy on her behind the rocks on the beach, where she screams and . . . They also say that she's not in her right mind. But I don't believe it. If she sees me, I'll pay her.

Sonia   Don't even think about it.

Efraín   Shut up, Sonia.

Márgara (*coming near to* **Renata**, *looks at her with interest, intensely*)   I don't want to talk to her. (*Moves away.*) I don't know her. Where's my knitting? I put it . . . where?

Efraín   She'll pay you.

Márgara   What?

Efraín   She'll pay you! Didn't you hear?

Renata   And if you don't accept money, I'll pay you in gratitude.

Efraín   No, she'll accept it, she'll accept it!

Márgara   Then will you stop hating me?

Efraín   I don't hate you, señora.

Márgara   I won't charge her.

Efraín (*becoming indignant*)   What am I doing here, surrounded by skirts? Sonia, finish up here soon. (*To the air, but obviously to* **Márgara**.) Idiot! (*Exits.*)

Márgara   I won't talk to her either.

Renata   Why don't you want to talk to me? I'll hardly bother you at all. Just one question.

Márgara   I was busy, knitting, I want to go on knitting! I was going to take a nap!

Sonia   Later, Mum.

Márgara   Ah, now it's later? Because it suits you, doesn't it. Don't disturb me! (*She finds her knitting. Nervously, she fumbles around with it, nervously she takes out the needles.*) Oh, I've dropped stitches! What a terrible shame!

Sonia   Mum, see what the lady wants. (*She goes to bring her.*) I don't know what she wants to tell you, but it'll only take a moment. And a moment for you to answer her.

Márgara   Didn't you say I'm a little deaf? (*Capricious.*) Didn't you hear me? I don't hear!

Sonia (*persuasively as she guides her*)   Maybe she wants you to knit her a scarf, a sweater . . .

Márgara   Yes! I'd love that! (*She digs her heels in.*) No. She doesn't want that! (*Aggressively, to* **Renata**.) I predict the future, my lady, but not here, not for you! Go somewhere else to get your cards read!

Renata   Where? If it's true that you know the future, don't hide it from me. My husband is sick. I want to know if he'll get better.

Márgara (*annoyed*)   I don't know!

Sonia   Mum . . .

Márgara   Silence!

Renata   He has a fever, pain. With his teeth clenched, his teeth have got bigger.

Márgara (*trying to avoid looking at her*)   He eats a lot! That's why!

Renata   He hasn't eaten in days. Before, the little he ate didn't reach his stomach either. He threw it up on the bedclothes. Before, he complained. Now he doesn't even do that. He no longer recognises me.

Márgara   And what do I have to see? I don't deal with these cases. I make prophesies to crowds! That's where I predict the future!

Renata   What is mine?

Márgara   Widow!

Renata (*she smiles weakly*)   No. My husband survive. Will he survive? I don't mind looking after him if in the end he opens his eyes, sits up in bed, murmurs my name.

Márgara (*like a child, she covers her face with her hands*)   I'm hiding. Márgara isn't in. I'm not here!

Sonia   Leave her. She gets agitated. She can't help you. Old age has caught up with her now, very fragile. She's rarely lucid.

Márgara (*uncovers her face, furious*)   What's wrong with my old age? It's not a state, it's a passage! I'm lucid, awake!

Renata   So tell me . . .

Márgara   Between these four walls I know nothing. Least of all about your husband. On the beach, that's where you have to listen to me. There I speak and I predict that thousands of little horses with their heads adorned with coloured plumes . . . Only there can your husband be saved.

Renata (*with a thin thread of a voice*)   Not in his bed? What are you saying? Don't predict his death for me. And if you predict it for me, let it be after, not before, my own. Whoever knows the future is forearmed and can change it.

Márgara   Very good! It's as if you've heard me!

Renata Will he survive?

Márgara (*looks at her. After a silence, categorical*) No. Not alone. With his head under the covers, he will not survive in his bed.

Renata What? What? Where then?

Sonia Mum . . . What are you talking about? Shut up.

Márgara You won't even be able to touch him with your hand. Keep your children away because what he has will reach other bodies. It will make them sick.

Renata Is this what you predict for me?

Márgara What do you want? I'm not the one who takes away your hope.

Sonia You do take it away, Mum!

Márgara No. It was her words. (*She touches her mouth. To* **Renata**.) You have to be careful! It's everything you said that killed hope. You signed the death sentence, my dear!

Renata You're blaming me? Why can't he recover? He was an oak! He was never ill. Not even a cold. (*Silence from* **Márgara**.) And now . . .? What's wrong with him? What disease can it be that he cannot be cured?

Márgara (*implacable*) A deadly one. I predict what I see. And now I don't see little horses. I see him under the ground.

Renata No. (*To* **Sonia**.) How can you allow . . .?

Márgara In less than . . . three days. Not a day more or a day less.

Renata (*to* **Sonia**) Look at her! She rejuvenated by predicting misery. She was an old woman. And now. . .! Her eyes are sparkling, she's happy to predict it.

Márgara I can't comfort you. You would also have hated me if I had predicted health for your husband and you had found him dead on your return.

Renata Shut up! Your eyes are sparkling! Tie your tongue in a knot, you be the one to die!

Márgara Don't get annoyed with me.

Renata With whom then? I had hope! Couldn't you lie to me? Even if only for a second to relieve me of this burden, this heavy load!

Sonia (*puts a hand on her shoulder, takes her towards the door*) Come. I'll come with you.

Renata He'll get better, won't he?

Sonia Yes. Don't pay any attention to her.

Renata (*turns her head back. To* **Márgara**) Why did you predict that misery for me? Are you gloating, does it make you happy?

Márgara   No. Neither happy nor unhappy. Sometimes I can straighten things out, but not always. Together we can save ourselves and help someone else to be saved. If everyone joins me, then I have the power of many hands, our breath, our unanimous will. With the many, madam, I can predict and determine. With death in a bed and someone crying only for that death, no, I can't! Go away!

Márgara *on the beach* (*deserted*).

Márgara   Oh, they come to hear me! All except for Sonia, who is forbidden to by Efraín. It doesn't matter. I will tell her my prophecies later, in her ear, like when she was little and I used to tell her stories about little horses, dragons, unicorns. And she slept with them because they appeared around her bed at night. (*Looks.*) So many, so many! For as far as the eye can see. Millions and millions. They're all there, even those with a secretly shadow spirit. Efraín, Efraín! Hope warms your body from head to foot. They await my prophecies. If they hear me, my prophecies will come true. It's like saying: together we will triumph! (*Laughs.*) Efraín! They drool because hope makes them drool with a bittersweet juice, they smile and look wide-eyed at my trotting little horses with their coloured plumes . . . Closer! Open your ears, spread your elephant ears, so you don't miss a word. I predict a light heart, such beautiful humanity. Not only do I prophesise, I decide! That a catastrophe will never fall upon them – not war, not famine, not abduction – They'll no longer suffer the capsising of a boat full of helpless creatures to share an impossible pact with happiness, they'll no longer be shipwrecked, they'll no longer appear swollen with water, eaten by fish. They're in the world and the world is no longer the enemy, it shelters them, protects them, heals and saves them. Mother, mother! Doors open to them, maternal and fraternal, nourishing them with all the good things egoism has deprived them of. All wounds have been cauterised. There will no longer be a reason for repentance to exist – for what? – atonement, we'll no longer show the obscene and satisfied figure of those who caused suffering to be more powerful, richer, more abhorrent, or the massacred faces of those who suffered at their hands. Our memory, even our memory, is clean because we recognise ourselves as good. Crime, they ask themselves, what was a crime? An act, a desire? To caress, to eat, to feel nostalgia? They won't know no matter how hard they try to remember because they've changed in such a way, so entirely, that they won't have the memory of an inconceivable act, there's no blood on their hands to be rinsed away without a trace under water. No longer any fear of some people or guilt or gloating over so much suffering for others, the concentration camps, the ovens in the night and the fog, the tortured bodies and the nameless graves, so much evil, so much evil . . . The one who granted me the gift of prophecy can do nothing against me, (*Points.*) they've been convinced! Efraín, Efraín! What's it like to look without hatred? How is it, to act without devastating the universe in each one that you wronged? Does your heart feel light now? Hear me. Everyone hear me!

I predict green and fertile plains to counter hunger, and pristine mountains, rivers and seas of transparent waters and a humanity given to the goodness of each gesture. And how the sun will shine! How the rains will come with precise regularity, the earthquakes will fall silent and the tsunamis will disappear because not even nature will dare to cloud the results of goodness. How we'll lose the fear of nothingness.

After a happy life, we'll go to bed and death will be the dream beneath clean sheets. Or if we insist, stubborn like those in the throes of death – sweetly –, we'll go serenely in silver ships crossing the sea, serenely. This I predict, this I foretell, oh with a light heart, with my incredibly beautiful humanity!

Efraín *enters, whistling, his face bright and clear.*

Efraín (*looks around, darkens little by little*)   What a house! If this is a home . . . Sadness and grime. Two women and neither one clean, one old and the other idle. (*He passes his hand over the table, he looks at it.*) It's not that dirty . . . And if I bought better furniture . . . A lamp there . . . A surprise for Sonia, some joy. She doesn't have much of that. And why should I give her joy? Who gives it to me? The old woman said that we should all abide by her prophecy: such beautiful humanity! All cultivate good sense and give ourselves to goodness. (*Ambiguous.*) Little birds, chicks, beetles . . . all good! We see each other and we kiss. I take the bread out of my mouth and give it to a poor wretch. I don't touch a weapon, they no longer exist! I don't cause suffering and nobody convinces me that hate is in my nature. The old woman predicted that kindness . . . and at that moment I almost . . . (*Laughs despite himself.*) I'm laughing like a fool! I did something incredibly stupid and it doesn't seem serious to me . . . I'm laughing . . .

Sonia (*enters*)   Efraín . . . were you whistling? I thought I heard . . . Was it you? (*He looks at her, smiles and whistles after a moment. He goes out to meet her and hugs her tightly.* **Sonia**, *suspicious.*) What's wrong?

Efraín   What needs to happen for me to embrace you?

Sonia   It's been a long time since . . .

Efraín   I went close to the beach. I heard the old woman. (*Laughs.*) She's always running away from you! Where is she now?

Sonia   In her bedroom.

Efraín   And what's she doing?

Sonia   She's sleeping.

Efraín (*ironically*)   Better that she rests, yes. She's out of sight! What a relief!

Sonia   I made food.

Efraín   Which is your duty, isn't it?

Sonia   I fulfilled it.

Efraín (*changes tone*)   She's sleeping. Is her room warm? She suffers with the cold. (*Stokes the fire.*) When she wakes up at least make it warm in here.

Sonia (*mistrustful*)   Do you care?

Efraín   Why wouldn't I? I gave away my boats, Sonia.

Sonia   What?

Efraín   I only have one left and I myself will set out, to sea, instead of watching them go, or instead of selfishly keeping my distance, doing the accounts, accumulating money I don't spend.

Sonia (*she smiles weakly*)   Really? It's not like you to . . .

Efraín   We were a multitude. And my heart became light, the rancor left, like a wild animal that sees the open door of its cage. And I didn't follow it. I let it go. And my men, the fishermen in my boats, who looked at me resentfully because they were taking risks for little pay, welcome me gratefully with open arms . . .

Sonia   Do you want to eat now? It's time to eat. Shall I bring you the food?

Efraín   I'd prefer a coffee. I'm not hungry.

Sonia   I'll make you one right away. (*She moves away*.)

Efraín   And my words gushed out to all of them, because the first thing that the absence of resentment brought me was words. Careful words. Only good words. (*Laughs*.) Oh, is this goodness? Is it that simple, does it cost so little? (*Quietly*.) Although Sonia irritates me and brought me that old woman . . . (*To* **Sonia**.) It was her, your mother. She made me sane, turned me from stone to water. Tame.

Sonia (*puts bread and the coffee on the table*)   The bread . . .

Efraín (*sits down, feels it*)   It's not fresh bread.

Sonia   I bought a lot yesterday and . . .

Efraín   And you didn't buy any today. You can't even calculate something so simple? The daily bread? (*Laughs*.) It doesn't matter. Thank you, did I used to say thank you before?

Sonia   Never.

Efraín   Well, now you will hear that word until you're tired of it. You'll say to me: enough thanks! Don't thank me so much! (*Tastes the coffee, grimaces*.)

Sonia   Is it okay?

Efraín   Cold. Don't worry. If it's cold I'll say I needed a summer drink. I'll drink it anyway.

Sonia   I'll warm it up.

Efraín   Reheating it is worse. Why are you frightened?

Sonia   You're irritable.

Efraín   No. I promise. (*Emphatic with fictional kindness*.) Thank you, Sonia. I'll drink this coffee you made for me with great pleasure . . . lovingly. Lovingly, right?

Sonia   Yes.

Efraín   If I don't like it, I'll put up with it. I'll drink this cup of coffee . . . (*He drinks, chokes*.) Bitter, acidic, cold! It's undrinkable! It tastes like an old dishcloth!

Pure poison! (*He throws the cup violently.*) When will you learn to make a hot coffee which tastes good? It's not that difficult, is it?

Sonia (*picks up the cup*)   I'll make another one. And this time . . .

Efraín   It'll be the same! Ah, I smother you with my demands! Poor dear!

Sonia   What do you expect from me? Apart from a coffee you can't drink.

Efraín   Nothing! I can't expect anything! When will you learn the bare minimum? To make a coffee, to cook? Not to join forces with your mother? When will you look at me with love? Because I don't have your love, I'm sure of it.

Sonia   I love you, Efraín.

Efraín (*gets up, turns over a chair*)   I don't need it either! Luckily for me! I don't need your love!

Sonia   In that case I'll take it back. Actually, it's already gone.

Efraín   Yes, with someone else. Anyone will do because deep down you're nothing but a frustrated whore.

Sonia   How could I be anything else with you?

Efraín   What? This is how you answer me, with that spite? Me, the one who supports you, the one who puts up with your mother?

Sonia   I'll take her away. I'll go to my brothers.

Efraín   Your brothers are like me, with little will for what they don't like. And now she's old, they don't like your mother. And you . . . what will you do . . . (*Stressing the words.*) with your brothers? Lead the high life! How are you going to pay for the bread they throw at you, the roof they don't want to offer you? Stupid woman! You're good and you have no strength, what a waste of goodness! No, Sonia. You will stay here, at home, and make no mistake, don't take it for granted because I could regret it. I would kick you out, though that door!

Sonia   I believe you. It wouldn't make much difference to you. In what way is this my house? When has it ever been?

Efraín   That's true. It's mine. All the same you'll stay here to respect me, to serve me – badly – without opening your mouth. I have quite enough with your mother, she's raving mad!

Sonia   The resentment didn't leave you. You have it deep inside, it doesn't matter against what, against whom. You embraced me, Efraín. Why? Was it your resentment? Did it move your arms, force you to be tender? Why, despite my disbelief, did you make me think . . .?

Efraín   What you wanted. You were never intelligent, Sonia. With as little intelligence as those who believe that I gave away the boats and wrote off their debts. You can't stand up to me. I breathe hate and you kindness. Shall we see who wins?

Sonia   You said . . .

Efraín   What I said was carried away on the wind! Rubbish! I'd burn you alive. (*He beats her.*)

Sonia *and* **Márgara**. **Sonia** *with the mark of having been hit on her face and a hardened expression. Outside, again a storm of wind and rain.*

Márgara (*picks up the shapeless knitting. Looks at it*)   I don't feel like knitting.

Sonia (*dryly*)   I don't know what you can entertain yourself with then.

Márgara   Thinking! No matter how much I think, I can't explain it. Do you understand this?

Sonia   What, Mum?

Márgara   The storm. This summer storm.

Sonia   It's not summer. It's cold. This dawn felled trees and tore away half the pier. It wreaked havoc.

Márgara   What?

Sonia   Efraín is furious.

Márgara   No, what's he got to be furious about! He's soft hearted, I saw him on the beach.

Sonia   Hard. Try sinking your teeth into that soft heart.

Márgara   I don't understand you. Nor do I understand this storm. I declared that not even nature would oppose kindness. It's strange, isn't it? That now . . .

Sonia (*impatient*)   Yes, Mum. Very strange.

The storm lets up. A pale sun crosses the window diagonally.

Márgara   The sun! Didn't I tell you? It was nothing more than a whim of . . . (*Points upwards.*) How's the town? It's changed, hasn't it?

Sonia   I didn't go out.

Márgara   Together they could prepare a big party to celebrate . . . With little horses going round the square . . .

Sonia   There are no little horses in the town, Mum.

Márgara   I'll lend them mine! Or if not . . . Are there pigs?

Sonia   Yes.

Márgara   They can be pigs with a ribbon . . . (*Points to the neck.*) It's enough that the neighbours dress up for the party, elegant. What shall we wear? Bake a cake. Your cakes are delicious!

Sonia (*looks at her darkly*)   Efraín doesn't like them.

Márgara (*doesn't hear*)   Who doesn't like them?

Sonia Efraín!

Márgara He doesn't have to eat them! For the ones who don't want anything there's always something. That's what they used to say to me when I was little. How miserable! I lived in one room and ate whatever was around. (*Laughs.*)

Sonia Tell that to Efraín.

Márgara I don't need to! He devours your food, he loves your desserts!

Sonia Since when?

Márgara From now on! Isn't he appreciative, doesn't he say thank you at every opportunity? And he has such generosity!

Sonia Don't talk nonsense, Mum.

Márgara I saw him! He listened to me embracing the crowd, struck dumb and with such a sweet expression! Didn't the sweetness last, eh? You see, Sonia? (*Takes a few steps dancing.*) My prophecies come true!

Sonia He hit me.

Márgara What? I can't hear you!

Sonia Yes, so sweet. With sweetness he fought with the men he gave the boats away to. He hadn't signed any papers, so he's still the skipper of the boats, they're still his, Mum. And today, despite the storm, the men swallowed the insult – because he ordered them to – and they set sail as if it was a peaceful day. They went out to sea. To the storm.

Márgara To fish!

Sonia To drown! If they're shipwrecked, at least I'll be happy that Efraín loses his boats.

Márgara (*disconcerted*) What are you saying to me, Sonia?

Sonia I'm lying to you (*Points to her cheek.*) and this bruise lies. (*Someone's knocking at the door.* **Sonia** *opens it.*) Renata?

Renata (*enters*) Are you alone? I came to ask forgiveness. From you. I took advantage the moment the rain stopped. I was so shocked the other day . . .

Sonia Your husband . . .?

Renata He's better.

Márgara Under the ground.

Sonia (*dismisses her with an impatient gesture*) I'm very happy, Renata.

Renata I was upset, so beside myself that . . .! She broke my heart with her prophecies. Prophet of doom. Twisted. (*To* **Sonia**.) I'm sorry.

Márgara Say sorry to me! You insulted me! Not her!

Renata   What do you expect? You were cruel to me. Your daughter comforted me, but you . . .!

Márgara (*defiant*)   I told you that with a dying man in his bed, in his room, I can do nothing. I only have power with a crowd. Yesterday, before a multitude, my prophecies were different, and they came true right there and then, señora. Why weren't you there?

The gale returns abruptly. A gust of wind opens the window.

Sonia (*runs and closes it*)   It's raining heavily. It's pouring down.

Márgara   I don't understand. I'm going to concentrate and . . . (*She closes her eyes.*)

Sonia   Have the boats come back? They must be on their way back by now, mustn't they?

Renata   You would know, only your husband's boats went out. And they haven't come back.

Márgara   A clear sky. A little cloud here, there . . .

Renata   The women are waiting on the beach. Soaked through, scanning the horizon which is a dark smudge. I pity them.

Márgara   With you two talking I can't concentrate. Please . . .!

Grumbling to herself she hears them with an expression which is sulky to begin with.

Renata   Luckily none of my family is out at sea. After what I went through, that anguish was the last thing I needed.

Sonia   Those fisherman are well seasoned. Foolhardy even? They didn't see the time, the threat the storm foretold?

Renata   They look to *Mr* Efraín. They depend on him.

Sonia   Blindly? Always?

Renata   When there's hunger on the one hand and the opportunity to make a living from someone else's assets on the other, there's nothing in between. Just need.

Sonia   Efraín wouldn't risk his boats.

Renata   He believed they were safe. At least, he believed that at worst he could lose one or two men taken off guard by a swell on deck. He was wrong.

Márgara   Relax. They'll return safe and sound! All of them. And they'll bring so many fish that the women in the factory will work day and night to get the sardines into cans.

Renata   I don't know why she winds me up.

Sonia   She's an old woman, don't pay any attention to her. She doesn't think straight, she can't speak or think sensibly. And she's deaf!

Márgara (*hears them incredulously*)   I heard that! I don't think straight? Everyone heard me yesterday, they kissed the hem of my robe. They recognised the joy that kindness brings, and so they left, kind, as I had predicted.

Renata (*acidic*)   You got it right.

Márgara (*vindictive*)   You believe I got it wrong? Are you sure that your man is getting better? There can been those little improvements just before death.

Renata   Shut up! (*To* **Sonia**.) Make her shut up!

Sonia   Mum . . . !

Márgara   Only those who dream together leave in silver ships looking serenely at the sea. The others, who want to die in their bed, die alone in their bed. And they're buried under the earth!

Renata (*to* **Sonia**)   Goodbye. Goodbye, señora. Thank you for meeting me.

Sonia   Don't go yet. Wait for the storm to stop.

Renata   It's almost finished. Anyway, better to face the storm than listen to your mother. She'll stir me up again. (*Leaves*.)

Márgara   What a terrible character! She's not evil! But kindness passes her by.

I was supposed to convince those who were close and I convinced those who were far away. But of course, it's never that effective . . . at a distance . . .

Sonia   Yes, Mum. Go to your room, rest a little. Leave me in peace!

Márgara   I'm cold. The fire isn't lit.

Sonia   Efraín didn't buy wood. He says summer's already coming. Do you see summer? (*Points*.)

Márgara   Oh, he didn't buy it because he's got a surprise. He'll come with a heater. With two! One for me.

Sonia   He'll keep the fishermen's homes. He has given them money and it wasn't a gift.

Márgara   Do you mean . . .

Sonia (*harshly*)   It is what it is! And it doesn't change. Soon you'll have to go back to my brothers. Efraín can't stand you, he doesn't want you here.

Márgara   You're wrong. He adores me. And you too! (**Efraín** *walks in*. **Márgara**, *happy*.) Efraín!

Efraín   Ah, the two of you together.

Sonia   What happened, Efraín?

Efraín   Does it interest you to find out?

Sonia   Why wouldn't it?

Efraín   Such satisfaction you give me!

Sonia   Please, Efraín . . .

Efraín   It only concerns me. Only I suffer losses. The boats didn't come back. Only some debris, strings, a piece of mast. That was omen enough. How could you not warn me, señora?

Sonia   My God . . ., no one . . . survived?

Efraín   They retrieved the oldest, the most expendable. He brought back as much water as a barrel of wine . . . diluted. The others sank. (*Points to* **Márgara**.) What luck you brought us!

Márgara   I didn't prophesise this! How is it possible? I prophesised a future without catastrophes! I decided on that future and everyone joined me, determined to live it with me. You were on the beach, you heard me!

Efraín (*to* **Sonia**)   Shut her up! Get her out of here because otherwise you will pay, Sonia. Get her away from me!

Sonia   Mum . . . go to your room.

Márgara   I don't want to!

Sonia (*takes the knitting, puts it in her hands*)   Go!

Márgara   I don't want to go to my room! Let alone knit. You're not going to order me around like an idiot!

Efraín   You don't want to go to your room? Then get out!

Sonia   No, Efraín!

Efraín   Get out!

The sound of stones being thrown against the outer wall is heard. It's a bombardment which lasts some minutes.

Márgara (*incredulous*)   What are they throwing? Are they throwing stones at us? (*Opens the window, looks out and steps back with the force of a stone hitting her.*)

Sonia   Mum! No! (*She closes it.*) Are you crazy?

Márgara (*dazed*)   What was that? (*She rubs her shoulder.*)

Sonia   A stone. Are you hurt?

Efraín   This is the result. This is how they respond. You got them fired up.

Márgara   Not against me! It's because your boats didn't come back!

Efraín   Really? Didn't you prophesise kindness for them? Good people understand, forgive. Why don't you face them! They won't do you any damage. (*He pushes her outside.*) Go away, señora. Don't wind me up. Go peacefully.

Sonia   No, Efraín. Leave her.

Efraín Get out of my way!

Sonia What has she ever done to you? Leave her.

Efraín You can go with her! Let her make prophecies to the men who drowned. I lost the boats. I told you I'd kick you out the door myself, through that door! You've worn me out. Get out the both of you! Think of some watertight excuses because they'll eat you alive, the good guys. Get lost. (**Márgara**, *scared, hides behind* **Sonia**.) You too, señora! Get out! (*He pushes them brutally.*)

Sonia Efraín, for God's sake!

Efraín *throws them out. Closes the door, locks it.* **Sonia***'s voice can be heard shouting 'Efraín, Efraín!' And some banging at the door which dies down and stops.*

Efraín (*with an air of shocked surprise*) I was so tough! Implacable. And how does it make me feel? Do I begin to suffer, my knees buckling beneath me, is my skin covered in a cold sweat? Do I feel ashamed, am I repentant? Do I open the door and call out after them? Sonia! Come back, Sonia! I need you both! (*A pause, he smiles*.) There's no point. There might have been if I weren't . . . because I feel . . . (*Opens his arms, shouts joyously*.) Fine!

Márgara *is on the beach, poised as if she's about to deliver a speech. But there's a long silence.*

Márgara He dared to throw us out! He was waiting for an excuse and I gave it to him, on a silver platter. Get out! He threw us to the wolves, those goody goodies who had reason to hate. They shoved us because they believed we shared his guilt and wealth in that house they threw stones at. It was just a few yanks of our hair, a few scratches. With their mouths full of curses and reproaches, they wanted him, Efraín. How long will the fury last? Not long, because Efraín will buy other boats and they'll swallow their pride to get work. They'll forget, forced to forget. The rain stopped but there are no crowds in front of me. And I don't call anyone. I don't want them to hear anymore. I still have the gift of prophecy but I won't use it. I'll let it rust like iron left out in the elements. What could I prophesise that doesn't contradict myself? That there'll be no more shipwrecks? No more hunger, war? That we'll forget even the name for crime, crime in its thousands of forms forgotten? What will I prophesise? That the water won't become poisoned and the white whales won't swim in pain, sick with cancer, cancer! Flipping their tail in an ocean that's deceptively transparent. What have they made of my prophecies? They looked at the little horses with coloured plumes going around a circus ring, they gathered up my words and being convinced by goodness lasted just a moment. Oh, they're not seduced by goodness, they don't want to be, they can't be doing with it. This is the issue. In love, they caress evil, they make it their own, and the terrible thing is that it gives them a sordid happiness, neither the powerful nor the weak reject it, regardless of their possibilities and resources. Sordid happiness? Meagre? What am I talking about? Enormous! Conceited. Why not, if they enjoy the uses of cruelty that the powerful perfect with merciless imagination. Oh, what inventiveness! What a fever of profit runs through them, what a delightful shudder when not a single mistake misses the target. (*She strikes her chest with her fist.*) Here! Here is shame. The clumsy, the great excuser, what can I do but be ashamed? Touched by guilt. But what am I going to find with shame, that stone washed clean, that rodent without teeth that doesn't put things right, doesn't make amends, that has no power to bargain with what's already been done. Ah! How credulous and arrogant I was, so arrogant as to believe that humanity would respond, halving that humanity into those who suffer and those who cause the suffering. I had wished the world was another one. Whoever gave me the gift of prophecy does not allow me to choose my prophecies. He chopped off my head with an axe.

Sonia *and* **Márgara**.

With an air of fatigue, **Sonia** *supports* **Márgara** *while they walk near the sea.*

Márgara   A shelter! (*There isn't one.*) Let's go under the shelter, Sonia. Let's sit. How calm the sea is! (*Laughs.*) Like us! How stormy! That's Efraín. (*She touches* **Sonia**'s *bruise*.) He hit you? With his fist?

Sonia   A stone hit you. Does it hurt? Let me look at you.

Márgara (*rubbing her shoulder*)   There's no point. With such thin skin, slow blood, I outdo you in bruises. Why look at them?

Sonia (*holds out her hand*)   To heal you.

Márgara (*pulls away*)   With what? Let them be. They'll go away on their own. Yours and mine.

Sonia   I couldn't stop him, Mum. Efraín . . .

Márgara   Don't make excuses for him! Don't even think about it! He kicked us out, Sonia! He won't get away with it. I will punish him. He'll wish he hadn't done it.

Sonia   Yes, Mum.

Márgara   I'll shoot him! Where are the bolts of lightning? (*Stretches out her hands with her fingers spread.*) Come out! Don't get in the way, little horses! I don't want you here. I want bolts of lightning! Punish the soulless. Strike him down! (*Waits. Disappointed.*) Nothing happens.

Sonia (*anguished, she crouches down on the ground*)   Come, Mum. Sit down. What will we do now? Where can I carry you to?

Márgara   To the train! On the first train, to the city! With your brothers.

Sonia   They don't want us.

Márgara   You think?

Sonia   I know them. They consider their duties already fulfilled as sons. They had you for a long time.

Márgara   Duty? They had me? Like a thing?

Sonia   No, Mum.

Márgara   If they don't want us, what, who is left for us then?

Sonia Nobody.

Márgara Renata! She holds a grudge against me, but she would help you. Definitely.

Sonia She can't. She feeds a lot of mouths.

Márgara Where two can eat, so can three. That's what poor people say, not rich people. At their opulent table only they eat.

Sonia If she helps me, what would happen with you, Mum?

Márgara (*with great force*) Ah, I, I . . .! I'm cold. (*She presses against* **Sonia**.) This is how we are. Why didn't they choose goodness? They pull and they pull and they stretch things to breaking . . . I can no longer decide. I can't even get out of the cold. I was an arrogant old woman, and so naive! (**Sonia** *breaks down in tears*.) Sonia, Sonia, what's wrong with you? Don't cry.

Sonia Mum, save me from Efraín, I'll have to go back to him, save me from my meekness, from my goodness without strength . . .

Márgara (*she takes her in her arms*) Shhhh . . . Shhhh . . . What's the matter with you? Don't cry. It distresses me to see you cry. Are you scared? You fell over? Ah, that's it, you fell over! (*She rubs her wrist*.) Let's kiss it better . . . All better! (*Laughs, starts to tickle her*.)

Sonia (*pushes her away in fits of laughter*) What are you doing, Mum? Get off me!

Márgara Why? Don't you like it? My mum, when I fell over or was sad, used to tickle me, she used to sing to me! How strange that I remember it. So many years . . . Laugh again. Please. Laugh, my little girl. (*Insists*.)

Sonia (*pushes her away roughly*) I'm not a little girl anymore. Mum, laughing like this is no good. You try to stitch together what's broken with weak threads, it doesn't work.

Márgara It's better than nothing, Sonia. Don't you get above yourself either. Perhaps it's in this, the goodness, in such . . . silliness. Small . . . if I liken it to a light heart, such beautiful humanity . . . I'm hungry.

Sonia This is desperate. What will I do, what will we do, Mum? I think and think, and I don't know. Who will help us?

Márgara Renata, I told you! Let's go to her house, let's go before I freeze. I'll be out of sight, I'll hide while you convince her. Assure her that I no longer make prophecies, she'll soften.

Sonia Why? We hardly know her. What reason does she have for welcoming us into her home, with her sick husband, her children, so many mouths to feed? She'll welcome us with open arms. What a gift we'd be!

Márgara You comforted her. She owes you one. (*Timidly*.) And I think she . . . is good. She'll give us shelter for a few days, Sonia, and then . . .

Sonia   Nothing. The weather. I can't take it anymore, Mum! I want to die! (*Cries.*)

Márgara   No, no. We can always bear more than we think, more grief, more pain. May God not dare think of sending us everything we can bear. (*Laughs weakly.*) Don't cry, Sonia. You make me feel old, I get sad . . .

Sonia (*she contains herself drying her tears*)   What did she sing to you, Mum?

Márgara   What?

Sonia   What did she sing to you?

Márgara   Who?

Sonia   Your mum!

Márgara   To me?

Sonia   When you were sad, what did she sing to you?

Márgara   She didn't sing to me, she had a squeaky voice. She also made me fried cakes! But before that she would kiss me (*She covers* **Sonia** *with kisses quickly and repeatedly.*) and then, whispered in my ear . . . she told me that in the sea, that sea! (*Points.*) a very small wave was saying hello to her mummy.

Sonia   And that used to comfort you?

Márgara   Of course! And I, who was already beginning to make prophecies, at the age of five! slept by her side and also whispered in her ear and predicted a long life, so happy . . . It didn't come true.

Sonia (*seeing her become saddened*)   What else? Tell me. What else did your mum used to say to you?

Márgara   Not my mum. The little wave. She spoke, she crept slowly across the sand and said: 'I am the smallest wave / from the sea / I offer you little drops / the freshest / from the sea.' I remember, Sonia! How I liked her to talk!

Sonia   Do you remember?

Márgara   As if I could hear her!
'I offer you droplets
the freshest
from the sea.
Dip your feet in, señora,
she used to say
to my mum.

That wave so small
kissed my mother's big toe
with a very round kiss.

My mum felt ticklish
her big toe laughed

with the smallest wave
from the sea.'

(*She looks at* **Sonia** *expectantly*.) And . . .? What did you think?

Sonia   Lovely . . .

Márgara   I remembered everything, Sonia! It comforted me so much! I didn't cry anymore. Of course I was only a little one! Today I don't know if . . . (*Shyly*.) And you? Do you . . .?

Sonia   It comforted me too, Mum. Me too.

Overwhelmed, she slides onto **Márgara**'*s lap, closes her eyes.* **Márgara** *strokes her head. After a moment, without them noticing,* **Renata** *reveals herself.* **Renata** *takes a few steps forward, stops, and looks at them. Slowly she raises her arm, slowly she opens her hand towards them as the light dies out.*

Curtain.

The phrase 'Together we can save ourselves and help someone else to be saved' belongs to Boris Pahor, from his book Necropolis.

Acknowledgements

I was first introduced to the work of Griselda Gambaro by writer, theatre translator and scholar Catherine Boyle when I began work on Out of the Wings, an AHRC-funded theatre-in-translation project which began in 2008 of which she is the director. Born out of a collaboration between its co-founders and the Royal Shakespeare Company's acclaimed Spanish Golden Age season, Out of the Wings was established in order to bring English translations of the theatre of Spanish- and Portuguese-speaking worlds to the UK. In 2011, as part of the Out of the Wings project, a production of my translation of *Siamese Twins* was performed at Theatro Technis, directed by Jorge Perez Falconi and Mara Lockowandt. Out of the Wings continues as a theatre collective and as an annual theatre festival, in which a rehearsed reading of *As the Dream Dictates* was performed in July 2016, directed by British theatre director Sue Dunderdale. I am hugely grateful to Catherine Boyle for starting me on this journey and for her continuing support. I am not alone in my good fortune of having had her inspirational mentorship.

In 2010 I was involved in the project 'Translating Cultural Extremity' which examined the *grotesco criollo* in its performative nature. The description of the *grotesco criollo* featured in the introduction to this volume was formulated for a presentation to the British actors who were preparing to work on the script of *Babilonia* (1925) by Armando Discépolo. Although they had read the play in advance of the workshop, ultimately the play was to be revealed by the process of examining the script dramaturgically, and through the actors' embodiment of it. It is particularly the case with the theatre of the *grotesco criollo* that it is not a theatre to be read, but to be performed. I am quite sure that what I observed in this project allowed me to understand and to perceive its legacy in the theatre of Griselda Gambaro, a vital insight without which my translations would have been all the poorer.

Several of the translations featured in his volume were read with the British theatre company, Presence Theatre under the direction of Simon Usher, and later also Colin Ellwood. In Presence, Gambaro's theatre has found a natural home. Their manifesto reads 'Presence Theatre believes that the theatre is an art form whose primary strength lies in the power of the actor and the word. We think this must remain the case even, and perhaps especially, when the form of a production is innovative or difficult. We embrace the classical and modern repertoire as well as new plays, with a particular interest in the avant-garde, and furthermore we seek to address the problem of the ever-shrinking repertoire in our mainstream theatres. [. . .] Openness is all.' This manifesto might be a description of Gambaro's theatre. Indeed the notion of openness offers a reception of the ambiguity and ambivalence in Gambaro's theatre which is immensely rich and creative. There is an inferred world in her plays, 'a shadow world' as Simon Usher has described it. I am grateful for the intuitive readings Simon, Colin and their extraordinarily talented actors have given over the years since I first brought Gambaro's work to them in 2015 when they recognised her greatness in an instant.

Finally I would like to thank my friend and colleague, Maria-José Blanco for her guidance in reading early drafts of my translations, and then for sitting through hours of me performing all parts of all of the plays whilst diligently reading the Spanish to check for accuracy.